Music Technology REFERENCE BOOK

Peter Buick and Vic Lennard

PC Publishing

PC Publishing
Export House
130 Vale Road
Kent TN9 1SP
UK

Tel 01732 770893
Fax 01732 770268
email pcp@cix.compulink.co.uk
website http://www.pc-pubs.demon.co.uk

First published 1995, reprinted 1997

ISBN 1 870775 34 1

British Library Cataloguing in Publication Data
A catalogue record for this book is available from the British Library

Printed in Great Britain by Bell and Bain, Glasgow

Preface

Success in the music business today can no longer be guaranteed by simply thrashing out a brilliant guitar performance on stage (if indeed it ever could) – the entertainment industry is changing.

Technology and society are now demanding more than simple musical brilliance and talent from their entertainers. Visual sophistication is now demanded by all sorts of delivery media, including cable TV, video and CD-ROM. Even interactive concerts and theme parks are becoming part of the norm. The traditional live performance music market is also shrinking. Kids play computer games, adults stay in and watch television, and record sales are slowly being eroded by more absorbing media, such as video and CD-ROM. Today's musician must search for new markets and be ready to satisfy them.

Coupled with this is the need to understand the technology involved in order to get the most from it, to be original and creative, not forgetting the need to get some actual work! A typical gig in the near future might involve a 3D animation for a back projection, creating original sounds through sound design, and writing the odd computer program in C to customise a system so that your MIDI music would control stage pyrotechnics. Of course, if you can afford it you can hire in all of these skills, but until you've "made it" by doing these things, you have to do it all yourself !

Welcome to the *Music Technology Reference Book*. This book came about because we were tired of looking through mountains of books to remember some detail we'd forgotten. Half of our development time was spent tidying up the bookcase!

This book is a reference book. It is not a replacement for traditional training and specialised text books, but a supplement, like course notes. It is (hopefully) a useful revision of the things you will need to use regularly. If you have an aptitude for the subject you may be able to learn from this book as well, although this isn't its function.

We can't guarantee that it will be all-encompassing, but we have tried to make it so. In any case, if we can save you even half an hour looking something up, or inspire you to go further, then we will have succeeded in our objective.

Foreword

So you thought your video recorder was a nightmare to program! How about the frustrations faced by the modern music maker and the huge amount of technical data he or she has to absorb before a single note can be produced from the great myriad of available black boxes linked by an inevitable spaghetti of cables?

Modern music technology seems more geared to rocket scientists than budding axesmiths trying to attain stardom at Wembley Stadium, but that's just a fact of life. If you're going to do anything in music these days, you have to accept that some of your time is going to be spent trying to find the right plug ... and reading technical manuals. That's where this book comes in.

All the technical information you could possibly want in one place – an absolute godsend for anyone working in MIDI rooms, broadcasting, rehearsal rooms, commercial or garage studios, wherever. It is a comprehensive guide to MIDI, recording techniques and acoustics, musical structure, computers in music and so on, and contains hundreds of useful snippets of information designed to reduce dramatically the amount of head scratching we have all had to put up with.

With the help of this book, we can obtain a better understanding of the *science* of modern music, and we can all benefit from the ability to devote more time to musical creation, without having to stare at our equipment continually and ask *Why?*

Alan Parsons

Alan Parsons is a renowned composer, record producer and sound engineer. His recording career started with The Beatles at Abbey Road, and his best known work as engineer is Pink Floyd's classic Dark Side of the Moon. *As well as a mountain of hits as producer with both British and American artists, his numerous albums as the Alan Parsons Project have earned him a string of gold and platinum awards and Grammy nominations. He is a directorate member of RePro, the Guild of Recording Directors, Producers and Engineers, and runs his own 48-track digital studio in Sussex.*

Contents

Contents

1

MIDI

MIDI in general

MIDI stands for Musical Instrument Digital Interface. It allows devices to communicate with each other and exchange data, but never contains any sound data directly. Although it may describe a sound, it can only achieve this through a sample dump or sound patch parameters, and not in real-time. It has been said that one purpose of the MIDI specification is to "publicise information and foster compatibility".

MIDI devices go way beyond the traditional keyboard, and include effects units, mixer automation, tape machine control, lighting and theatre prop control. MIDI controllers include MIDI-equipped guitars, drum kits/pads, wind controllers, retro-fitted pianos, virtual reality sensors (light and pressure sensors), and control pads using sliders and buttons.

> **INFORMATION**
>
> *Some manufacturers refer to a single sound by different names: Sound – Patch – Timbre – Tone. Additionally, a collection of sounds accessible as a keyboard split/layer or as a multi-timbral set-up are also referred to by different names: Combi – Multi – Patch – Performance. Refer to the specific model to determine its nomenclature standard. This can even change between models from the same manufacturer.*

MIDI messages

There are two different types of MIDI message:

Channel messages

A channel message is sent on a specific MIDI channel. This divides further:

- *Channel voice* message, such as notes on and off, pitch bend and patch changes.
- *Channel mode* message, such as the MIDI mode (1-4) – Poly on/off and Omni on/off, Local on/off and Reset All Controllers (Controller #121).

System messages

System messages are not channelised and so are intended for all devices. However, only some devices will interpret the commands, such as with a System Exclusive message that is addressed to a particular device by using a manufacturer and unit device number ID.

These also divide further into:

- *System Exclusive* message, such as a specific device's parameter settings.
- *System Common* message, such as Song Select, Song Position Pointer and MIDI Time Code (MTC).
- *System Real-time* message, such as MIDI Clock, Song Start and Active Sensing. Real-time messages may be interleaved with System Exclusive messages.

MIDI channels

Some MIDI messages can be sent on a single channel of the available 16 MIDI channels. This allows instructions to address one of 16 possible devices.

> **CONVENTIONS**
>
> *Many of the numbers in this book use hexadecimal numbering (base 16) rather than the decimal (base 10 system). This is denoted by an "H" after the figure (e.g. 40H) or the abbreviation "Hex". Decimal figures are denoted with no annotation or the abbreviation "Dec".*
>
> *Remember that computers count 0 as the first number in a series, hence bank 1 is the second bank; bank 0 is the first.*

Additional individually addressable MIDI ports can increase the effective number of MIDI channels.

System Exclusive data is not normally MIDI channel dependent, but uses a system of manufacturer ID and device ID numbers (0-127) to identify a particular unit. On some systems, however, the MIDI channel can then further divide the device ID into 16 possible units, although this is not common.

MIDI bytes

There are two types of MIDI byte:

- *Status byte.* Essentially an instruction and always larger than 128 decimal, 80H (bit 8 is set to 1). The range is 80H to FFH.
- *Data byte.* The value to be acted upon with a maximum range of 0 to 127 (bit 8 is always 0). If a value higher than 127 is needed, extra data bytes are sent. The range is 00H to 7FH.

Running Status

A MIDI message usually comprises one or more bytes, the first of which is always a status byte. However, as it is superfluous to send the same type of status byte repetitively, the Running Status scheme was devised where a status byte is sent only once. It is then assumed that any following data bytes refer to that status byte. Once the message type changes, the relevant status byte is sent.

While this system reduces the demand on the MIDI bus, some devices cannot cope with this scheme and need a full MIDI message (including the status byte) every time. Such units include the Korg DDD1, Ensoniq Mirage and IT Plus48.

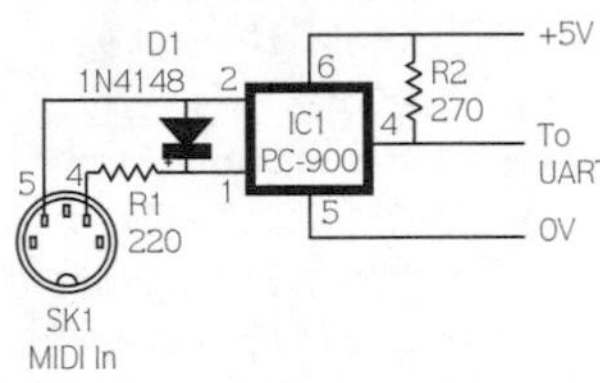

Circuit for MIDI In

MIDI ports

There are three types of MIDI port. MIDI In receives data (listens like an ear); MIDI Out transmits data (like a mouth). The MIDI Thru repeats the data received at the MIDI In (like a parrot repeating what it hears).

From this it should be apparent that, like real life, there is no point in two people speaking (out to out, thru to out, thru to thru, or out to thru) or both listening (In to In): one person has to be speaking while the others listen.

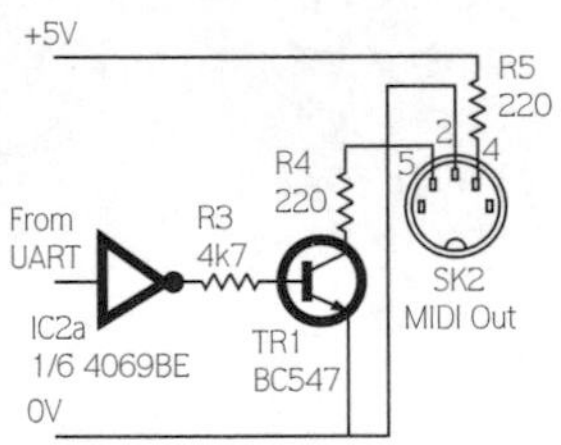

Circuit for MIDI Out

MIDI Hardware Specification

The MIDI Specification states the following:

- A 5-pin din (180 degree) socket type, using pins 4 and 5 with 2 as screen.
- The screen should not be connected to chassis and should not be connected on In sockets.
- Transmission speed of 31.25 KBaud (±1%), 8 bits plus 1 start and 1 stop bit. Each byte takes 320μs to send.
- The connections are opto-isolated (less than 2μs transient response) and use a 5mA current loop.
- Maximum cable length is 50 feet (15m) and should use screened, twisted-pair cable.
- It is recommended that not more than three devices are daisy-chained via MIDI Thrus due to the accumulation of buffer delays.
- Each MIDI port should be connected to only one other, unless via suitable buffering.

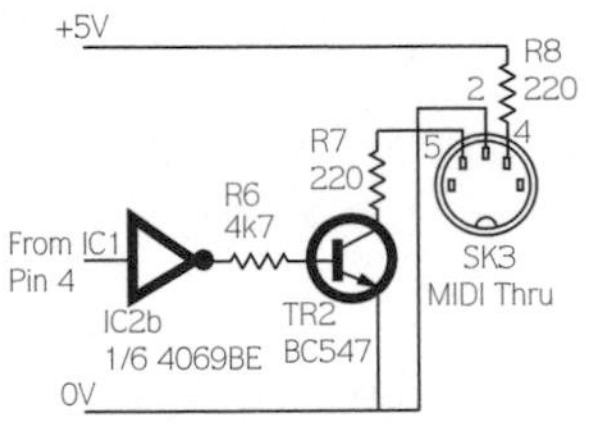

Circuit for MIDI Thru

MIDI system connections
The figure shows a typical MIDI sequencing system showing how units can be connected via a "daisy chain" of MIDI Thru to MIDI In.

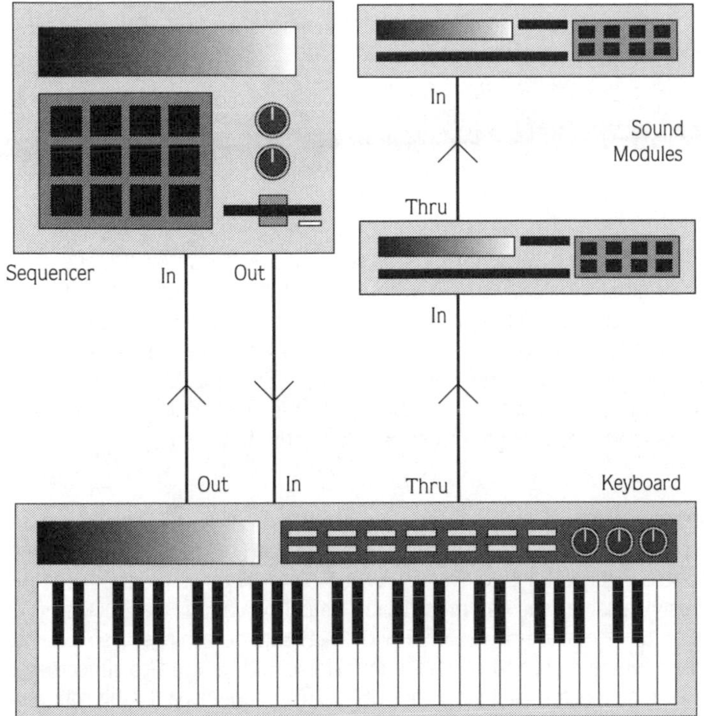

A typical MIDI sequencing system set up

MIDI modes
A MIDI device can be in one of four receiving modes, the most common being Mode 3 which is used in a multi-timbral set-up. The modes are derivations of Omni on/off and Polyphonic/Monophonic as shown.

Mode	*Omni*	*Poly/mono*
1	on	poly
2	on	mono
3	off	poly
4	off	mono

Channel voice messages

Function	*Hex*	*No of data bytes*	*Description*
Note On	9n kk vv	2	n = MIDI channel (0 to F) kk = note number (00 to 7F) vv = velocity (00 to 7F)
Note Off	9n kk 00 or 8n kk 00	2 2	
Polyphonic aftertouch	An kk aa	2	kk = note number aa = pressure value (00 to 7F)
Channel aftertouch	Dn aa	1	aa = pressure value (00 to 7F)
Controller change	Bn cc vv	2	cc = control number (00 to 65) vv = value (00 to 7F)
Program change	Cn pp	1	pp = program number (00 to 7F)
Pitch bend change	En ll mm	2	ll = LSB, mm = MSB centre = En 00 40
Mode change	Bn mm vv	2	mm = mode number (79 to 7F) vv = value (00 to 7F)

Important controllers recently added to the MIDI Specification

Function	Hex	Description
Bank select (patch change)	Bn 00 MM	n = MIDI channel, MM = MSB value
	Bn 20 LL	LL = LSB value
All sounds off (per channel)	Bn 78 00	n = MIDI channel
Legato footswitch	Bn 44 vv	n = MIDI channel
		vv < 40 = normal, vv ⩾ 40 = legato
Portamento (for following single note)	Bn 54 kk	kk = note to slide from

Note off

The reason for having two methods of sending a Note Off lies in the following. The original version with a Note Off status (8n) allows for Note Off velocity to change a sound dependent on a player's key release as well as the attack of the key. However, this requires an extra status byte so reducing any bandwidth advantage of using Running Status. Using the same status byte as Note On (9n) but with a velocity of zero is employed to solve this problem. A MIDI device should be capable of using either method.

MIDI controllers

A MIDI controller is used to modify a parameter or function of a device. These controls can take two forms: switch (for instance, sustain pedal) or continuously variable (such as modulation wheel or volume pedal). Using only one data byte, a maximum resolution of 128 can be achieved, so a scheme was devised where a second related controller could be used to send the LSB, with the original controller being the MSB. This produces a 14-bit value with a resolution of 16,384 steps. The relationship between the controllers is that 0–31 are related to 32–63 (add 32 to the first controller number). If the extra resolution is not required, then the LSB controller need not be sent. The LSB byte can be sent on its own for a fine adjust only. If an MSB byte is sent, the device should assume the LSB is zero.

The original MIDI Specification defined controllers 64–69 (decimal) as switches but they can also be used as continuous types. All controllers can be implemented as continuous (0–127) or switches (0–63 = off, 64–127 = on. It is preferred that 0 = off and 127 = on).

MIDI controller numbers

Hex	Dec	Controller	Hex	Dec	Controller
00	0	bank select MSB	0B	11	expression (volume accent)
01	1	modulation wheel	0C	12	effect control 1
02	2	breath controller	0D	13	effect control 2
03	3	undefined/old Yamaha DX7 pressure	0E	14	undefined
04	4	foot controller	0F	15	undefined
05	5	portamento time	10	16	general purpose 1
06	6	data entry MSB	11	17	general purpose 2
07	7	volume	12	18	general purpose 3
08	8	balance (between two sources)	13	19	general purpose 4
09	9	undefined	14	20	undefined
0A	10	pan (between outputs)	15	21	undefined

Hex	Dec	Controller
16	22	undefined
17	23	undefined
18	24	undefined
19	25	undefined
1A	26	undefined
1B	27	undefined
1C	28	undefined
1D	29	undefined
1E	30	undefined
1F	31	undefined
20	32	LSB for controller 0
21	33	LSB for controller 1
22	34	LSB for controller 2
23	35	LSB for controller 3
24	36	LSB for controller 4
25	37	LSB for controller 5
26	38	LSB for controller 6
27	39	LSB for controller 7
28	40	LSB for controller 8
29	41	LSB for controller 9
2A	42	LSB for controller 10
2B	43	LSB for controller 11
2C	44	LSB for controller 12
2D	45	LSB for controller 13
2E	46	LSB for controller 14
2F	47	LSB for controller 15
30	48	LSB for controller 16
31	49	LSB for controller 17
32	50	LSB for controller 18
33	51	LSB for controller 19
34	52	LSB for controller 20
35	53	LSB for controller 21
36	54	LSB for controller 22
37	55	LSB for controller 23
38	56	LSB for controller 24
39	57	LSB for controller 25
3A	58	LSB for controller 26
3B	59	LSB for controller 27
3C	60	LSB for controller 28
3D	61	LSB for controller 29
3E	62	LSB for controller 30
3F	63	LSB for controller 31
40	64	damper pedal (hold/sustain)
41	65	portamento on/off
42	66	sostenuto
43	67	soft pedal
44	68	legato switch (>40 = legato on)
45	69	hold 2
46	70	sound controller 1/sound variation
47	71	sound controller 2/timbre/harmonic intensity
48	72	sound controller 3/release time
49	73	sound controller 4/attack time
4A	74	sound controller 5/brightness
4B	75	sound controller 6
4C	76	sound controller 7
4D	77	sound controller 8

Hex	Dec	Controller
4E	78	sound controller 9
4F	79	sound controller 10
50	80	general purpose 5
51	81	general purpose 6
52	82	general purpose 7
53	83	general purpose 8
54	84	portamento control (e.g., Bn 54 kk where kk = note to slide from to the next note played)
55	85	undefined
56	86	undefined
57	87	undefined
58	88	undefined
59	89	undefined
5A	90	undefined
5B	91	external effects depth/effects depth 1
5C	92	tremolo depth/effects depth 2
5D	93	chorus depth/effects depth 3
5E	94	celeste detune depth/effects depth 4
5F	95	phaser depth/effects depth 5
60	96	data increment
61	97	data decrement
62	98	non registered lsb
63	99	non registered msb
64	100	registered parameter lsb
65	101	registered parameter msb
66	102	undefined
67	103	undefined
68	104	undefined
69	105	undefined
6A	106	undefined
6B	107	undefined
6C	108	undefined
6D	109	undefined
6E	110	undefined
6F	111	undefined
70	112	undefined
71	113	undefined
72	114	undefined
73	115	undefined
74	116	undefined
75	117	undefined
76	118	undefined
77	119	undefined

Channel mode messages (controller codes reserved for Channel mode messages).

Hex	Dec	Controller
78	120	all sound off
79	121	reset all controllers (send value 0)
7A	122	local control on (127)/off (0)
7B	123	all notes off (0)
7C	124	omni mode off (0)
7D	125	omni mode on (0)
7E	126	mono mode on (no of channels or 0 for maximum of device)
7F	127	poly mode on (0)

Roland implement the Bank Change message in a non-standard way, reversing the MSB and LSB. This refers to bank 1 as 128, 2 as 256 and so on.

Patch Change/Bank Select

It is possible to select a new patch (sometimes called a program or memory) in a device, remotely over MIDI by use of the *Patch Change* command. This makes the device recall a certain patch location. Note, however, that it has no control over what is in that patch location (for instance if a new bank of sounds has been loaded).

The system needn't be limited to keyboards and can apply equally to effects units, drum machines (pattern selection) and to recall "scene" changes on a lighting or audio mixer.

The original MIDI Specification provided for only 128 patches which has now been updated to 16,384 banks of 128 patches using the *Bank Select* command (Controllers 00 and 20 in addition to the regular patch change):

Bn 00 mm
Bn 20 ll
Cn pp

For example, Bn 00 00, Bn 20 00, Cn 30 would select patch 30H in bank 0. Bn 00 01, Bn 20 00, Cn 40 would select patch 40H in bank 128.

Patch Change/hex to binary table

Dec 0	Dec 1	Hex	Binary	Roland
0	1	00	0000 0000	11
1	2	01	0000 0001	12
2	3	02	0000 0010	13
3	4	03	0000 0011	14
4	5	04	0000 0100	15
5	6	05	0000 0101	16
6	7	06	0000 0110	17
7	8	07	0000 0111	18
8	9	08	0000 1000	21
9	10	09	0000 1001	22
10	11	0A	0000 1010	23
11	12	0B	0000 1011	24
12	13	0C	0000 1100	25
13	14	0D	0000 1101	26
14	15	0E	0000 1110	27
15	16	0F	0000 1111	28
16	17	10	0001 0000	31
17	18	11	0001 0001	32
18	19	12	0001 0010	33
19	20	13	0001 0011	34
20	21	14	0001 0100	35
21	22	15	0001 0101	36
22	23	16	0001 0110	37
23	24	17	0001 0111	38
24	25	18	0001 1000	41
25	26	19	0001 1001	42
26	27	1A	0001 1010	43
27	28	1B	0001 1011	44
28	29	1C	0001 1100	45
29	30	1D	0001 1101	46
30	31	1E	0001 1110	47

Dec 0	Dec 1	Hex	Binary	Roland
31	32	1F	0001 1111	48
32	33	20	0010 0000	51
33	34	21	0010 0001	52
34	35	22	0010 0010	53
35	36	23	0010 0011	54
36	37	24	0010 0100	55
37	38	25	0010 0101	56
38	39	26	0010 0110	57
39	40	27	0010 0111	58
40	41	28	0010 1000	61
41	42	29	0010 1001	62
42	43	2A	0010 1010	63
43	44	2B	0010 1011	64
44	45	2C	0010 1100	65
45	46	2D	0010 1101	66
46	47	2E	0010 1110	67
47	48	2F	0010 1111	68
48	49	30	0011 0000	71
49	50	31	0011 0001	72
50	51	32	0011 0010	73
51	52	33	0011 0011	74
52	53	34	0011 0100	75
53	54	35	0011 0101	76
54	55	36	0011 0110	77
55	56	37	0011 0111	78
56	57	38	0011 1000	81
57	58	39	0011 1001	82
58	59	3A	0011 1010	83
59	60	3B	0011 1011	84
60	61	3C	0011 1100	85
61	62	3D	0011 1101	86
62	63	3E	0011 1110	87
63	64	3F	0011 1111	88
64	65	40	0100 0000	
65	66	41	0100 0001	
66	67	42	0100 0010	
67	68	43	0100 0011	
68	69	44	0100 0100	
69	70	45	0100 0101	
70	71	46	0100 0110	
71	72	47	0100 0111	
72	73	48	0100 1000	
73	74	49	0100 1001	
74	75	4A	0100 1010	
75	76	4B	0100 1011	
76	77	4C	0100 1100	
77	78	4D	0100 1101	
78	79	4E	0100 1110	
79	80	4F	0100 1111	
80	81	50	0101 0000	
81	82	51	0101 0001	
82	83	52	0101 0010	
83	84	53	0101 0011	
84	85	54	0101 0100	
85	86	55	0101 0101	
86	87	56	0101 0110	
87	88	57	0101 0111	
88	89	58	0101 1000	
89	90	59	0101 1001	

Dec 0	*Dec 1*	*Hex*	*Binary*
90	91	5A	0101 1010
91	92	5B	0101 1011
92	93	5C	0101 1100
93	94	5D	0101 1101
94	95	5E	0101 1110
95	96	5F	0101 1111
96	97	60	0110 0000
97	98	61	0110 0001
98	99	62	0110 0010
99	100	63	0110 0011
100	101	64	0110 0100
101	102	65	0110 0101
102	103	66	0110 0110
103	104	67	0110 0111
104	105	68	0110 1000
105	106	69	0110 1001
106	107	6A	0110 1010
107	108	6B	0110 1011
108	109	6C	0110 1100
109	110	6D	0110 1101
110	111	6E	0110 1110
111	112	6F	0110 1111
112	113	70	0111 0000
113	114	71	0111 0001
114	115	72	0111 0010
115	116	73	0111 0011
116	117	74	0111 0100
117	118	75	0111 0101
118	119	76	0111 0110
119	120	77	0111 0111
120	121	78	0111 1000
121	122	79	0111 1001
122	123	7A	0111 1010
123	124	7B	0111 1011
124	125	7C	0111 1100
125	126	7D	0111 1101
126	127	7E	0111 1110
127	128	7F	0111 1111
128	129	80	1000 0000
129	130	81	1000 0001
130	131	82	1000 0010
131	132	83	1000 0011
132	133	84	1000 0100
133	134	85	1000 0101
134	135	86	1000 0110
135	136	87	1000 0111
136	137	88	1000 1000
137	138	89	1000 1001
138	139	8A	1000 1010
139	140	8B	1000 1011
140	141	8C	1000 1100
141	142	8D	1000 1101
142	143	8E	1000 1110
143	144	8F	1000 1111
144	145	90	1001 0000
145	146	91	1001 0001
146	147	92	1001 0010
147	148	93	1001 0011
148	149	94	1001 0100

Dec 0	*Dec 1*	*Hex*	*Binary*
149	150	95	1001 0101
150	151	96	1001 0110
151	152	97	1001 0111
152	153	98	1001 1000
153	154	99	1001 1001
154	155	9A	1001 1010
155	156	9B	1001 1011
156	157	9C	1001 1100
157	158	9D	1001 1101
158	159	9E	1001 1110
159	160	9F	1001 1111
160	161	A0	1010 0000
161	162	A1	1010 0001
162	163	A2	1010 0010
163	164	A3	1010 0011
164	165	A4	1010 0100
165	166	A5	1010 0101
166	167	A6	1010 0110
167	168	A7	1010 0111
168	169	A8	1010 1000
169	170	A9	1010 1001
170	171	AA	1010 1010
171	172	AB	1010 1011
172	173	AC	1010 1100
173	174	AD	1010 1101
174	175	AE	1010 1110
175	176	AF	1010 1111
176	177	B0	1011 0000
177	178	B1	1011 0001
178	179	B2	1011 0010
179	180	B3	1011 0011
180	181	B4	1011 0100
181	182	B5	1011 0101
182	183	B6	1011 0110
183	184	B7	1011 0111
184	185	B8	1011 1000
185	186	B9	1011 1001
186	187	BA	1011 1010
187	188	BB	1011 1011
188	189	BC	1011 1100
189	190	BD	1011 1101
190	191	BE	1011 1110
191	192	BF	1011 1111
192	193	C0	1100 0000
193	194	C1	1100 0001
194	195	C2	1100 0010
195	196	C3	1100 0011
196	197	C4	1100 0100
197	198	C5	1100 0101
198	199	C6	1100 0110
199	200	C7	1100 0111
200	201	C8	1100 1000
201	202	C9	1100 1001
202	203	CA	1100 1010
203	204	CB	1100 1011
204	205	CC	1100 1100
205	206	CD	1100 1101
206	207	CE	1100 1110
207	208	CF	1100 1111

Dec 0	*Dec 1*	*Hex*	*Binary*
208	209	D0	1101 0000
209	210	D1	1101 0001
210	211	D2	1101 0010
211	212	D3	1101 0011
212	213	D4	1101 0100
213	214	D5	1101 0101
214	215	D6	1101 0110
215	216	D7	1101 0111
216	217	D8	1101 1000
217	218	D9	1101 1001
218	219	DA	1101 1010
219	220	DB	1101 1011
220	221	DC	1101 1100
221	222	DD	1101 1101
222	223	DE	1101 1110
223	224	DF	1101 1111
224	225	E0	1110 0000
225	226	E1	1110 0001
226	227	E2	1110 0010
227	228	E3	1110 0011
228	229	E4	1110 0100
229	230	E5	1110 0101
230	231	E6	1110 0110
231	232	E7	1110 0111
232	233	E8	1110 1000
233	234	E9	1110 1001
234	235	EA	1110 1010
235	236	EB	1110 1011
236	237	EC	1110 1100
237	238	ED	1110 1101
238	239	EE	1110 1110
239	240	EF	1110 1111
240	241	F0	1111 0000
241	242	F1	1111 0001
242	243	F2	1111 0010
243	244	F3	1111 0011
244	245	F4	1111 0100
245	246	F5	1111 0101
246	247	F6	1111 0110
247	248	F7	1111 0111
248	249	F8	1111 1000
249	250	F9	1111 1001
250	251	FA	1111 1010
251	252	FB	1111 1011
252	253	FC	1111 1100
253	254	FD	1111 1101
254	255	FE	1111 1110
255	256	FF	1111 1111

Registered Parameter Numbers

LSB (Controller 64H	MSB Controller 65H)	Function
00	00	pitch bend sensitivity for each direction (cents/semitones)
01	00	fine tuning
02	00	coarse tuning
03	00	tuning program select
04	00	tuning bank select

Universal System Exclusive codes

Use	Hex	Decimal
non commercial	7D	125
non real-time	7E	126
real-time	7F	127

System Common messages

Hex	Function	Notes
F1 mv	MIDI time code (MTC) quarter frame message	m = message type (0mmm), v = value. See MTC section (page 27) for details.
F2 ll mm	song position pointer	ll = LSB, mm = MSB. mmll is a 14-bit counter: 1 count is 6 timing clocks = 1 semiquaver
F3 ss	select song number	ss = song number (00 to 7F)
F4	undefined	
F5	undefined	
F6	tune request	

System Real-time messages

Hex	Function	Notes
F8	MIDI clock	24 times crotchet rate
F9	undefined	
FA	song start	
FB	song continue	
FC	song stop	
FD	undefined	
FE	active sensing	
FF	system reset	

Active Sensing

Active Sensing is an optional message used to detect the disconnection of a system. Once an Active Sensing message is received, the device expects to receive some MIDI information within 300ms or should assume the transmitter has been disconnected and reset its status. If no other MIDI information is being sent, the transmitter employing Active Sensing should send the Active Sensing message within 300ms.

Active Sensing is sent every 300ms at maximum. If never received, the system should work as normal. If it has been received and then disappears, the receiving device should turn off all voices and return to normal status.

System Reset

A System Reset can be used to initialise a system at any point. It should instigate the following conditions in any receiving devices:

- Set omni mode, poly mode and local to on if applicable.
- Turn off any sounding voices and reset controllers.
- Stop play-back and set song position to zero.
- Clear Running Status.
- Reset any instruments to their power-up condition.

Device inquiry message

Sent: F0 7E nn 06 01 F7
Returned: F0 7E nn 06 02 id lf mf lm mm rv rv rv rv F7

where nn = channel number
id = manufacturer's System Exclusive ID
lf = LSB of family code
mf = MSB of family code
lm = LSB of family member code
mm = MSB of family member code
rv = software revision code

Notation markers

Bar and time messages may be sent in real time as follows (taking effect from the next MIDI clock received):

F0 7F ID 03 01 ll mm F7

where ID = 7F for all devices or unique
03 = sub ID – notation information
01 = sub ID – bar number message
ll mm = bar number (LSB first)

where 00 40 = not running
01 40 - 00 00 = count in
01 00 - 7E 3F = bar number in song
7F 3F = running bar number unknown or less than 8K.

Time signature changes

F0 7F ID 03 S2 ln nn dd cc bb (nn dd) F7

where ID = 7F for all or unique
03 = sub ID – notation information
S2 = sub ID – 02 for immediate change, 42 delayed change

ln = number of data bytes to follow (default = 4, rises in 2s for each extra sig. change per bar)
nn = number of beats – numerator
dd = beat value – denominator (negative power of 2)
cc = number of MIDI clicks in metronome
bb = number of notated 32nd notes per MIDI quarter note
(nn dd) = additional pairs of time signatures for compound time

Master volume
F0 F7 ID 04 01 ll mm F7

where ll=LSB and mm=MSB of volume. (00 00 = volume off)

Master balance
F0 F7 ID 04 02 ll mm F7

where ll=LSB and mm=MSB of balance. (00 00 = hard left, 7F 7F = hard right)

System Exclusive messages
F0 Start of System Exclusive message
F7 EOX: End of System Exclusive message

Manufacturer's ID
Each manufacturer is allocated a special ID with which to identify System Exclusive messages that are intended for their own products.

If the first byte of the ID is 00, then the following two bytes also form part of the ID (using the three-byte system), otherwise the first byte is the whole ID number.

Certain single ID numbers are reserved for special purposes: 7D is for educational and research use only, 7E (non real-time) and 7F (real-time) are used for extensions to the MIDI Specification.

Patch change vs System Exclusive
A patch change is a MIDI instruction for a device to recall a storage (sound, effects patch or mix data) location. It cannot know if the correct sound is in this place – this may have been changed since you last used it, such as by loading a new bank of sounds.

A System Exclusive message is an instruction describing the parameters that made up a storage location (such as a sound or effect parameters). System Exclusive is unique for each model and make of machine and is neither understandable nor transferable between other devices which are unlikely to have the same type, number or range of parameters. By sending a System Exclusive message to a (certain location) of a device, the patch can be assured of containing the correct data. The disadvantage is the length of time taken.

A System Exclusive message is made up as follows:

F0 ID MN UN db... db F7

where F0 = start of System Exclusive message
ID = manufacturer's ID
MN = model number
UN = unit number
db = data bytes
F7 = end of exclusive

Because of the time System Exclusive takes, it is best to use System Exclusive to set up devices initially and then use the much quicker patch changes to alter the pre-loaded locations.

Many devices take time to patch change, and mute their outputs while this occurs. For this reason it is best to send patch changes during silence or before the beat where the effect won't be so noticeable. Shifting a patch change event back 10 ticks (or a 64th note) can cure this problem. (It is also possible to send a patch change for one device while another is playing, so masking the effect.)

MIDI ID # country ranges

Country	1 byte	3 byte
USA	01 – 1F	00 00 01 – 00 1F 7F
Europe	2F – 3F	00 20 00 – 00 3F 7F
Japan	40 – 5F	00 40 00 – 00 5F 7F
Other	60 – 7C	00 60 00 – 00 7F 7F
Special	7D – 7F	

USA/Canada

Company	Hex	Decimal
Sequential	01	1
IDP	02	2
Octave Plateau	03	3
Moog	04	4
Passport	05	5
Lexicon	06	6
Kurzweil	07	7
Fender	08	8
Gulbransen	09	9
AKG Acoustics	0A	10
Voyce Music	0B	11
Waveframe Corp.	0C	12
ADA	0D	13
Garfield	0E	14
Ensoniq	0F	15
Oberheim	10	16
Apple Computers	11	17
Grey Matter Response	12	18
Digidesign	13	19
Palm Tree Inst.	14	20
JL Cooper	15	21
Lowrey	16	22
Adams-Smith	17	23
EMU systems	18	24
Harmony Systems	19	25
ART	1A	26
Baldwin	1B	27
Eventide	1C	28
Inventronics	1D	29
	1E	30
Clarity	1F	31
(3 byte system)		
Warner New Media	00 00 01	0 0 1
	00 00 02	0 0 2
	00 00 03	0 0 3
	00 00 04	0 0 4
	00 00 05	0 0 5
	00 00 06	0 0 6
Digital Music Corp	00 00 07	0 0 7
Iota Systems	00 00 08	0 0 8
New England Digital	00 00 09	0 0 9
Artisyn	00 00 0A	0 0 10
IVL Technologies	00 00 0B	0 0 11
Southern Music Systems	00 00 0C	0 0 12
Lake Butler Sound	00 00 0D	0 0 13
Alesis	00 00 0E	0 0 14
	00 00 0F	0 0 15
DOD Electronics	00 00 10	0 0 16
Studer-Editech	00 00 11	0 0 17
	00 00 12	0 0 18
	00 00 13	0 0 19
Perfect Fretworks	00 00 14	0 0 20
KAT	00 00 15	0 0 21
Opcode	00 00 16	0 0 22
Rane Corp	00 00 17	0 0 23
Spatial Sound	00 00 18	0 0 24
KMX	00 00 19	0 0 25
Allen & Heath Brenell	00 00 1A	0 0 26
Peavey Electronics	00 00 1B	0 0 27
360 Systems	00 00 1C	0 0 28
Spectrum Design	00 00 1D	0 0 29
Marquis Musi	00 00 1E	0 0 30
Zeta Systems	00 00 1F	0 0 31
Axxes	00 00 20	0 0 32
Orban	00 00 21	0 0 33
	00 00 22	0 0 34
	00 00 23	0 0 35
KTI	00 00 24	0 0 36
Breakaway Technologies	00 00 25	0 0 37
CAE	00 00 26	0 0 38
	00 00 27	0 0 39
	00 00 28	0 0 40
Rocktron	00 00 29	0 0 41
PianoDisc	00 00 2A	0 0 42
Cannon Research Corp	00 00 2B	0 0 43
	00 00 2C	0 0 44
Rogers Instruments	00 00 2D	0 0 45
Blue Sky Logic	00 00 2E	0 0 46
Encore Electronics	00 00 2F	0 0 47
Uptown	00 00 30	0 0 48
Voce	00 00 31	0 0 49
CTI Audio	00 00 32	0 0 50
S&S Research	00 00 33	0 0 51
Broderbund software	00 00 34	0 0 52
Allen Organ Co.	00 00 35	0 0 53
	00 00 36	0 0 54
Music Quest	00 00 37	0 0 55

Company	Hex	Decimal	Company	Hex	Decimal
Aphex	00 00 38	0 0 56	InterMIDI Inc	00 00 4F	0 0 79
Gallien Krueger	00 00 39	0 0 57		00 00 50	0 0 80
IBM	00 00 3A	0 0 58		00 00 51	0 0 81
	00 00 3B	0 0 59		00 00 52	0 0 82
Hotz Instrument Tech	00 00 3C	0 0 60		00 00 53	0 0 83
ETA Lighting	00 00 3D	0 0 61		00 00 54	0 0 84
NSI Corporation	00 00 3E	0 0 62	Lone Wolf	00 00 55	0 0 85
Ad Lib Inc	00 00 3F	0 0 63		00 00 56	0 0 86
Richmond Sound Design	00 00 40	0 0 64		00 00 57	0 0 87
Microsoft	00 00 41	0 0 65		00 00 58	0 0 88
The Software Toolworks	00 00 42	0 0 66		00 00 59	0 0 89
RJMG/Niche	00 00 43	0 0 67		00 00 5A	0 0 90
Intone	00 00 44	0 0 68		00 00 5B	0 0 91
	00 00 45	0 0 69		00 00 5C	0 0 92
	00 00 46	0 0 70		00 00 5D	0 0 93
Groove Tube Electronics	00 00 47	0 0 71		00 00 5E	0 0 94
	00 00 48	0 0 72		00 00 5F	0 0 95
	00 00 49	0 0 73		00 00 60	0 0 96
	00 00 4A	0 0 74		00 00 61	0 0 97
	00 00 4B	0 0 75		00 00 62	0 0 98
	00 00 4C	0 0 76		00 00 63	0 0 99
	00 00 4D	0 0 77	Musonix	00 00 64	0 0 100
	00 00 4E	0 0 78			

Europe

Company	Hex	Decimal	Company	Hex	Decimal
Passac	20	32	Digigram	3D	61
SIEL	21	33	Waldolf Electronics	3E	62
Synthaxe	22	34	Quasimidi	3F	63
	23	35	Dream	00 20 00	0 32 0
Hohner	24	36	Strand Lighting	00 20 01	0 32 1
Twister	25	37	Amek Systems Ltd	00 20 02	0 32 2
Solton	26	38		00 20 03	0 32 3
Jellinghaus MS	27	39	Dr Bohm	00 20 04	0 32 4
Southworth (CTM)	28	40		00 20 05	0 32 5
PPG	29	41	Trident Audio	00 20 06	0 32 6
JEN	2A	42	Real World Studio	00 20 07	0 32 7
SSL Ltd	2B	43		00 20 08	0 32 8
Audio Veritrieb	2C	44	Yes Technology	00 20 09	0 32 9
	2D	45	Audiomatica	00 20 0A	0 32 10
SoundTracs	2E	46	Bontempi/Farfisa	00 20 0B	0 32 11
Elka/General Music	2F	47	FBT Electronica	00 20 0C	0 32 12
Dynacord	30	48		00 20 0D	0 32 13
	31	49	Larking Audio	00 20 0E	0 32 14
	32	50	Zero 88 Lighting Ltd	00 20 0F	0 32 15
Clavia Digital Instruments	33	51	Micon Audio GMBH	00 20 10	0 32 16
Audio Architecture	34	52	Forefront Technology	00 20 11	0 32 17
General Music Corp	35	53		00 20 12	0 32 18
	36	54	Kenton Electronics	00 20 13	0 32 19
	37	55		00 20 14	0 32 20
	38	56	ADB	00 20 15	0 32 21
Soundcraft Electronics	39	57	Jim Marshall Products	00 20 16	0 32 22
	3A	58	DDA	00 20 17	0 32 23
Wersi	3B	59	TC Electronics	00 20 18	0 32 24
AVAB Electronik AB	3C	60		00 20 19	0 32 25

Company	Hex	Decimal	Company	Hex	Decimal
TC Electronics (cont)	00 20 1A	0 32 26	TC Electronics (cont)	00 20 1D	0 32 29
	00 20 1B	0 32 27		00 20 1E	0 32 30
	00 20 1C	0 32 28		00 20 1F	0 32 31

Japan

Company	Hex	Decimal	Company	Hex	Decimal
Kawai	40	64	Matsushita Electric	50	80
Roland	41	65	Fostex	51	81
Korg	42	66	Zoom	52	82
Yamaha	43	67	Midori Electronics	53	83
Casio	44	68	Matsushita Comms	54	84
	45	69	Suzuki Musical Inst	55	85
Kamiya Studio	46	70		56	86
Akai	47	71		57	87
Japan Victor	48	72		58	88
Meisosha	49	73		59	89
Hoshino Gakki	4A	74		5A	90
Fujitsu Elect	4B	75		5B	91
Sony	4C	76		5C	92
Nisshin Onpa	4D	77		5D	93
TEAC Corp.	4E	78		5E	94
System Product	4F	79		5F	95

Universal System Exclusive Real-time (7F) ID numbers

Sub ID 1	Sub ID 2	Function
00		Undefined
01		MIDI Time Code
	01	full message
	02	user bits
02		MIDI Show Control (MSC)
	00	MSC extensions
	01	general lighting
	02	moving lights
	03	colour changers
	04	strobes
	05	lasers
	06	chasers
	07	
	08	
	09	
	0A	
	0B	
	0C	
	0D	
	0E	
	0F	
	10	general sound

Sub ID 1	Sub ID 2	Function
	11	music
	12	CD players
	13	EPROM play-back
	14	audio tape machines
	15	intercoms
	16	amplifiers
	17	audio effects devices
	18	equalisers
	19	
	0A	
	20	general machinery
	21	rigging
	22	flys
	23	lifts
	24	turntables
	25	trusses
	26	robots
	27	animation
	28	floats
	29	breakaways
	2A	barges
	30	general video
	31	video tape machines
	32	video cassette machine
	33	video disc players
	34	video switchers
	35	video effects
	36	video character generators
	37	video still stores
	38	video monitors
	39	
	3A	
	40	general projection
	41	film projectors
	42	slide projectors
	43	video projectors
	44	dissolvers
	45	shutter controls
	46	
	47	
	48	
	49	
	4A	
	50	general process control
	51	hydraulic oil
	52	water
	53	carbon dioxide
	54	compressed air
	55	natural gas
	56	fog
	57	smoke
	58	cracked haze
	59	
	5A	
	60	general pyrotechnics
	61	fireworks
	62	explosions
	63	flame
	64	smoke pots

Sub ID 1	*Sub ID 2*	*Function*	
	65		
	66		
	67		
	68		
	69		
	6A		
	7F	global – all devices	
03		Notation Information	
	01	bar number	
	02	time signature – immediate	
	03	time signature – delayed	
04		Device control	
	01	master volume	
	02	master balance	
05		Realtime MTC cueing	
	00	special	
	01	punch-in point	
	02	punch-out point	
	03	reserved	
	04	reserved	
	05	event start point	
	06	event stop point	
	07	event start plus extra info	
	08	event stop plus extra info	
	09	reserved	
	0A	reserved	
	0B	cue points	
	0C	cue point plus extra info	
	0D	reserved	
	0E	event name plus extra info	
06		MIDI Machine Control commands. Most functions (except play) exit from record rehearse.	
	00	reserved for extensions	
	01	stop	
	02	play (immediate)	
	03	deferred play (wait for locate)	
	04	fast forward	
	05	rewind	
	06	record strobe (record/rehearse toggle)	
	07	record exit	
	08	record pause	
	09	pause	
	0A	eject (or end of reel)	
	0B	chase (chase lock enable)	
	0C	command error reset (required after an error to continue)	
	0D	MMC reset (resort to power up conditions)	
	0E		
	0F		
		(# of data bytes to follow)	
	40	n	write (loads data in to an info field – count, name, data)
	41	n	masked write (to address specific bytes only – count, name, byte no., mask (1s permit), new data.)
	42	n	read requests info in field – count, name.
	43	n	update (to update field info – re-transmit internal update list)
	44	n	locate (locate timecode either "00 GP08" or "01 hr mm ss fr sf")
	45	3	enter variable play speed of (3 bytes – sh sm sl)

Sub ID 1	Sub ID 2	Function
46	3	search mode at speed of sh sm sl with monitoring.
47	3	shuttle (as search but without monitoring)
48	1	step to 0dss ssss (where d = sign – 1 reverse)
49	1	assign system master of device ID now sent
4A	1	generator command. 00 = stop, 01 = run, 0 = copy/jam
4B	1	produce MTC command. 00 = off, 02 = follow TC defined by MTC info field
4C	2	move information from one field to another – 4C, count, destination, source
4D	3	add info fields – 4D, count, destination, source 1, source 2
4E	3	subtract (as above but subtract fields)
4F	1	drop frame adjust (convert field from 30 frame to drop frame format)
50	n	procedure – define a set of procedures followed by sub id and procedure name. 00 = assemble the following as NAME as a procedure 01 = delete procedure 02 = set name of procedure to appear after next read of response field 03 = execute this procedure
51	n	define event is 51 followed by type 00. Format is 51 type event flag's source name command where event = event name (00-7E) and flags = 0d0s00tt d = 0 for delete, 1 to remain s = 0 for trigger when at speed, 1 for anytime tt = 00 for trigger when forwards, 01 when in reverse,10 when moving in either direction. Source = info field name for TC source 00 = extensions, 01 = selected TC, 02 = selected master, 06 = generator TC, 07 = MTC name = field name for trigger time. 00 = reserved, 08 is GP0, 09 is GP1, 0A is GP2, 0B is GP3... command = any single command plus data or procedure Other types are 51 followed by: 01 = delete 02 = set 03 = test (trigger without deletion). Format is 51 count type event_name (00-7E)
52	n	group commands. 52 followed by type 00 is define device. 52 count 00 group_no device_IDs_to_include 01 is dis-assign (as above)
53	n	command segment – allows a command longer than 48 byte maximum to be sent in segments. 53 count 0snnnnnn where s = 1 for first segment, 0 for subsequent. nnnnnn = segment number descending order
54	3	deferred variable play. As 45 except waits for locate
55	3	record strobe variable. Record/rehearse toggle for variable play speed
56		
57		
58		
59		
5A		
7C		wait (F0 7F ID mcr 7F F7)

Sub ID 1	Sub ID 2	Function	
	7F	resume (after a wait)	
07		MIDI Machine Control responses (# of data bytes to follow)	
	00	5	reserved for extensions
	01	5	selected time code – hh mm ss ff sf
	02	5	selected master code to chase – hh mm ss ff sf
	03	5	requested TC offset. (non drop frame) hh mm ss ff sf
	04	5	actual TC offset. non drop frame, Selected minus master
	05	5	lock deviation. Selected TC minus master TC minus required offset
	06	5	generator time code (current value) – hh mm ss ff sf
	07	5	MIDI Time Code input (most recent MTC value received)
	08	5	gp0/locate point – hh mm ss ff sf
	09	5	gp1
	0A	5	gp2
	0B	5	gp3
	0C	5	gp4
	0D	5	gp5
	0E	5	gp6
	0F	5	gp7
	21-2F	2	short form versions of 01-0F
	40	n	signature. Bitmapped response to all commands. 1 for supported
	41	1	update rate, minimum between tx as a 7-bit frame count
	42	n	response error. A group of unsupported requests sent once
	43	n	command error. Bitmap of error response. 43 count flags level error_code count offset string where error_code is:
			01 receive buffer overflow
			02 SysEx length error
			03 command count error
			04 info field error
			05 illegal group name
			06 illegal procedure name
			07 illegal event name
			08 illegal name extension
			09 segmentation error
			20 update list overflow
			21 group buffer overflow
			22 undefined procedure
			23 procedure buffer overflow
			24 undefined event
			25 event buffer overflow
			26 blank time code
			40 unsupported command
			41 unrecognised sub command (type)
			42 unrecognised command data
			43 unsupported info field – data
			44 unsupported info field – procedure
			45 event source unavailable
			46 nested procedure
			47 recursive procedure
			48 nested event
			49 procedure with event error

Sub ID 1	Sub ID 2	Function
		60 write to unsupported field 61 write tor read only field 62 unrecognised info field during write-data 63 unsupported info field name during write-data
44	1	command error level. ignore errors below set level, 44 01 level
45	1	time code standard used, 45 01 type where type is 00 = 24, 01 = 25, 10 = 30df, 11 = 30
46	1	selected TC source for info field, 46 01 id where id is 00 = LTC, 01 = VITC, 02 = tape counter (tacho), 04 = auto
47	9	contains selected TC user bits, 47 09 (u1-u9)
48	3	motion control tally, 48 03 ms mp ss where ms is 00 = extensions, 01 = stop, 02 = play, 04 = fast forward,05 = rewind, 09 = pause, 0A = eject, 45 = varispeed play, 46 = search, 47 = shuttle, 48 = step. mp is 00 = extensions, 0B = chase, 44 = locate, 7F = none (default) ss is 0sss 0ppp where sss = mcs command success level and ppp = mcp command success as follows: 000 = transition, 001 = stopped, 010 = failure, 011 = deduced, 101 = play not resolved, 100 = active, 110 = parked.
49	3	velocity tally, 49 03 sh sm sl
4A	1	stop mode audio monitor, 4a 01 mm where mm is 00 = disable, 01 = enable, 7F = local
4B	1	fast wind modes audio monitor (as above)
4C	1	record mode, 4c 01 mm where mm is 00 = disable, 01 = record (insert), 02 = record (assemble), 04 = rehearse, 05 = record (crash/full record), 06 = rec/pause, 7F = local
4D	1	actual record status – last nibble as above
4E	n	bitmap of actual track record status. 1 = recording
4F	n	bitmap to set track record ready/enable. 1 = record
50	1	global monitor, 50 01 mm where mm is 00 = sync playback (default), 01 = input, 02 = repro playback, 7F=local
51	1	record monitor for tracks in sync mode only, 51 01 mm where mm is 00 = record only, 01 = record/non play, 02 = record/ready, 7F = local
52	n	bitmap to select/read sync playback monitor status
53	n	bitmap of select/read track input monitor. 00 = all off
54	1	step length, 54 01 sf where sf = sub frames (default f/2)
55	1	play speed reference. 00 = internal, 01 = external, 7F = local
56	1	set/read fixed speed. 3F = next lower, 41 = next higher, 40 = standard, 7F = local.
57	1	lifter defeat. 00 = no defeat, 01 = defeat, 7F = local
58	1	remote control disable. 00 = enable, 01 = disable (local), 7F = local
59	1	resolve play speed to TC. 00 = not resolved, 01 = free resolve, 7F = local
5A	1	chase mode resolve between selected and master TC. 00 = data dependent, 01 = independent (resolve)

Sub ID 1	*Sub ID 2*	*Function*	
	5B	2	generator mode command tally, 5b 02 gc ss where gc is 00 = stop, 01 = run, 02 = copy/jam and ss is 00rt0lll where r = loss of frame reference, b = loss of TC, lll = success level (001 = success, 010 = failure)
	5C	3	generator set up, 5c 03 0rrr0jjj src mode where rrr is reference for run mode. 000 = internal, 001 = external, 010 = internal drop A, 011 = internal drop B, 111 = local and jjj is reference for jam mode – 000 = TC frame edges, 001 = external, 111 = local
	5D	9	generator user bits, 5d 09 (u1-u9)
	5E	2	MTC command tally, 5e mm 0000 0lll where mm is 00 = off, 02 = follow MTC. lll is success level – 000 = transition, 001 = success, 010 = failure.
	5F	1	MTC generator set up, 5f 02 00fedcba src where f is 0 = transmit on mmc response cable, 1 = don't. e is 0 = no userbits, 1 = transmit userbits. d = fast data type. 0 = quarter frame, 1 = full MTC message. c = MTC fast tx. 0 = inhibit MTC at high speed. 1 = don't. b = MTC stop type. 0 = quarter frame messages sent, 1 = full messages sent. a = MTC stop tx. 0 = inhibit MTC in stop mode. 1 = don't
	60	n	read back procedure response. 60 count procedure (command #)
	61	n	read back event response. 61 count event flags source hhmmssffsf command
	62	n	Bitmap of track mutes. 1 = muted. 00 = all unmuted
	63	3	VITC insert enable. 63 03 cc h1 h2 where cc is 00 = disable control, 01 = enable, 7F = local. h1 = first horizontal line for VITC insertion. h2 = second horizontal line for VITC insertion
	64	n	response segment. As before.
	65	n	catastrophic failure of device. 65 count ASCII_message
	66		
	67		
	68		
	69		
	6A		
	7C	wait	
	7F	resume	
08		MIDI tuning standard	
	02	note change	

MSC commands (sub ID 3)

00	Reserved MSC extensions as defined by specific applications and manufacturers
01	
02	
03	
04	

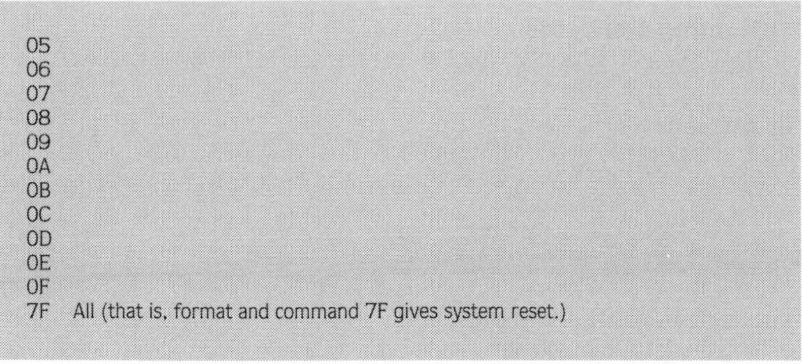

05	
06	
07	
08	
09	
0A	
0B	
0C	
0D	
0E	
0F	
7F	All (that is, format and command 7F gives system reset.)

Universal System Exclusive non Real-time (F0 7E cc id1 id2 F7) ID numbers

Sub ID 1	*Sub ID 2*	*Function*
00	–	Undefined
01	–	Sample dump header (see details below)
02	–	Sample data packet
03	–	Sample dump request (F0 7E cc 03 ll mm F7)
04		MIDI time code
	00	special
	01	punch in point
	02	punch out point
	03	delete punch in point
	04	delete punch out point
	05	event start point
	06	event stop point
	07	event start plus extra info
	08	event stop plus extra info
	09	delete event start point
	0A	delete event stop point
	0B	cue points
	0C	cue point plus extra info
	0D	delete cue point
	0E	event name plus extra info
05		sample dump extensions
	01	multiple loop points
	02	loop points request
06		General information
	01	device request
	02	device reply
07		File dump
	01	header
	02	data packet
	03	request
08		MIDI tuning standard
	00	bulk dump request
	01	bulk dump reply
09		General MIDI
	01	GM mode on
	02	GM mode off
7B	–	End of file
7C	–	Wait for sample F0 7E cc 7C pp F7
7D	–	Cancel for sample F0 7E cc 7D pp F7
7E	–	NAK for sample F0 7E cc 7E pp F7
7F	–	ACK for sample F0 7E cc 7F pp F7

MIDI dump standards

Files (MIDI data or otherwise) may also be transmitted between devices:

File dump header

FO 7E IDd 07 dt IDs type length name F7

where IDd = destination ID
07 = sub ID – file dump
dt = dump message type
01 header
02 data packet
03 request
IDs = source ID
type = four 7-bit ASCII type
length= un-encoded file length, LSB first.
name = 7-bit ASCII name terminated with F7

File dump data packets

FO 7E IDd 07 dt packet# byte_count data checksum F7

where IDd = destination ID
07 = sub ID – file dump
dt = dump message type
01 header
02 data packet
03 request
packet # = one byte packet count. Starts from 0 and resets to 0 after 7F
byte_count = one byte packet size (encoded data bytes minus one)
data = the encoded data
checksum = one byte checksum (XOR from FO)

File dump request

FO 7E IDs 07 03 IDd type name F7

where IDs = ID of source
IDd = ID of destination
type = four 7-bit ASCII bytes denoting type of file
(with recommended DOS file extension shown)
"MIDI" – MIDIfile (.MID)
"MIEX" – MIDIex file (.MEX)
"ESEQ" – ESEQ file (.ESQ)
"TEXT" – Text file (.TXT)
"BIN " – Binary file (.BIN)
"MAC " – Macintosh file (.MAC)
name = filename in 7-bit ASCII bytes terminated by F7.

File dump handshake
F0 7E IDs hm pp F7

where IDs = source ID
hm = handshake message
7B = EOF
7C = Wait
7D = Cancel
7E = NAK
7F = ACK
pp = packet number

MIDI sample dump standard
Request: F0 7E cc 03 ss ss F7

where cc = channel number
ss = requested sample number (LSB first)

Acknowledge (ACK): F0 7E cc 7F pp F7

where cc = channel number
pp = the sample packet number that was received correctly

Not-acknowledged (NAK): F0 7E cc 7E pp F7

where cc = channel number
pp = the sample packet number that was not received correctly

Cancel: F0 7E cc 7D pp F7

where cc = channel number
pp = sample packet number to abort sending

Wait: F0 7E cc 7C pp F7

where cc = channel number
pp = wait for an ack before sending further sample packets

Sample dump header: F0 7E cc 01 ss ss ee ff ff ff gg gg gg hh hh hh ii ii ii jj F7

where cc = channel number
ss = sample number (LSB first)
ee = sample bit format (8-28)
ff = sample period (1/sample rate) in nanoseconds (LSB first)
gg = sample length in words (LSB first)
hh = sustain loop start point word number (LSB first)
ii = sustain loop end point word number (LSB first)
jj = loop type (00 forward, 01 alternating)

Sample dump data packet: F0 7E cc 02 kk (120 bytes) ll F7

where cc = channel number
kk = running packet count (0-127 – restarts from 0 after 127)
ll = XOR checksum (XOR of 7E to end of data bytes)

Sample dump sequence
- Request sample dump
- Sample dump header sent from sampler
- Time out period – (two seconds)

If no response, assumes open loop system and continues
If a CANCEL is received, dump is aborted
If ACK is received, assumes closed loop system and continues

- Send data packets with ACK for each (WAIT will wait) for a closed loop system. If NAK is received, it sends the packet again

Note: The sample dump is sent in 120-byte packets to allow the system to respond to other messages in between. These packets (MSB first) form sample words, the number of which will depend on the sample format (30, 40 or 60 words).

Sample dump data packet structure

Sample bit format	Number of 7-bit words sent
1-7	one (7-bit) word
8-14	two bytes form a word
15-21	three bytes form a word
22-28	four bytes form a word

Note: each 7-bit byte is left justified. Unused bits are filled with zeros.

SMDI

There is also a system added recently that allows the transmission of MIDI sample dump information over the SCSI bus (normally used to connect hard drives).

As a parallel interface using a higher transmission rate, the SMDI protocol can provide much faster data transfer.

MIDI tuning standard

This part of the MIDI specification allows real-time sharing and changing of micro-tuning between devices, as well as real-time tuning of individual notes. Up to 128 tuning memory locations are supported with a resolution of 100 cents/2^{14} = 0.0061 cents.

A three-byte 7-bit message is used consisting of the nearest equal-tempered semitone below followed by two bytes for the fraction of cents above that semitone.

Note that 7F 7F 7F is reserved as a "no change" message.

Bulk tuning request: F0 7E ID 08 00 tt F7

where F0 7E = universal non real-time SysEx header
ID = ID of target device
08 = sub ID – MIDI tuning standard
00 = sub ID – bulk dump request
tt = tuning program number (0-127)
F7 = EOX

Bulk tuning dump: F0 7E ID 08 01 tt name (fs fm fl) checksum F7

where ID = ID of receiving device
08 = sub ID – MIDI tuning standard
01 = sub ID – bulk dump reply
tt = tuning program number (0-127)
name = 16 ASCII character tuning name
(fs = nearest semitone below in equal tempered scale
fm = tuning fraction of cent above MSB
fl = tuning fraction of cent above LSB –
repeated for each note in scale.)
checksum = XOR from 7E

Single note real-time tuning change: F0 7F ID 08 02 tt ll (kk fs fm fl) F7

where ID = target ID
08 = sub ID – MIDI tuning standard
02 = sub ID – single note change
tt = tuning program number (0-127)
ll = number of changes
(kk = MIDI key number
fs = nearest equal tempered semitone
fm = tuning fraction above MSB
fl = tuning fraction above LSB (repeated for number of changes.)
F7 = EOX

Tuning program change
It is possible to select micro-tuning programs remotely by sending a data entry followed by an increment or decrement command:

Bn 64 03 65 00 06 tt (data entry)
Bn 64 03 65 00 60 7F (data increment)
Bn 64 03 65 00 61 7F (data decrement)

where n = basic MIDI channel number
tt = tuning program number

A tuning bank change is also provided:

Bn 64 04 65 00 06 bb (data entry)
Bn 64 04 65 00 60 7F (data increment)
Bn 64 04 65 00 61 7F (data decrement)

where n = basic MIDI channel number
bb = tuning bank number

MIDI time code (MTC)
Quarter frame messages:

F1 mv MIDI time code (MTC) quarter frame message

where m = message type (0mmm), v = value

message types: 0 = frame count LS nibble
1 = frame count MS nibble
2 = second count LS nibble

3 = second count MS nibble
4 = minute count LS nibble
5 = minute count MS nibble
6 = hours count LS nibble
7 = hours count MS nibble

value types: for frames = 0S0vvvvv (0-29)
for seconds = 0Bvvvvvv (0-59)
for minutes = 0Cvvvvvv (0-59)
for hours = 0TTvvvvv (0-23) where T = frame rate type
0 (00) = 24, 1 (01) = 25, 2 (10) = 30df, 3 (11) = 30
C = 0 for non colour frame, 1 for colour frame.
S = SMPTE signed bit: 0 = +ve, 1 = -ve.
B = for MMC, a 0 indicates normal, 1 means timecode has not been loaded into this field since power up or MMC reset.

MIDI time code (MTC) quarter frame information

In addition to control functions, MTC is a way of encoding SMPTE time for direct use in a MIDI system. Eight quarter-frame messages (sent over two frames) are required to indicate the actual SMPTE position, transmitted as F1 0v to F1 7v.

Messages are sent in reverse order. These messages should not be sent during shuttle, but a full message sent when positioned. F1 0v and F1 4v must indicate actual frame boundaries. F1 0V indicates the actual instantaneous frame position in all cases.

MTC full message

An MTC full message is employed after shuttling and positioning to save clogging the data bus with continual quarter-frame messages.

The MTC full message contains the SMPTE time in one complete message and takes 10 bytes as follows:

F0 7F nn 01 si hr mn sc fr F7

where nn = channel number
01 = sub ID – MTC message
si = sub ID – 01 for full MTC message
time format hr, mn, sc, fr as per MTC quarter frame messages

Time is assumed to be running after receipt of the next quarter frame message.

MTC user bits

32 user bits can be included in a SMPTE message and can be used for reel or date identification.

They are consistent throughout the reel. These are portrayed in MTC as follows:

F0 7F nn 01 02 (u1 to u9) F7

where nn = channel number
01 = sub ID – MTC
02 = sub ID – user bits
u1 to u8 = 0000vvvv (zeros must be used as shown) to form four 8-bit characters.
u9 = 000000vv is the two binary group bit flags as defined by SMPTE.

MTC set up/cueing messages

MTC can also be used for set up and control messages:

F0 7E nn 04 si hr mn sc fr ff el em info... F7

where7E = non real-time event
nn = channel number
si = 00 for special global parameters. The special type takes the place of the event number el em as follows:

00 00 = time code offset
01 00 = enable event list
02 00 = disable event list
03 00 = clear event list
04 00 = system stop (tape end)
05 00 = event list request from SMPTE time given

01 = punch in point – event number gives track
02 = punch out point – event number gives track
03 = delete punch in point of time and event number
04 = delete punch out point of time and event number
05 = event start point. Event number refers to slave device
06 = event stop point. Event number refers to slave device
07 = event start (as above) plus extra info
08 = event stop (as above) plus extra info
09 = delete event start point
0A = delete event stop point
0B = cue points (single one shot event)
0C = cue point plus extra info
0D = delete cue point
0E = event name plus extra info

hr to fr = time format as described previously
ff = sub frames 0-99 (1/100th of a frame) – 0vvvvvvv
el = LSB of event number
em = MSB of event number
info... = additional information sent as nibblized MIDI data stream with LS nibble first, except 0E event name, sent in nibblized ASCII codes LS nibble first. (for example, 7F is sent as 0F 07)

MTC Real-time cueing

F0 7F ID 05 S2 el em (info) F7

where F0 = start of System Exclusive
7F = universal real-time SysEx header
ID = target device
05 = sub ID – MTC cueing messages
S2 = event type

00 = special event (04 00 = system stop)
01 = punch in points
02 = punch out points
03 = reserved
04 = reserved

S2 = event type (cont)

05 = event start point
06 = event stop point
07 = event start extra info
08 = event stop extra info
09 = reserved
0A = reserved
0B = cue points
0C = cue points extra info
0D = reserved
0E = event name extra info

el em = event number, LSB first then MSB
info = nibblized as per MTC specification
F7 = EOX

MIDI machine control (MMC)

MMC is intended to link MIDI equipment with more traditional equipment such as audio and video tape machines and multimedia computer devices. MMC is based on the universal real-time System Exclusive protocol using sub ID 06.

The system can be used as an open or closed loop type, the latter expecting a response from a command, while the former has to assume that it has happened.

The general format is as follows:

F0 7F ID 06 (commands or responses) (count) (data) F7

where ID = device ID (7F for all)
06 = MMC sub ID
commands and responses = rx and tx codes
count = length of data to follow where implemented
data = must be less than 48 bytes long

See section on universal real time codes for details of commands and responses.

MIDI machine control (MMC) time references

MTC often has a reference to SMPTE times and, like the MSC implementation, there are two modes of coding of the sub frames: frame and status. These modes are signalled by the third bit of the frame byte – 0 for subframes, 1 for status.

Frame mode uses sub frame accuracy (1/100th of a frame). Status mode puts extra information in the sub frame section (identical to MSC implementation) as follows:

0 e i v c 0 0 0

(note zeros must be used as shown.)

where e = 0 for normal time code, 1 for control/tach generated
i = 0 for valid, 1 of invalid/error
v = 0 for no field info, 1 for first frame in 4/8 field sequence
c = 0 for time code read, 1 for time coded never read

MMC short time code

To save MIDI bandwidth, a short time code message can also be used containing only frame and sub frame information (as other changes only happen every second).

This format is identical to the full format, except that it contains only frame and sub frame information.

MMC other

There are other protocols for user bits and variable speed encoding, but these are beyond the scope of this book. Refer to the full 100-page MMC documentation from the IMA (address on page 134) for more details if necessary.

MMC commands

The MTC protocol generally works on a system of commands (06) and responses (07), which break down into subsets of message types as follows: communication, control, event, generator, I/O, sync, math, MTC, procedure, time. See the section on real-time System Exclusive (page 16) for further details of these commands and responses.

MMC and MTC cueing comparison

In the following table we can see where the two protocols overlap and differ:

MMC	*MTC*
MMC events only trigger other MMC commands	MTC events trigger event sequences, cues and track punch in/out
Events are defined by the event command	Events are defined by MTC set-up messages
Each event is unique and identified by a 7-bit name	The same event number can be triggered at different times and is selected by a combination of trigger time and event number
The source of the time code stream is specified with each event	The time code source is not specified and assumed to be MTC
Additional flags are contained in events to denote triggering in relation to play speed and direction	No motion restrictions are specified
For compatibility with the ESbus systems, events may be deleted after triggering	Events are not deleted after triggering
No global enable/disable event is defined	Event enable/disable affects event status without affecting the list itself
Error trapping is used to check for illegal event names and undefined events at the time of trigger	No error trapping is used

MIDI show control (MSC)

MSC is intended to control dedicated equipment in theatre, live performance, multimedia and audio visual applications. MSC is based on the universal real-time System Exclusive format, using sub ID number 1 (02 hex). The general format is as follows:

F0 7F ID 02 cmd_format cmd data F7

where ID = device ID (00-6F = individual, 7F = all, 70-7E = groups 1-15)

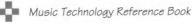

02 = MSC sub ID
cmd_format = 01-7F. 00 is reserved for future extensions
cmd = 01-7F. 00 is reserved for future extensions
data is in machine-specific format but less than 128 bytes long

See section on real-time System Exclusive controllers (page 16) for details of specific cmd_format and command codes.

MSC cue numbers
When cue numbers are sent as data, additional data fields may be specified (Q_list and Q_path) each delimited by 00. These data fields contain numbers 0-9 represented by 30H-39H and a decimal point 2E used to delineate sections.

MSC time code references
Time information can also be included in MSC commands using the same protocol as MTC set-up messages, with a few additions. There are two modes: frame mode is as MTC using sub frame (1/100th frame) accuracy; status mode uses status data in place of the sub frame information. This mode is signalled by the third bit of the frame value – 0 = sub frames, 1 = status.

If the mode is status, then the sub frame value has the following significance:

0 e i v c 0 0 0

(Note zeros must be used as shown.)

where e = 0 for normal time code, 1 for control/tach generated
i = 0 for valid, 1 of invalid/error
v = 0 for no field info, 1 for first frame in 4/8 field sequence
c = 0 for time code read, 1 for time code never read

MSC safety information
It will be seen that MIDI can be used to control potentially dangerous systems and adequate manual and automatic safety cut out precautions must be taken. However it is envisaged that the repeatability and accuracy of such automation, given the correct safety conditions, will produce more elaborate and safe phenomena. The digital communication benefits to control such devices should also prove more reliable.

MSC minimum command sets
A range of minimum commands have been suggested. After the command, a cue number, list and path may be sent (delineated with zero, zero). If no cue number is specified, the next cue or all devices respond.

General

Hex	*Command*	*Data bytes*	*Function*
00	extensions		
01	GO	variable	starts a transition or fade to on
02	STOP	variable	stops a transition or fade
03	RESUME	variable	resumes transitions from last point
04	TIMED GO	variable	followed by time in hh mm ss ff sf and then cue list

Hex	Command	Data bytes	Function
05	LOAD	variable	places a cue in standby mode in preparation
06	SET	4 or 9	sets a device parameter by value or time. 06 lc mc hr mm ss fr sf where lc = lSB control number and mc = msb control number
07	FIRE	1	followed by preprogrammed macro number
08	ALL_OFF	0	turns all functions and outputs off but leaves settings
09	RESTORE	0	returns operating state to previous condition
0A	RESET	0	initialises to power up conditions
0B	GO_OFF	variable	starts a transition of fade to off

Sound (all have number of data bytes as variable)

Hex	Command	Function
10	go/jam clock	starts a transition and forces time to that of cue
11	standby_+	next cue to standby
12	standby_–	previous cue to standby
13	sequence_+	next parent cue to standby
14	sequence_–	previous parent cue to standby
15	start_clock	starts or continues clock count
16	stop_clock	stops clock count
17	zero_clock	resets clock to zero
18	set_clock	sets clock to following time sent
19	MTC chase on	sets clock to incoming MTC time
1A	MTC chase off	clock stops chasing MTC, but continues in state
1B	open cue list	activates cue list for access
1C	close cue list	closes and removes cue list access
1D	open cue path	followed by cue_path, makes it available
1E	close cue path	followed by cue_path closes cue path.
1F	–	

Note: If a cue number is sent, command affects only that cue or loads next/previous cue as applicable. If no cue number is sent, command affects all cues or prepares next available.

General MIDI Level 1

General MIDI may be turned on and off remotely on some devices as follows:

F0 7E ID 09 01 F7 (General MIDI mode on)
F0 7E ID 09 02 F7 (General MIDI mode off)

General MIDI sound grouping for all MIDI channels except 10

1-8	pianos	65-72	reed
9-16	chromatic percussion	73-80	pipe
17-24	organ	81-88	synth lead
25-32	guitar	89-96	synth pad
33-40	bass	97-104	synth effects
41-48	strings	105-112	ethnic
49-56	ensemble	113-120	percussive
57-64	brass	121-128	sound effects

General MIDI sound voicing

Prog	Voice	Prog	Voice	Prog	Voice
1	acoustic grand piano	44	contrabass	87	lead 7 fifths
2	bright acoustic piano	45	tremolo strings	88	lead 8 bass + lead
3	electric grand piano	46	pizzicato strings	89	pad 1 new age
4	honky tonk piano	47	orchestral harp	90	pad 2 warm
5	electric piano 1	48	timpani	91	pad 3 polysynth
6	electric piano 2	49	string ensemble 1	92	pad 4 choir
7	harpsichord	50	string ensemble 2	93	pad 5 bowed
8	clavi	51	synth strings 1	94	pad 6 metallic
9	celesta	52	synth strings 2	95	pad 7 halo
10	glockenspiel	53	choir aahs	96	pad 8 sweep
11	music box	54	voice oohs	97	fx 1 rain
12	vibraphone	55	synth voice	98	fx 2 soundtrack
13	marimba	56	orchestra hit	99	fx 3 crystal
14	xylophone	57	trumpet	100	fx 4 atmosphere
15	tubular bells	58	trombone	101	fx 5 brightness
16	dulcimer	59	tuba	102	fx 6 goblins
17	drawbar organ	60	muted trumpet	103	fx 7 echoes
18	percussive organ	61	French horn	104	fx 8 sci-fi
19	rock organ	62	brass section	105	sitar
20	church organ	63	synth brass 1	106	banjo
21	reed organ	64	synth brass 2	107	shamisen
22	accordion	65	soprano sax	108	koto
23	harmonica	66	alto sax	109	kalimba
24	tango accordion	67	tenor sax	110	bagpipe
25	acoustic guitar nylon	68	baritone sax	111	fiddle
26	acoustic guitar steel	69	oboe	112	shanai
27	electric guitar jazz	70	English horn	113	tinkle bell
28	electric guitar clean	71	bassoon	114	agogo
29	electric guitar muted	72	clarinet	115	steel drums
30	overdriven guitar	73	piccolo	116	woodblock
31	distorted guitar	74	flute	117	taiko drum
32	guitar harmonics	75	recorder	118	melodic tom
33	acoustic bass	76	pan flute	119	synth drum
34	electric bass finger	77	blown bottle	120	reverse cymbal
35	electric bass pick	78	shakuhachi	121	guitar fret noise
36	fretless bass	79	whistle	122	breath noise
37	slap bass 1	80	ocarina	123	seashore
38	slap bass 2	81	lead 1 square	124	bird tweet
39	synth bass 1	82	lead 2 sawtooth	125	telephone ring
40	synth bass 2	83	lead 3 calliope	126	helicopter
41	violin	84	lead 4 chiff	127	applause
42	viola	85	lead 5 charang	128	gunshot
43	cello	86	lead 6 voice		

General MIDI drum map (MIDI channel 10)

Note	No	Sound	Note	No	Sound	Note	No	Sound
C-2	0		G1	43	High floor tom	D5	86	
C#-2	1		G#1	44	Pedal high hat	D#5	87	
D-2	2		A1	45	Low tom	E5	88	
D#-2	3		A#1	46	Open high hat	F5	89	
E-2	4		B1	47	Low mid tom	F#5	90	
F-2	5		C2	48	High mid tom	G5	91	
F#-2	6		C#2	49	Crash cymbal 1	G#5	92	
G-2	7		D2	50	High tom	A5	93	
G#-2	8		D#2	51	Ride cymbal	A#5	94	
A-2	9		E2	52	Chinese cymbal	B5	95	
A#-2	10		F2	53	Ride bell	C6	96	
B-2	11		F#2	54	Tambourine	C#6	97	
C-1	12		G2	55	Splash cymbal	D6	98	
C#-1	13		G#2	56	Cowbell	D#6	99	
D-1	14		A2	57	Crash cymbal 2	E6	100	
D#-1	15		A#2	58	Vibraslap	F6	101	
E-1	16		B2	59	Ride cymbal 2	F#6	102	
F-1	17		C3	60	Hi bongo	G6	103	
F#-1	18		C#3	61	Low bongo	G#6	104	
G-1	19		D3	62	Muted hi conga	A6	105	
G#-1	20		D#3	63	Open hi conga	A#6	106	
A-1	21		E3	64	Low conga	B6	107	
A#-1	22		F3	65	High timbale	C7	108	
B-1	23		F#3	66	Low timbale	C#7	109	
C0	24		G3	67	High agogo	D7	110	
C#0	25		G#3	68	Low agogo	D#7	111	
D0	26		A3	69	Cabasa	E7	112	
D#0	27		A#3	70	Maracas	F7	113	
E0	28		B3	71	Short whistle	F#7	114	
F0	29		C4	72	Long whistle	G7	115	
F#0	30		C#4	73	Short guiro	G#7	116	
G0	31		D4	74	Long guiro	A7	117	
G#0	32		D#4	75	Claves	A#7	118	
A0	33		E4	76	Hi wood block	B7	119	
A#0	34		F4	77	Low wood block	C8	120	
B0	35	Acoustic bass drum	F#4	78	Muted cuica	C#8	121	
C1	36	Bass drum 1	G4	79	Open cuica	D8	122	
C#1	37	Side stick	G#4	80	Muted triangle	D#8	123	
D1	38	Acoustic snare	A4	81	Open triangle	E8	124	
D#1	39	Hand clap	A#4	82		F8	125	
E1	40	Electronic snare	B4	83		F#8	126	
F1	41	Low floor tom	C5	84		G8	127	
F#1	42	Closed high hat	C#5	85		G#8	128	

System expansion

In any MIDI system there can be a number of problems to overcome and some devices can be used to solve them:

MIDI Thru

Firstly, it is not recommended that more than three MIDI units are daisy-chained together using the Thru to In type connection. Also, some units may not feature a MIDI Thru connector (although these can go last in the chain if necessary). To overcome this, a MIDI Thru box can be used, which provides a parallel buffer.

MIDI switchers

With most systems there is a need for two-way communication between devices at different times – for instance, when editing a sound module via computer. In this case, a simple MIDI switcher can reconnect the various MIDI Outs of your equipment to the computer's MIDI In as required so saving time (and confusion) re-patching.

These devices are also useful when working with multiple controllers such as keyboard, drum pad and MIDI guitar. As these are not used simultaneously, they can be switched. If simultaneous use is required (such as when jamming with other MIDI musicians), a MIDI merge box will be required.

MIDI merge

A MIDI merge box is used to combine two MIDI Outs for simultaneous use. There are few needs for this that can't be solved with a simple MIDI switcher, other than when jamming with other MIDI musicians simultaneously.

These devices need to be intelligent to handle the two data streams, otherwise garbled messages can result. It should be remembered that MIDI is a serial data stream using a set of related MIDI bytes and that these cannot just be mixed using a parallel strip. In particular, the treatment of MIDI clock, System Exclusive messages, MIDI controllers and general priorities can cause many problems.

MIDI patchbays

An alternative to the simple MIDI switcher is the MIDI patchbay, an active device offering MIDI switching and thru facilities. They often include MIDI merging and MIDI filtering and processing options as well as the ability to be MIDI controlled themselves through patch changes. Some MIDI patchbays offer a manual physical patching system using patch chords, but the electronic options are usually more effective.

MIDI labelling

As with any system, it is important to label all leads and terminal points to save confusion at a later date.

MIDI earthing

MIDI should provide an optically isolated means of interconnection, but some problems in the past have been traced to a remaining earth connection on the centre pin or the chassis. This aids electrical screening which works most effectively with a complete circuit. However in practice, a single connection at one end only can suffice if required at all. An adaptor with this pin removed can help to trace these problems quickly.

MIDI synchronisation

It is possible for a number of devices to be synchronised together. One system is that of MIDI clock and song pointer, with one device acting as the master and the rest as slaves.

Firstly, a song position pointer should be sent. Each pointer relates to 6 MIDI clocks, a 16th note as the MIDI clock rate is defined as 24ppqn (pulses per quarter note). Therefore the receiving device (sequencer) should multiply the pointer figure by 6 to determine the result.

If the receiving device uses a greater resolution than this, a sequencer must multiply the pointer figure by 6 and then by its internal time base. For instance, SPP = 100: 100 x 6 = 600 MIDI clocks into the song. But if sequencer resolution is 96ppqn then there are 96/24 internal ticks per quarter note = 4. Therefore 600 x 4 = 2,400 ticks into the sequence.

A song continue message can then be sent (a Start command would default the SPP to 0). On receipt of the next clock pulse (F8) the receiver should start playback.

Any clock pulses received between the SPP and before starting should be included in the position calculation.

MTC synchronisation

MTC (MIDI time code) is a way of encoding SMPTE time code (which is an audio signal) for use in a MIDI system. There is also provision for commands to be used in the MTC protocol – see the relevant section for more details.

The most important aspect of MTC is that it is an intelligent system that updates its current position. So even if some timing information is missing or corrupted, the system can chase to the correct position a short time later.

In addition to the SMPTE location, quarter frame messages can also be sent – 4 every 1/25 second (at 25 fps) = every 10ms.

SMPTE

SMPTE time code is a special audio signal used to encode a tape machine (audio or video) with a time reference. This time reference is in the form of a 24-hour clock, but also includes a frame division in addition to seconds. The number of frames used is dependent on the application and country of usage as follows:

Usage and country	*Frame rate per second*	*Time per frame*
UK and European film industry	24	41.66ms
UK and European video and TV	25	40.00ms
USA B/W TV and video	30	33.33ms
USA colour TV and video	30 drop frame (29.97 approx.)	33.37ms

A SMPTE synchroniser generates and records the SMPTE audio signal onto the highest edge track of the tape recorder (usually between -7 and -3 VU). On playback, the time code is converted into MIDI timing information (MIDI clock and song pointer) using an internal tempo map that is programmed to contain the song start position, tempo, time signature and any changes. Some devices do this by "hearing" the song once using MIDI timing information from the sequencer. System Exclusive programming over MIDI is another option as are buttons on the unit itself.

The latest trend is for SMPTE to MTC synchronisers that convert the audio SMPTE time code into MTC, its MIDI counterpart, which is then used by the sequencer. The advantage of this system is that the tempo map information in the sequencer can be used directly (and is saved with each song automatically). On a computer-based sequencer, this can allow visual programming and interpretation of the tempo map.

The so called EBU (European Broadcast Union) SMPTE time code standard is a special version of the 25 fps standard, with particular tolerances specified for waveform shape and timing. For most purposes, these differences can be ignored.

Absolute timing reference

There can be compatibility problems between SMPTE synchronisers (particularly from those of different manufacturers) owing to the absolute timing reference used. For instance, is 120 BPM equal to 120.001 or 119.944? Even with these crystal-locked devices, such errors can be significant especially over longer periods. There isn't an easy solution to this problem, although it is possible to calculate a new tempo or find it empirically. It could also be suggested that a more common reference source of SMPTE could be used – DSP-generated or perhaps an audio sample CD.

FSK devices

Some manufacturers have devised their own synchronisation codes using FSK coding (frequency shift keying). These generally have to have their tempo map programmed when laying the code and cannot be altered afterwards. Although generally cheaper than their SMPTE counterparts, there is no guarantee of any exchangeability between devices or systems, so it is recommended that these be avoided in favour of SMPTE devices.

Standard MIDI files

A MIDI file is a standard way of exchanging MIDI sequence data through a disk file. Tempos, time signature information and track names are also included. The Running Status protocol is used and SysEx messages can also be embedded.

There are three MIDI file formats as follows:

Format	*Description*
0	one multi-channel track (no. of tracks is always 1)
1	one or more simultaneous tracks (linear)
2	one or more sequentially independent track patterns

The data is sent in "chunks" headed by a four-byte (character) ASCII description, followed by a byte length and then a four-byte value (32-bit). There are two types of chunk: header (MThd) and track (MTrk). The format for the header is:

Header length format no_of_tracks ppq_clock_division

If bit 15 of ppq_clock_division is 1 then ppq is in SMPTE time format instead – see the full MIDI Specification for further details.

The format for a track chunk is essentially the MIDI data preceded by a delta time (a variable length quantity) which states when it occurs in ticks after the previous event. Simultaneous events have a delta time of 0. The format for the track chunk is:

Header length (delta_time event)...

Example format 1:

4D 54 68 64	MThd
00 00 00 06	this chunk length
00 01	MIDI file format 1

00 02	two tracks
00 60	96ppqn
4D 54 72 6B	MTrk
00 00 00 1A	chunk length (26 bytes)
FF 58 04 04 02 18 08	time sig of 4/4
FF 51 03 07 A1 20	tempo
00 C0 05	patch change to 6
00 90 3C 64	Note On C3 (60) channel 1, velocity 100
60 90 60 00	Note Off C3, quarter note later
83 00	end of track
4D 54 72 6B	MTrk
00 00 00 0E	chunk length (14 bytes)
00 C0 0A	patch change to 11
00 91 40 64	Note On E3 (64) channel 2, velocity 100
83 00 90 60 00	Note Off E3, one bar later
83 00	end of track
4D 54 72 6B	MTrk
00 00 00 12	chunk length (18 bytes)
00 91 4C 60	half Note On E4 (76) channel 2, velocity 96
60 90 45 30	then a 1/4 note later a quarter note on A4 (69) channel 1, velocity 48
60 91 4C 00	Note Off E4
00 90 60 00	Note Off A4
83 00	end of track

Non MIDI events (called meta events) can also be sent in the format:

FF type_no length info

Currently defined type_no include:

00 = sequence number
01 = ASCII text message (lyric...)
02 = copyright notice including "©"
03 = sequence/track name
04 = instrument name
05 = lyric
06 = song marker
07 = cue point

20 01 cc = MIDI channel reference for SysEx and meta events
2F 00 = end of track (mandatory)
51 03 tttttt = set tempo (in µs/ppqn)
54 05 hh mm ss ff sf = SMPTE offset
58 04 nn dd cc bb = time signature where nn and dd = time sig (Note: dd is expressed as a power of two. For instance, for 6/8 time – 8 is the third power of 2, giving 06 03.)
cc = number of MIDI clicks per metronome beat
bb = number of notated 32nd notes in a quarter note
59 02 sf kk = key signature, where sf = no. of sharps (+) or flats (–) and kk is major (0) or minor (1) key
7F length data = sequencer specific (where the first byte/s of data is the manufacturer's ID)

Variable length quantities

One important aspect of MIDI files is the need for variable length values, which means that the number of bytes used to represent a value cannot be defined. To overcome this, each value is sent in a number of bytes (up to a maximum of a 32-bit number) but only the last data byte has bit 7 set to 1; all other bytes have bit 7 set to 0. It is necessary to look for this bit to determine if it is the last byte of a value.

MIDI troubleshooting

The most common causes for MIDI problems are as follows:

- MIDI channels between transmitter and receiver different
- Audio leads not connected or audio volume down
- MIDI device in omni mode, hence responding to all MIDI messages
- MIDI device is in wrong mode
- All MIDI channels set to same sound – particularly home keyboards that require a MIDI patch change sent down each MIDI channel and can't be changed from front panel
- Keyboard transmits on more than one MIDI channel at once – especially home organs and pianos
- Controller messages (like sustain) affecting devices from another sequencer track
- Device cannot use Running Status (check sequencer options)
- Notes left hanging caused by slow opto-isolators/buffering in device – put at end of chain or use MIDI Thrus or extra MIDI ports.

MIDI planning

Although MIDI is a very open-ended system with almost endless flexibility, this can also be its downfall. It is important in a MIDI system to standardise on a method of working. This could include using a consistent drum map, keeping certain tracks associated with certain MIDI channels and laying out sounds in a synthesiser's memory in a consistent way.

An empty song template is an excellent idea as is labelling all tracks with sound name information. It is very easy to upgrade a system and then not be able to play back old songs easily through lack of labelling. Notes should also be taken and saved with the song file on equipment and sound usage, lyrics, synchronisation and mixing notes. It is also very important to keep back-up files of any important data.

Keep documentation that will allow a third party to pick up where you left off. This is particularly important for commercial studios and writing teams.

MIDI PLANNER

Please photocopy and use this planner

Name ______________________ *Date* ____________

Site address ______________________

____

____

____

Project ______________________

Artist ______________________

Composer ______________________

Engineer ______________________

Producer ______________________

Programmer ______________________

Session people ______________________ ______________________

______________________ ______________________

______________________ ______________________

______________________ ______________________

______________________ ______________________

Production notes

Equipment list

		Sound bank	*Stored in memory/file on disk*
Drums			
Sampler			
Synth 1			
Synth 2			
Synth 3			
Synth 4			
Synth 5			

MIDI Planner (cont)

Project ______________________________

Port A

MIDI channel	*Sound name*	*Instrument*	*Sep o/ps*	*Patch*	*Notes (mixer channel/patchbay)*
1					
2					
3					
4					
5					
6					
7					
8					
9					
10					
11					
12					
13					
14					
15					
16					

Port B

MIDI channel	*Sound name*	*Instrument*	*Sep o/ps*	*Patch*	*Notes (mixer channel/patchbay)*
1					
2					
3					
4					
5					
6					
7					
8					
9					
10					
11					
12					
13					
14					
15					
16					

MIDI Planner (cont)

Project ____________

Drum map

Instrument	*Note no/channel*	*Remapping*	*Tuning/outputs*
kick 1			
kick 2			
kick 3			
kick 4			
snare 1			
snare 2			
snare 3			
snare 4			
side stick			
rim shot			
electronic snare			
hand clap			
closed high hat			
open high hat			
pedal high hat			
low floor tom			
low tom			
low mid tom			
high floor tom			
high mid tom			
high tom			
crash cymbal 1			
crash cymbal 2			
ride cymbal 1			
ride cymbal 2			
splash cymbal			
chinese cymbal			
ride bell			
tambourine			
cowbell			
vibraslap			
high bongo			

MIDI Planner (cont)

Project ______________________

low bongo			
muted hi conga			
open hi conga			
low conga			
high timbale			
low timbale			
high agogo			
low agogo			
cabasa			
maracas			
short whistle			
long whistle			
short guiro			
long guiro			
claves			
high wood block			
low wood block			
muted cuica			
open cuica			
muted triangle			
open triangle			

Information	*Files/storage*	*Back-up location*
Sequencer		
Synth sounds		
Sampler		
Lyrics		
Drum patterns		
Invoice		
Statement		
Audio DAT		
Audio cassette		
Audio multi-track		
Hard disk/backup		

2 Synthesis and sequencing

Types of synthesis

There are three main categories of synthesis:

- *Subtractive*, where a rich source is filtered and enveloped to produce the desired result.
- *Additive*, where component waveforms (usually pure sine waves) are added together (each with its own amplitude envelope) to produce the composite sound.
- *Direct*, such as FM and sample based.

With FM (patented by Yamaha), an oscillator (*modulator*) is used to frequency modulate another oscillator (*carrier*), producing a type of ring modulated result containing new frequencies. Each oscillator is called a *partial* and the arrangement (serial/parallel connections) is called an *algorithm*.

With sample-based synthesis, an actual recording of a sound is held digitally and then further modified, usually with a subtractive method.

Synthesis structure

Subtractive

Firstly, an oscillator waveshape that complements the sound is chosen and has filter and amplitude envelopes applied to it. A pitch envelope may need to be added to simulate an effect (like the sharp attack of brass). Finally, any performance factors are added such as velocity and brightness changes over keyboard ranges (called scaling).

Additive

With additive synthesis, the opposite approach is taken. Sounds are built from a large number of simple sine wave components (minimum 32, ideally 256), each with its own envelope generator. With Fourier analysis, it can be shown that all sounds can be broken down into sine wave components; the reverse is true, although a little unwieldy.

Direct

FM (frequency modulation) is a patent owned by Yamaha, although designed originally in a British university. Two (or more) oscillators (operators in Yamaha terms) interact to create new frequencies, much like ring modulation, but with the addition of the original and other harmonics. Oscillators are employed in two states depending on the algorithm. A carrier contributes its output to the audio directly, whereas a modulator changes the output of any carrier it is modulating.

Sample based

With sample-based synthesis, an actual digital recording (sample) of a sound is made. This may then be processed further, usually with some subtractive synthesis features, although there is little doubt that other synthesis functions will be introduced in the near future, such as re-synthesis (see Chapter 3 on Sampling (page 60) for more details).

Synthesis in detail

Subtractive synthesis

Each basic type of subtractive waveform has its own character. The sawtooth wave is quite bright and can be used for brass, strings (with lower VCF), guitar and harmonica. The square wave has a hollow, bright sound and can be used for clarinet, organ and harp-type sounds. The pulse waveform is quite thin as it has a weak fundamental, and resembles instruments with a small resonator body such as oboe, electric piano, koto, sitar and vibraphone. The sine and triangle waves are very pure (with no harmonics in sine and only a few in triangle) and are used for the likes of whistle and recorder.

Noise is quite an important sound source. Noise is an un-pitched sound comprising many random frequencies. It can be used as a basis for sound effects and percussion as well as adding realism, such as breath noise, to a sound. White noise consists of all frequencies at equal strengths and appears as an energetic high-pitched hissing sound, like tape hiss. Pink noise has a deeper passive sound (like rain) and consists of frequencies of equal strength in each octave band. Pink noise can largely be derived by filtering white noise.

With resonance, a peak is placed near the cut-off point of the filter to boost harmonics. This gives a very characteristic sound, essential to many bass and vocal timbres. It also helps to add movement in a sound if it is modulated, such as with LFO or velocity.

With ring modulation, two oscillators are used: one frequency modulates the other to produce sum and difference frequencies, while removing most of the original fundamentals. This gives it an un-pitched effect useful for gong and bell sounds and, if used more subtly, harp, sax, koto and guitar-type sounds. For example, 400Hz plus 100Hz provides 500Hz and 300Hz at the output.

INFORMATION

With subtractive synthesis, it is common to add a second, low-level oscillator at a particular frequency to boost certain harmonics in the first. This technique can also be used for adding extra depth and subtlety to a sound.

Sound	Waveform	Filter cutoff	Resonance	VCA ASR	VCF ASR	Notes
voice	25% pulse	60%	high	SFM	SFM	
bass	square	30%	off	FMF	FMF	
piano	15% pulse	50%	slight	FMM	FSM	
clavinet	80% pulse	60%	off	FMF	FFF	
string	sawtooth	40%	off	SMM	SMM	
brass	sawtooth	70%	off	FMF	FMF	
flute	triangle	25%	off	MMM	FFF	(+noise)

TIP

Layering a brass and string sound in octaves, or with a slight detune, can give an ensemble or chorus effect.

Additive synthesis

With additive synthesis, basic waveshapes (like sawtooth and pulsewidth as used in subtractive synthesis), as well as complex waveshapes, can be produced simply by adding the relevant harmonic frequencies at the correct amplitudes. The envelope generator per oscillator allows for tonal changes over time.

FM

With frequency modulation, the frequencies produced depend upon the interaction of two (or more) oscillators, but are not easily predicted. There are however some guidelines.

Oscillator use	*Change in level*	*Change in frequency*
carrier	sound volume	sound pitch
modulator	number of harmonics	spread of harmonics

The frequency ratio between a modulator and carrier is responsible for a large part of the result. As a rough guide, the following table illustrates this:

Frequency ratio	*Effect*	*Example*
1:1	all harmonics produced	sawtooth
2:1	only odd harmonics produced	square
3:1	only every third harmonic (starting with fourth) produced	pulse

In general, harmonics are created starting from C+M with a spacing of M (where C is carrier frequency and M is modifier frequency). For example with 1kHz and 3kHz, harmonics start from 4kHz (C+M) and then appear at 7kHz (4kHz + 3kHz), 10kHz (7kHz + 3kHz) and so on. The level of the modulator is responsible for the number of harmonics generated. To complicate this issue, lower sidebands are also created (for instance, C-M) and at zero, these then invert phase 180 degrees and go in a positive direction.

In some ways the modulator behaves like a VCF EG (envelope generator) and the carrier like a VCA EG in subtractive synthesis. The use of additional carriers to strengthen certain harmonic frequencies behaves like resonance in subtractive synthesis.

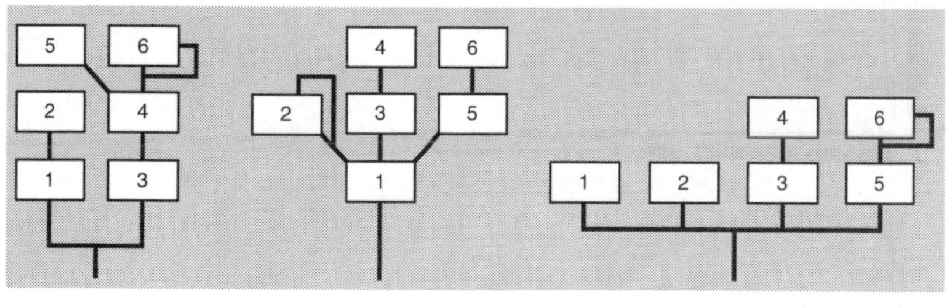

For two key element sounds, e.g. piano with click

For quite complex sounds, e.g. evolving bass with harmonics

For less complex but rich sounds, e.g. thick organ

As you can see from the diagrams on this page, we can view FM synthesis in conventional subtractive terms. The ratio (level and frequency) between the operators will effectively create different waveforms (as shown), and then the ways these are linked in the algorithm (a selection are shown) gives us the final result. Each operator can have its own envelope, which then changes this result over time.

Sine wave

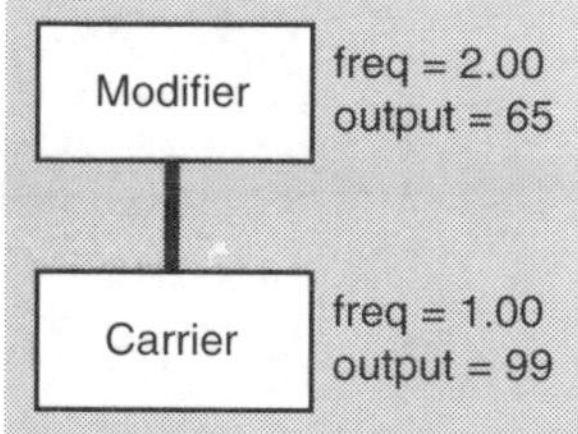

Square wave

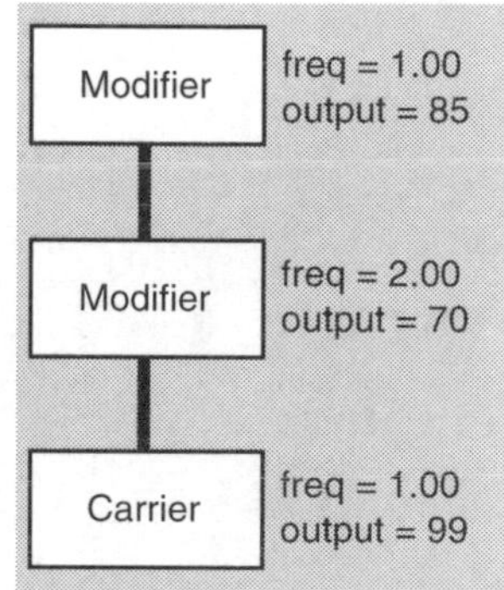

Pulse wave

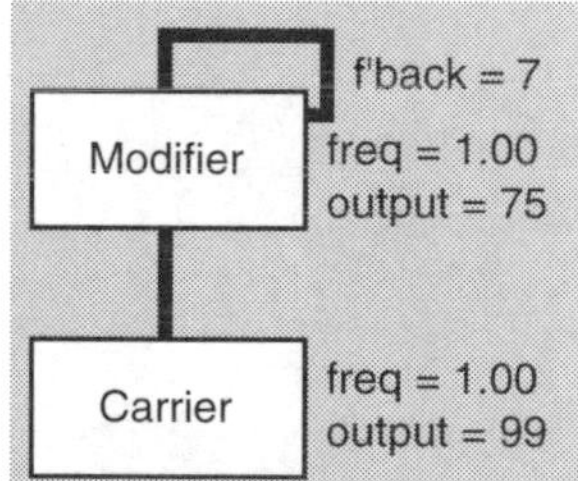

Sawtooth wave

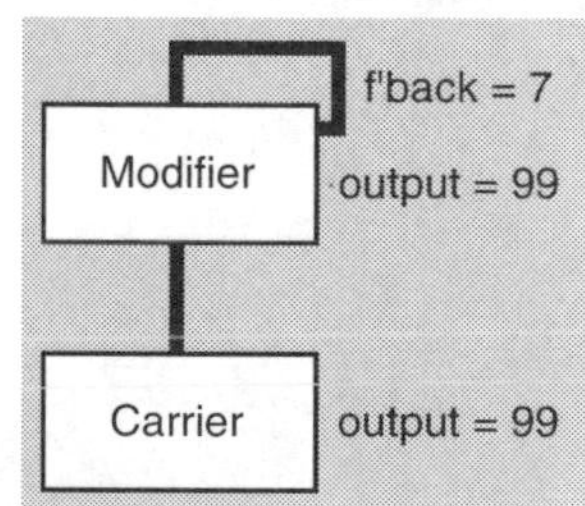

White noise. Experiment with integer and non-integer frequencies for differing effects. Using feedback of around 5 can produce sawtooth type waveforms

Typical envelopes for piano (top), a plucked instrument (second), guitar (third) and brass/strings (bottom).

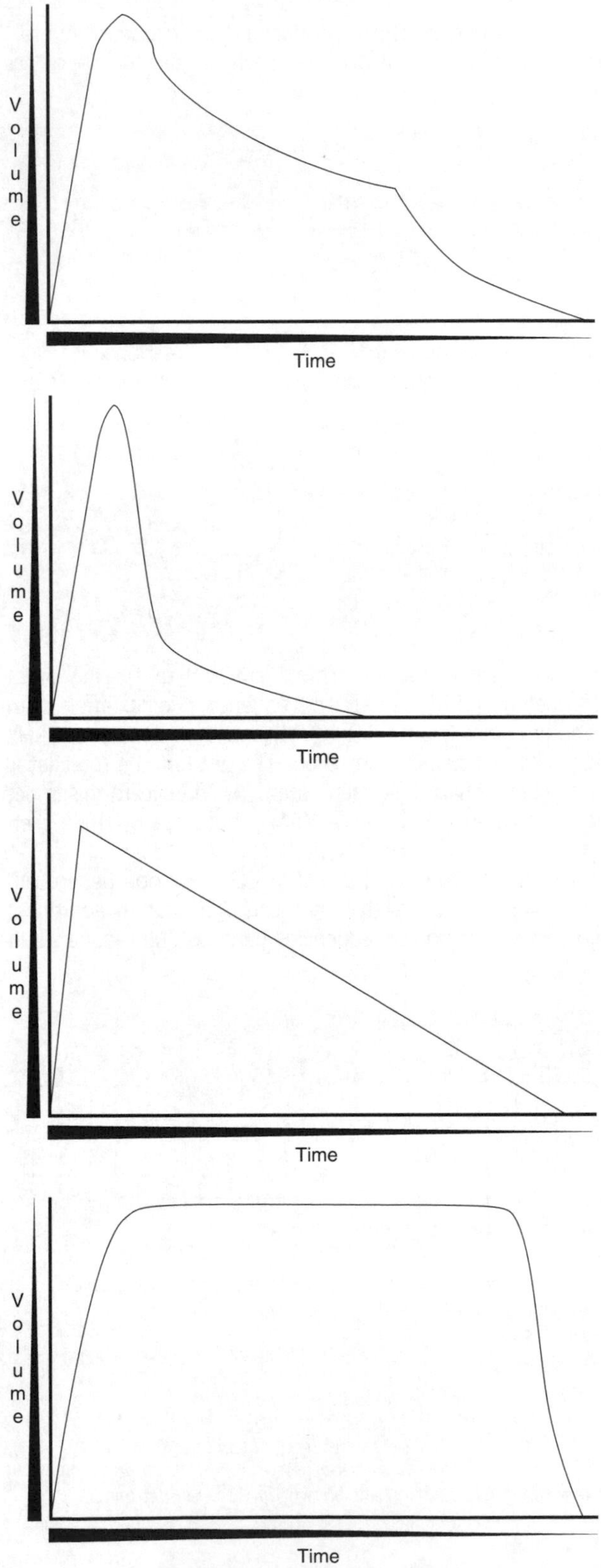

Oscillator descriptions

Waveshape	*Harmonic content*	*Sonic quality*	*Example*
sine	fundamental only	pure	whistle, test tone
triangle	odd harmonics only, at decreasing intensity	duller than square wave	recorders, woodwind
square	odd harmonics only, at reducing intensity	hollow, woody	clarinet, brass
pulse	odd and even harmonics, at variable intensity	nasal, spikey	clavinet
sawtooth	odd and even harmonics, at reducing intensity	rich, bright	string, brass
resonant	odd harmonics only, with one strong harmonic		synth bass, vocal formant
white noise	all frequencies at equal strength	high pitched hiss	tape hiss, laser sounds
pink noise	all frequencies, each octave band of equal strength	smooth	rain
ring modn.	sum and difference frequencies	complex overtones	gongs, bells

Synthesis quick edit comparison

Synthesis	*Pitch*	*Timbre*	*Volume*
subtractive	VCO/DCO	waveform and filters	VCA/DCA
additive	freq of oscs.	EGs of oscillators	level of oscillators
FM	carrier freq	modulator freq and level	carrier level
Casio PD	DCO	waveshape and DCW depth	DCA
sampling	DCO	sample, keymapping, filter	VCA

Six different types of audio waveform. From top: sine wave, triangle, square, pulse, sawtooth and resonant

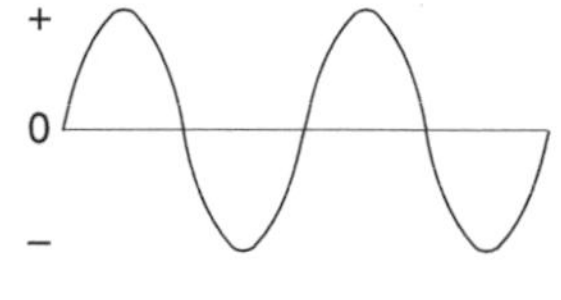

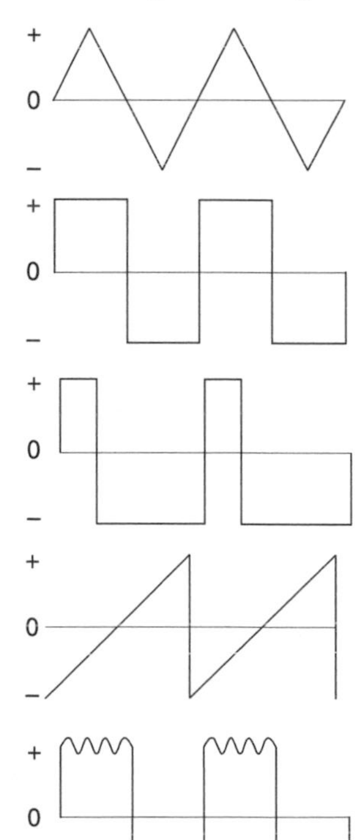

LFO descriptions

Effect	*Waveshape*	*Routing*	*Result*
vibrato	sine	VCO	smooth variations in pitch
trills	square	VCO	clear-cut pitch changes
tremolo	sine	VCA	volume tremolo
wah wah	sine	VCF	changes tone

Sound analysis

When analysing or programming sounds, it is helpful to break them down into categories. The following are suggested, but are by no means de facto or mandatory:

- quiet or loud
- pitched high or low
- pitched or non pitched
- thick or thin texture (rich or simple)
- amplitude envelope (fast attack, plucked, smooth)
- sustaining or fast decay
- evolving texture or static
- bright or dull
- component frequencies close or spread
- acoustic or electronic in origin
- worldly or unearthly
- solo or chorus/ensemble
- environment – acoustics, reverb, reflections...

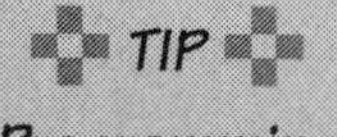

Programming techniques

Route LFO to filter envelope to add life and movement

Layer and detune oscillators for an ensemble effect

In terms of performance style:

solo or chordal
rhythmic or pad
legato or staccato
dynamic or compressed
ranging and note movement (big or small jumps, slides)
playing action (plucked, bowed, hammered, blown, strummed, slapped)

Filters

An active filter is basically a frequency selective amplifier except that it will boost some frequencies and attenuate others. There are four types of filter:

- LPF. In synthesis, the most common filter is the *low pass filter* which allows all frequencies below the cut-off point to pass, while attenuating higher ones.
- HPF. The *high pass filter* has the opposite effect to the LPF, in that it allows higher frequencies to pass while attenuating lower ones. A typical application of this is to remove low frequency rumble from microphone and record sources.
- BPF. The *band pass filter* is a combination of the LPF and HPF above, letting the (middle) range not covered by either to pass unhindered. This can be useful for simulating telephone type circuits and to restrict the bandwidth in both directions.
- BSF. The *band stop filter* has the opposite effect to the BPF above. If the frequency band allowed is very small and the filter very steep, it can become a notch filter, allowing the removal of a specific frequency such as a tone or noise.

The response or effectiveness of a filter is often measured in dBs per octave. So for each octave range, those frequencies would be attenuated by the stated amount:

1 pole – 6dB
2 pole – 12dB
4 pole – 24dB
6 pole – 36dB

The word *pole* comes from the number of elements in the electronic circuitry required to provide that effect.

Instruments/sound physics

- The larger the resonator, the lower the pitch.
- The stronger the vibration, the more the harmonic content.
- A doubling or halving in frequency/pitch represents an octave.
- Generally there are more harmonics at the beginning of a sound than at the end.

SUBTRACTIVE SYNTHESIS PATCH CHART

Music Technology Reference Book

Please photocopy and use this chart

	VCO1	*VCO2*
Oscillator waveform		
Pulse width (if any)		
Oscillator level		
Amplitude ADSR:		
- A		
- D		
- S		
- R		
EG amount		
Filter ADSR:		
- A		
- D		
- S		
- R		
EG amount		
Filter frequency		
Resonance		
Noise		
Ring modulator		
LFO routing		
LFO shape/speed		
Keyboard scaling:		
amplitude		
filter		
envelope to		
Oscillator sync		
Portamento		
Pitch EG		
Sub oscillators		

ADDITIVE SYNTHESIS PATCH CHART

Please photocopy and use this chart

Music Technology Reference Book

Oscillator	*Frequency*	*Level*	*Envelope* *A*	*D*	*S*	*R*	*Notes (* sync/shape)
1							
2							
3							
4							
5							
6							
7							
8							
9							
10							
11							
12							
13							
14							
15							
16							
17							
18							
19							
20							
21							
22							
23							
24							
25							
26							
27							
28							
29							
30							
31							
32							

Pitch EG ____

LFO notes ____

FM SYNTHESIS PATCH CHART

Please photocopy and use this chart

Algorithm

LFO notes

Operator	*1*	*2*	*3*	*4*	*5*	*6*
Waveshape						
Level						
Frequency mode						
Frequency coarse						
Frequency fine						
Detune						
Envelope rate:						
- A						
- D						
- S						
- R						
Envelope level:						
- A						
- D						
- S						
- R						
Feedback						
Key scaling						
Scaling notes						
Pitch EG						
Key sync						

INFORMATION

Many keyboards quote a polyphony figure, assuming the use of only a single oscillator per note. Many sounds require a number of oscillators to create a given sound. For instance, the Roland D110 was quoted as 32-note polyphonic, but if using 4 partial (oscillator) sounds, this reduced to only 8 notes. The allocation is usually carried out dynamically, making the effective polyphony much higher as most notes are not all required at once and any missing notes/oscillators would be masked by the others sounding.

Synth information

Keyboard modes

A keyboard can usually work in a number of playing modes as follows:

- Whole – one sound across the entire keyboard.
- Split – a number of sounds, each with its own key range.
- Layer – a number of sounds with overlapping key ranges.
- Multi – a number of sounds with individual key ranges but assigned to different MIDI channels (that is, not all from local keyboard control).
- Performance – any combination of the above modes.

Parts and polyphony

Modern keyboards are effectively a number of separate instruments housed in a single case (keyboard or rack housing). The number of separately usable instruments is often referred to as the number of *parts*. Although early keyboards could produce a number of sounds (such as piano, brass and strings), they could only do one at a time. With modern keyboards, several sounds are available simultaneously (usually 8 or 16 instruments/parts). Any one of these parts can be set to any one of the available sounds.

Within the whole instrument, however, will be a finite number of oscillators that can sound simultaneously. These are usually split on a dynamic allocation (last come, first served) basis. Older systems required the allocation of notes per part beforehand and on some modern keyboards, the number of oscillators per note can also be set beforehand.

Instrument ranges

Instrument	*Score*	*MIDI notes*	*Frequency range (fundamental in Hz)*
trumpet	E2-B♭4	52-82	82-466
slide trombone	G1-B♭3	43-70	49-233
French horn	F2-B♭3	53-70	87-233
brass ensemble	D0-B♭4	26-82	18-466
clarinet	D3-F6	62-101	146-1396
oboe	B♭3-G6	70-103	233-1568
saxophone	D♭3-A♭3	49-80	69-415
flute	C4-C7	72-108	261-2093
grand piano	A1-C8	21-120	14-4186
harpsichord	F0-F5	29-89	22-698
electric piano	F0-C7	29-108	22-2093
pipe organ	C2-C10	0-127	4-6271
accordion	F2-A4	53-81	87-440
acoustic guitar	E1-B4	40-83	41-493
electric guitar	E1-E5	40-88	41-659
electric bass	E0-E♭3	28-63	131-155
acoustic bass	E0-D3	28-62	131-146
violin	G3-B5	67-95	196-988
cello	C2-G4	48-79	65-392
string ensemble	E1-B5	40-95	41-988
marimba	C2-C6	48-96	65-1046
vibraphone	F2-D5	53-86	87-587

Micro-tuning

In western music, the tuning relationship between notes is a standard that has evolved over time. Yet in many other countries, and with a growing following from all over the world, alternate micro-tunings are in use. They are purported to give more musical results and to change the effect of the music. Less flexible in terms of key changing and selection, and a particular tuning has to be chosen for each micro-tuned scale. In terms of fretted instruments, these have to be of a moving design, or use different fret boards per scale.

The so-called *equal temperament* uses a fixed ratio between notes (2 to the 12th root) of 1.059 from the previous. Facilitating playing in all keys, and for key changes with minimal detrimental effects, this is very much a western taste and the benefits of micro-tuning should not be ignored.

Equal temperament frequency to note pitch table

A4 is assumed to be A above middle C, with a MIDI note number of 69 and a frequency of 440Hz.

In the equal temperament scale, each note is a fixed ratio of 1.059 (12th root of two) apart from the next. An octave spacing is a doubling, or halving, of pitch from which the following table can be derived:

Piano note	*Note*	*MIDI Note*	*Frequency*	*CV voltage*	
				log	*lin*
4	C1	36	32.703		
5	C#1	37	34.648		
6	D1	38	36.708		
7	D#1	39	38.891		
8	E1	40	41.203		
9	F1	41	43.654		
10	F#1	42	46.249		
11	G1	43	48.999		
12	G#1	44	51.913		
13	A1	45	55.000		
14	A#1	46	58.270	0.083	1.000
15	B1	47	61.735	0.166	1.059
16	C2	48	65.406	0.250	1.122
17	C#2	49	69.296	0.333	1.189
18	D2	50	73.416	0.416	1.260
19	D#2	51	77.782	0.500	1.335
20	E2	52	82.407	0.583	1.414
21	F2	53	87.307	0.666	1.498
22	F#2	54	92.499	0.750	1.587
23	G2	55	97.999	0.883	1.682
24	G#2	56	103.83	0.916	1.782
25	A2	57	110.00	1.000	1.888
26	A#2	58	116.54	1.083	2.000
27	B2	59	123.47	1.166	2.119
28	C3	60	130.81	1.250	2.245
29	C#3	61	138.59	1.333	2.378
30	D3	62	146.83	1.416	2.520
31	D#3	63	155.56	1.500	2.670
32	E3	64	164.81	1.583	2.828
33	F3	65	174.61	1.666	2.996
34	F#3	66	185.00	1.750	3.175
35	G3	67	196.00	1.833	3.383
36	G#3	68	207.65	1.916	3.563

Piano note	Note	MIDI note	Frequency	CV voltage log	CV voltage lin
37	A3	69	220.00	2.000	3.775
38	A#3	70	233.08	2.083	4.000
39	B3	71	246.94	2.166	4.756
40	C4	72	261.63	2.250	(Middle C)
41	C#4	73	277.18	2.333	
42	D4	74	293.66	2.146	
43	D#4	75	311.13	2.500	
44	E4	76	329.63	2.583	
45	F4	77	349.23	2.666	
46	F#4	78	369.99	2.750	
47	G4	79	392.00	2.833	
48	G#4	80	415.30	2.916	
49	A4	81	440.00	3.000	
50	A#4	82	466.16		
51	B4	83	493.88		
52	C5	84	523.25		
53	C#5	85	554.37		
54	D5	86	587.33		
55	D#5	87	622.25		
56	E5	88	659.26		
57	F5	89	698.46		
58	F#5	90	739.99		
59	G5	91	783.99		
60	G#5	92	839.61		
61	A5	93	880.00		
62	A#5	94	932.33		
63	B5	95	987.77		
64	C6	96	1046.5		
65	C#6	97	1108.7		
66	D6	98	1174.7		
67	D#6	99	1244.5		
68	E6	100	1318.5		
69	F6	101	1396.9		
70	F#6	102	1480.0		
71	G6	103	1568.0		
72	G#6	104	1661.2		
73	A6	105	1760.0		
74	A#6	106	1864.7		
75	B6	107	1975.5		
76	C7	108	2093.0		
77	C#7	109	2217.5		
78	D7	110	2349.3		
79	D#7	111	2489.0		
80	E7	112	2637.0		
81	F7	113	2793.8		
82	F#7	114	2960.0		
83	G7	115	3136.0		
84	G#7	116	3322.4		
85	A7	117	3520.0		
86	A#7	118	3729.3		
87	B7	119	3951.0		
88	C8	120	4186.0		
	C#8	121	4434.9		
	D8	122	4698.6		
	D#8	123	4977.9		
	E8	124	5273.9		
	F8	125	5587.5		
	F#8	126	5919.8		

Piano note	Note	MIDI note	Frequency	CV voltage	
				log	lin
	G8	127	6271.7		
	G#8				
	A8				
	A#8				
	B8				

Micro-tuning formula

Tuning is based on a ratio between notes. The ratio used is the variable in micro-tuning, the formula being as follows:

log i x (K/log 2) = pitch interval

where i is the interval ratio as a decimal and K is an integer to create convenient-sized units.

Micro-tuning tables

Note	Equal freq.	Cent settings			
		Equal	Pythagoras	Aristoxenus	Zarlino
C4	261.63	0	0	0	0
D4	293.66	200	204	204	204
E4	329.63	400	408	386	386
F4	349.23	500	498	498	498
G4	392.00	700	702	702	702
A4	440.00	900	906	906	884
B4	493.88	1100	1110	1088	1088
C5	523.26	1200	1200	1200	1200

Note	Cent deviation							
	Equal	Class. Just	Harmonic	Wemeister	Indian Raga	Arabic	Tibetan	CarlosAlpha
C4	0	0	0	0	0	0	0	0
C#4	100	-29	5	-8	-10	30	-42	-12
D4	200	4	4	-3	4	-20	32	-44
D#4	300	16	-2	-3	-6	-50	10	-66
E4	400	-14	-14	-7	-16	-45	-22	-88
F4	500	-2	-29	0	-2	2	22	-110
F#4	600	-10	-49	-9	-12	23	18	-132
G4	700	-2	2	-1	2	6	25	-164
G#4	800	14	41	-6	-8	-14	-27	-176
A4	900	-16	6	-6	-18	-43	-4	-198
A#4	1000	18	-31	-1	-4	-70	19	-220
B4	1100	-12	-12	-9	-14	10	-14	-242

(Note: there are 100 cents in a semitone.)

It is possible to experiment with micro-tuning, even on MIDI keyboards that do not support this feature, by recording each note on a separate MIDI channel and adding the required amount of pitch bend. The piano is not the best sound to attempt micro-tuning on. A sustained pad sound such as strings is better. Also, playing closely in one octave can help you to tune in to the effect.

The key thing to remember about micro-tuning is that it is mainly concerned with the interaction between notes. Some effects may be subtle, but help to create the mood of the piece. There are a number of micro-tuning scales that use more or less than the normal 12 notes per octave.

Interval names

In musical terms, each semitone interval is given a name in relationship to its scale. Following is the one for C:

C	tonic
C#	minor 2nd
D	major 2nd
D#	minor 3rd
E	major 3rd
F	perfect 4th
F#	tritone
G	perfect 5th
G#	minor 6th
A	major 6th
A#	dominant 7th
B	major 7th
C	Octave (tonic)

Slow down the tempo to add difficult performances. Pitch will not be affected.

- *Try playing a part differently – at different speeds (half or double), using a different sound (drum part on a synth sound), transposed (in octaves or in harmonies), with different quantisation values, or with inversed velocities or pitches, or reverse the note order.*
- *Try copying a part to a new track and impose different features on it, as suggested above.*

Sequencing

MIDI sequencing

MIDI sequencing allows MIDI data (such as a keyboard performance) to be recorded, manipulated and then played back. MIDI sequencers include dedicated hardware units and most computer platforms with the appropriate sequencing software and MIDI interface. Common sequencer concepts follow.

A sequencer can provide a linear or pattern-based style, or sometimes a mixture of both. A linear sequencer works like tape in that events are placed in a straight line order to arrange them. A pattern-based sequencer works like a drum machine and musical sections are created in blocks (patterns) that are then later chained together to form an arrangement. The former is best suited to studio production and the latter to composition, so neither single method is ideal.

MIDI performance

The MIDI performance needn't be limited to musical input from a MIDI keyboard, MIDI guitar, MIDI microphone, MIDI wind controller or MIDI percussion device. It can also include the recording of audio or lighting mixer control movements (such as faders or buttons) or input from virtual reality sensors (e.g. mats, interpreted camera images, etc.).

Step time and real time

The performance can be entered in real time, by performing live, or in step time. Step time is a mathematical way of entering data step by step, allowing for very precise (and often not re-creatable live) performances.

Operating a sequencer

Selecting a track A track is simply a place where data is stored. It can usually consist of one or more MIDI channels of information.

Selecting a MIDI channel The MIDI channel selects which physical MIDI instrument that track's data will go to. If there is an Any, or No mode, then the track's data is sent out on the original MIDI channels.

Selecting a sound Can either be done locally on the instrument or remotely over MIDI by sending a patch change from the sequencer.

Location Some form of location will be provided often in bars (musical) and in time. Often a locator system is provided which can provide automatic punch ins, cycling or recording.

As well as the recording and play back of MIDI performances, other sequencer functions which can be applied to a selected region usually include the following;

Copying The selected chunk of data can be copied instantly without having to perform it again.

Transposing The pitch of a chunk can be changed to a new key.

Quantising A process where events are moved on, or nearer, to a predefined timing grid. This can make music sound mathematically perfect but lack feel (i.e. robotic). The latest quantising options include swing and humanise which deliberately shift the timing randomly a small amount to introduce a human feel factor. Other quantising tools can include groove or template quantising, where the feel of one performance can be imposed upon another. Often the degree of quantisation (strength or depth) is adjustable, so that stages of "correctness" can be applied.

Event editing Event editing allows any factor of the event to be changed, including its timing, duration or values, or even the type of event itself.

Arrangement Some form of song arrangement is usually provided where it is easy to organise the structure of the song, often with the inclusion of muting, transposing and even MIDI channel assignment.

Muting and level control The sequencer often provides facilities for controlling non-note data such as volume, panning, muting, etc., providing a degree of automation to the mixing process. This may be by MIDI control of the instrument (often affecting the noise performance) or via an external device such as an audio VCA or mixer.

Logical or Boolean editing Some sequencers allow advanced manipulation of events. This can include transforming any event, or any aspect of it, into any other event or aspect. This can be done within defined limits. For instance, any note of C3 above a velocity of 100 on MIDI channel 10 could be turned into a MIDI volume command on channel 16. The applications are harder to develop than the skills to perform them.

Randomisation Often a sequencer can randomise or improvise on data to create a variation or original version. Treated as an inspirational tool, it can be very effective.

• Always overdub a controller performance (e.g. pitch bend or modulation) on a different track so that you can process it more easily.

• Keep all controllers (such as volume and patch changes) on separate tracks, so that they can be muted easily for track laying or mixing, or using a different instrument setup.

• Always record the MIDI performance too when recording audio to a hard disk system. You might decide to layer or change the sound on mixing.

• Use logical edit or transform to turn the velocities of one part into MIDI volume commands applied to a part on another channel. This can create pseudo gating or dynamic grooving effects.

• Label everything and annotate which instruments and banks of sounds you use. If you return to the project later and/or your instrument setup has changed you will appreciate this efficiency. Save any data with the song files – lyrics, sysex bank data (on a separate track at 60 BPM) and drum machine and SMPTE data.

3 Sampling and tapeless recording

General sampling information

Look after your ears, you only get one pair per life! See the safe hearing chart (page 113) for suggested levels

Analogue-digital

All modern samplers and hard disk recording systems use a process involving digital technology controlled by some form of computer (in dedicated hardware or otherwise). This means that the sound (analogue) must be converted into digital form via an A/D (analogue to digital) converter.

In essence, the analogue waveform is analysed in a number of time slices, where the level at that point is noted. This is then stored as a digital number to memory or disk. For playback purposes, the reverse of the process is carried out, using a D/A (digital to analogue) converter.

The number of times per second that the sound is analysed is called the *sampling rate*. This determines the highest audio frequency that can be recorded (sampling rate = 2.2 x highest audio). Any frequencies above this must be filtered out or a misrepresented frequency will be produced, an effect called *aliasing*. The filters are responsible for a large part of the quality of the sound, as is the A/D converter itself.

Another factor in the conversion is how many level steps can be used. Computers count in binary and a single 8-bit word can only give 2 to the power of 8 (256) levels. Anything between one of these levels has to be rounded up, producing an error which is heard as quantising noise, a high frequency break up of the sound. This is particularly noticeable on bass sounds at low levels.

Bits to levels chart

Bits	Levels	Application
1	2	example only
2	4	example only
4	16	example only
8	256	many internal computer sound systems and Fairlight 2
12	4,096	Akai S900/950 series samplers, 1980s delay units, Kurzweil K250 and Roland S330
16	65,536	compact disc audio, DAT and recent samplers like Roland S760
24	16,777,200	often used for internal digital processing (like when multiplying two 16-bit numbers) and an emerging high quality digital audio standard. Also allows the broadcast colour standard of 16 million colours in digital video.
32	4.2949 Gig	the most likely new standard for digital audio in the 21st century.

Dynamic range to bits

Bits	Levels	Theoretical best dynamic range/noise (dB) (20 Log 1 bit error/no. of bits)	Typical distortion
8	256	48.16	0.5%
12	4,096	72.25	0.1%
16	65,536	96.33	0.002%
24	16,777,200	144.49	–
32	4.2949 Gig	192.66	–

Recording time formula
time (mono in seconds) = memory (in words)/sampling rate (in Hz)

Instrument frequency range
When sampling or recording digitally, it is usually not possible to record at full bandwidth all of the time owing to cost and storage factors. The following chart will aid the selection of an appropriate sampling rate, although your ears must be the final judge of what is acceptable.

Highest frequency response	Fundamental (Hz)	Highest harmonics (kHz)
kick	500	8-12
snare	2000	12-18
hihats	4000	15-19
cymbals	4000	14-19
toms	3000	11-15
percussion	4000	13-16
marimba	1000	14-16
xylophone	2000	14-15
acoustic bass	200	10-12
electric bass	200	13-15
synth bass	300	12-15
acoustic guitar	500	11-14
electric guitar	700	12-15
grand piano	5000	14-16
electric piano	2500	12-14
pipe organ	6000	12-16
violin	100-3000	14-16
other strings	60-4000	10-15
trumpet	100-1000	14-17
French horn	50-1000	13-15
saxophone	100-1000	12-16
other brass/woodwind	20-2000	14-17
timpani/gongs/tubular bells	60-5000	12-17
synthesiser	10-6000	12-19
lead vocal	60-2000	12-14
harmony vocals	60-2000	11-14
speech	100-2000	6-15
telephone quality	300-3400	3-4
FM radio	30-15000	–
ferric cassette	50-11000	–
chrome cassette	40-13000	–
compact disc	20-20000	–
human hearing (child)	18-20000	–
human hearing (adult)	30-15000	–

INFORMATION

Level is of prime importance in a digital system, as working at a lower level than maximum effectively reduces the bit rate of a system and reduces signal-to-noise and distortion performance. For instance, using only 10% of a 12-bit system (4,096 levels) reduces the available quantising steps to 409 levels, akin to a 9-bit (512 level) system at 80% of full level.

INFORMATION

Digital clipping is a major problem in digital systems. There are no numbers above the maximum – headroom is 0dB. In fact, with digital clipping, cycling occurs where the difference between the maximum and required greater level is presented as the signal. This occurs on each pass through of the maximum level causing extreme changes that present themselves as click-type noises. For instance, a level of 4,098 on a 12-bit system would be presented as a level of 2.

There is also some evidence that harmonics above 20kHz make a difference even to older people whose hearing tests at a lower rate. High frequencies also represent themselves in the steepness of the attack of sonic transients (wave fronts).

Hard disk recording time chart

MBytes of 8-bit memory	Sample rate					
	48kHz		44.1kHz		32kHz	
	Mono	Stereo	Mono	Stereo	Mono	Stereo
0.5	5.33	2.66	5.80	2.90	8.00	4.00
1.0	10.66	5.33	11.61	5.81	16.00	8.00
2.0	21.32	10.66	23.22	11.61	32.00	16.00
4.0	42.64	21.32	46.44	23.22	64.00	32.00
5.0	53.33	26.67	58.05	29.02	160.00	80.00
8.0	85.28	42.64	92.88	46.44	128.00	64.00
10	106.66	53.34	116.10	58.04	320.00	160.00
16	170.56	85.28	185.76	92.88	256.00	128.00
32	341.12	170.56	371.52	185.76	512.00	256.00
64	682.24	341.12	743.04	371.52	1024.00	512.00
128	1364.48	682.24	1486.08	743.04	2048.00	1024.00

For hard disk recording at 44.1kHz in mono, approximately 5 Mbytes of hard disk space is required per mono track minute (or 10 Mbytes per stereo minute). The highest audio frequency that can be recorded is approximately just under half of the sampling rate. The actual formula is: highest audio = sampling rate/2.2. With tapeless recording, a linear recording time is not necessarily representative as segments can be re-used without wasting additional disk space. Also remember that times quoted are usually for mono (or stereo) tracks, not multi-tracking.

INFORMATION

A similar effect to instrument resonances is true with reverb and delay based effects where the spacing between the events is also transposed with the original sound. So an octave up, the reverb time is halved. If multisampling is not possible and a wide range is required, it is better to sample without effects and add them on playback. It is usually better to transpose a sample down rather than up, so that a greater range can be achieved before characterisation becomes too prevalent.

Mapping

A sampler can usually hold a number of samples in memory at once. These can be accessed in a variety of ways, either by assigning each sound to a separate MIDI channel or restricting its playable range to certain keys, or both of these techniques. This process is called *mapping*.

In addition to assigning a certain key range to a sample, it may also be assigned a certain velocity window from which to play. This can be treated as a velocity switch (abrupt change) or a velocity crossfade (a slow change or fade). Normally a second sample would be assigned to the remaining velocity areas, allowing, say, for two different snare drum sounds to be triggered, one soft strike with lower velocity triggering and a harder version triggered by a stronger velocity trigger. In this way not only does the level change with velocity, or even the sound of the sample (through filter control), but also the actual sample used.

A sample cannot be transposed far beyond its natural pitch without adopting a new character since, in the acoustic world, resonances of the instrument body are at fixed frequencies regardless of the note played. When sampled, these resonances are also transposed in a similar ratio and sound out of character.

Velocity crossfades are usually more effective than velocity switches. Use can also be made of assigning the samples to different outputs (for stereo panning), using different samples with and without an effect (like reverb, EQ or reverse), or even a totally different sound.

Looping

To save massive memory usage for long sustained sounds, a technique called *looping* is employed which repeats a section of the sound for as long as required, with the possibility of further synthesis applied to it (filtering or an amplitude envelope). Ideally the loop is undetectable.

Short loops tend to have a pitch, which may or may not match the note being played. Also short loops are quite noticeable unless the original sound creates the same effect, such as with a pure sound such as brass. Most auto-looping software creates such short loops and these need to be manually ranged over a suitable distance.

The loop is supposed to form in a section of the sound that would naturally repeat and still retain the character of the sound. Although one whole cycle may indicate the complete pitch, it will not be representative of the evolving nature of any sound (other than a pure tone or sine wave), and a large number of cycles will need to be taken.

The volume of the sample should not be changing at these points. The actual loop points themselves need to match in level, phase and gradient, otherwise a glitch (click) may be heard. Zero-crossing looping will only fade a zero level match and will not necessarily match the other two criteria. Crossfade looping can be a good way of creating a human-engineered match at the sample point, but may corrupt the sound irretrievably unless a backup or undo function is present.

The best looping results can often be obtained by backing up the end point a few samples and then finding a loop point. Start with the loop point after the initial attack (and character of the sound), usually around the last third of the sound, but not often less than a tenth. A visual sample editor, as provided with a computer system, can aid the process of looping significantly.

•

A good method of looping is to take long enough samples so as to avoid looping entirely. Two seconds will last a bar at 120BPM and should meet most needs. With restricted sample memory, the option of recording each sample/instrument to tape is a possibility.

Looping chart

Instrument	*Loop length*	*Loop type*
vocals	long	alternating (bidirectional)
piano	short	forward
string	medium	forward
brass	medium	forward
flute	short	forward

WAV file format

The WAV (WAVE) file format, as defined by Microsoft Corporation, is now quite common among computers and is a standard way of storing digitised sound samples to disk. WAV files are part of the RIFF family, related in structure to the Electronic Arts IFF file format. The file is broken down into identified chunks, a chunk structure being:

Chunk_ID (four letter code right-padded with spaces)
Chunk_size (32-bit (4 byte) unsigned number not including the chunk_ID, chunk_size or any pad byte at the end of the chunk_data field)
Chunk_data (signed or unsigned) including a pad byte of zero if necessary at the end to word align to an even number of bytes.

Any unexpected chunks should be ignored. The file format follows:

File header

"RIFF"	"WAVEfmt"	'form type
	INAM	'file name
	ICMT	'comment field
	ICOP	'copyright notice
	INFO	'other user information
	(fmt-ck)	'waveform format chunk: see below
	(wave-format) – see below	
	(format-specific) – see below	
	(data-ck)	'waveform data chunk: see below
	(data)	

Wave format

Word	wFormatTag	(1 for PCM format – only current option)
Word	nChannels	(1 for mono, 2 stereo...)
Dword	nsamplesPerSec	(sampling rate in samples/sec.)
Dword	nAvgBytesPerSec	(data transfer rate. If PCM, rate = nchannels*nBitsPerSec/8)
Word	nBlockAlign	(block alignment in bytes for buffer purposes. If PCM then = nChannels*nBitsPerSample/8)

Format specific

Uint	nBitsPerSample	'sample bit resolution. Same for each channel. 'stereo and multi-channel samples are interleaved 'low byte, high byte then next channel.

Data chunk

For 1 to 8 bits: unsigned integers are used, range 0-255 (00H-FFH), mid-point 128, 80H. For 9 and over: signed integers are used, range -32,768 to 32,767 (8000H-7FFFH), midpoint 0, 00H. The number of bytes required depends on the nBitsPerSample field above, with spare bits set to zero.

Notes:

- Word is a 16-bit unsigned quantity in Intel format (LSB first).
- Dword is a 32-bit unsigned quantity in Intel format (LSB first).
- Uint is a 16-bit unsigned quantity in Intel format (LSB first).
- The header "RIFF" means Intel format is used (LSB first), while "RIFX" uses Motorola format of MSB first. Otherwise they are identical.
- The letter codes used to designate each chunk must contain four (upper case if registered) letters, right padded with ASCII 32 if necessary.
- After each chunk header is a four byte size length.
- After a string, a modifier can be included as follows:
  none: no null terminator or size prefix
  Z: string is null terminated
  B: string has an 8-bit size prefix
  W: string has a 16-bit size prefix
- A RIFF format MIDI file is the same as a standard MIDI file except that it is enclosed in a RIFF RMID chunk.

MIDI file and dump formats

See Chapter 1 for further details.

HARD DISK RECORDING CHART

Please photocopy and use this chart

Music Technology Reference Book

Project	__________	Artist	__________
Client	__________	Studio	__________
Engineer	__________	Assistant	__________
Programmer	__________	Producer	__________

Equipment details and software versions

Project start date __________

Last update date __________

Drive __________

Cartridge __________

Last defrag date __________

Back-up date __________

Back-up media no. __________

Track	*Instrument*	*Filename/location*	*Mix Notes*	*Bounced*	*Backed-up*
1					
2					
3					
4					
5					
6					
7					
8					
9					
10					
11					
12					
13					
14					
15					
16					

Other notes __________

Useful advice

Sound effects tips

Interesting sound effects can be achieved by taking sounds and playing them out of pitch context. By sequencing and layering samples, even more textures can be created. Using 24 tracks of sounds is common when creating film sound effects such as dinosaurs and mechanical trousers!

Sound	*Octaves up*	*Octaves down*	*Equivalents*
kick drum			balloon pop
snare			door slam
snare			crisp packet
heartbeat			throat gulp
gunshot			door handle/slam
tambourine		submarine	
paper tearing		rock slide	
paper crumpling	fire		
percussion			mouth/body noises
maracas			coffee jar
Vandergraf generator			air ioniser

Checklist

Here are some key points to consider before purchasing or upgrading a tapeless system.

- Sonic quality: integrity and flexibility
- Side effects of any data compression (with multiple processes or platforms)
- Sampling rates provided
- Resampling option
- Number of virtual tracks
- Number of simultaneous record and playback tracks
- Bounce-down facilities
- Stereo and quadraphonic source handling
- Sufficient analogue and digital outputs (SP/DIF coaxial or optical, or AES)
- Physical output routing and provision for including external sources such as external effects
- Drive size: assuming 5Mbytes per mono minute
- Sufficient for single song, album project or DAT editing: hence required time
- How many projects to run concurrently?
- Back-up facilities, media and streaming time (often real time per mono track)
- Automated mixing of level, EQ and effects
- On-line processing
- Off-line processing (speed*?)
- Synchronisation: MIDI and SMPTE chase lock
- Expandability: software modules, tracks and interfacing
- Upgradeability for new technology
- Ergonomics and external remote control facilities (MIDI, hardware options)
- Reliability and power protection (how much is lost on power cut? e.g. Autosave)
- Downtime, maintenance and alignment costs
- Cost: value for money and re-saleability

4 Music

Chord information

Chord basics

A chord is a group of notes taken from a scale. Chords can be determined by taking the following intervals:

Chord	*Intervals*	*Example*
Major triad	root, third, fifth of major scale	C E G
Minor triad	root, third, fifth of minor scale	C D♯G

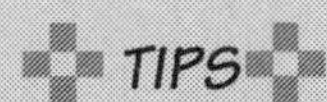

Moving one interval of the 3rd leads to the minor (interval down) or suspended 4th (interval up) form of a chord.

•

Moving the interval of the fifth leads to the augmented fifth (interval up) form of a chord.

•

A diminished chord can be played by moving the third and fifth an interval down and moving the original fifth a tone up.

Chord names

Chord name	*Notes*	
C	C E G	C major
C7	C E G B♭	
C-5♭	C E G♭	flattened fifth
Caug5	C E G♯	augmented fifth
Cm	C E♭ G	C minor
Cm7	C E♭G B♭	
C6	C E G A	
Csus4	C F G	C suspended fourth
Cmaj7	C E G B	C major seventh
Cmaj9	C E G B D	C major ninth
C9	C E G B♭ D	
C11	C E G B♭ D F	
C13	C E G B♭ D F A	
C13+11	C E G B♭ D F♯A	
C9sus4	C F G B♭ D	
C7-9	C E G B♭ D♭	C seventh, flattened ninth
C7-10	C E G B♭ E♭	
C6/7	B♭ E G A	
Cm9	C E♭G B♭ D	
Cmaj9	G B D E	
Cm6	C E♭ G A	
C13+11	B♭ E F♯A	not all notes are shown
Cm maj7	C E♭ G B	C minor, major seventh
C7-9	G B♭D♭ E	
C♯dim	C♯E G B♭	is also Edim, Gdim and B♭dim
Cdim	E♭ G♭ A C	is also E♭dim, G♭dim, Adim

- An inversion of a chord is simply the same chord with one (or more) of the notes played in another octave. The first inversion takes the lowest note and moves it up an octave. The second inversion takes the remaining lowest note from this and transposes it up an octave, and so on – C4 E4 G4; E4 G4 C5; G4 C5 E5…
- An inversion can dramatically change the effect of a chord sequence and should always be considered.
- Chords are patterns of intervals, using certain positions within the scale. If you apply this pattern, you should be able to determine any chord by knowing the scale. Usually any note from the scale will fit harmonically in terms of orchestration/arrangement, although better results can be expected by taking notes from the chord.

Note: by transposing the notes intervals shown on page 67, other chords can be formed (for instance, C11 to D11 by transposing all notes up two semitones).

Keys and relative minors

Major	*Rel minor*	*No of incidentals*	*Incidentals*	*Interval/notes*						
				T	*T*	*S*	*T*	*T*	*T*	*S*
C	Amin	0		C	D	E	F	G	A	B
G	Emin	1♯	F♯	G	A	B	C	D	E	F♯
D	Bmin	2♯	F♯ C♯	D	E	F♯	G	A	B	C♯
A	F♯ min	3♯	F♯ C♯ G♯	A	B	C♯	D	E	F♯	G♯
E	C♯ min	4♯	F♯ C♯ G♯ D♯	E	F♯	G♯	A	B	C♯	D♯
B	G♯ min	5♯	F♯ C♯ G♯ D♯ A♯	B	C♯	D♯	E	F♯	G♯	A♯
F♯	D♯ min	6♯	F♯ C♯ G♯ D♯ A♯ E♯	F♯	G♯	A♯	B	C♯	D♯	E♯
F	Dmin	1♭	B♭	F	G	A	B♭	C	D	E
B♭	Gmin	2♭	B♭ E♭	B♭	C	D	E♭	F	G	A
E♭	Cmin	3♭	B♭ E♭ A♭	E♭	F	G	A♭	B♭	C	D
A♭	Fmin	4♭	B♭ E♭ A♭ D♭	A♭	B♭	C	D♭	E♭	F	G
D♭	B♭min	5♭	B♭ E♭ A♭ D♭G♭	D♭	E♭	F	G♭	A♭	B♭	C

Abbreviations and meanings

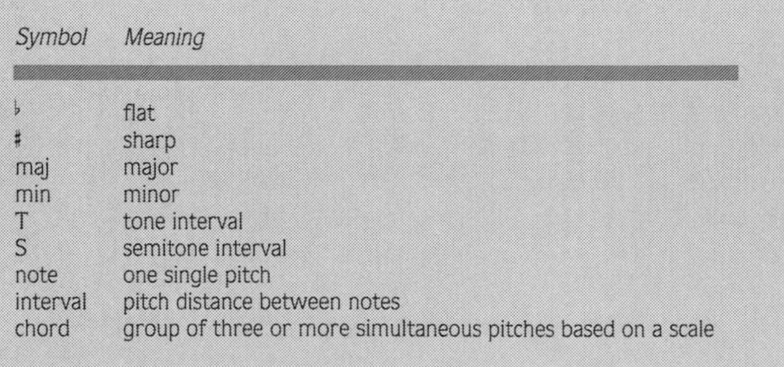

Symbol	*Meaning*
♭	flat
♯	sharp
maj	major
min	minor
T	tone interval
S	semitone interval
note	one single pitch
interval	pitch distance between notes
chord	group of three or more simultaneous pitches based on a scale

The relative minor of a major scale starts at either a sixth up or a third down on the major scale.

Guitar /keyboard chords

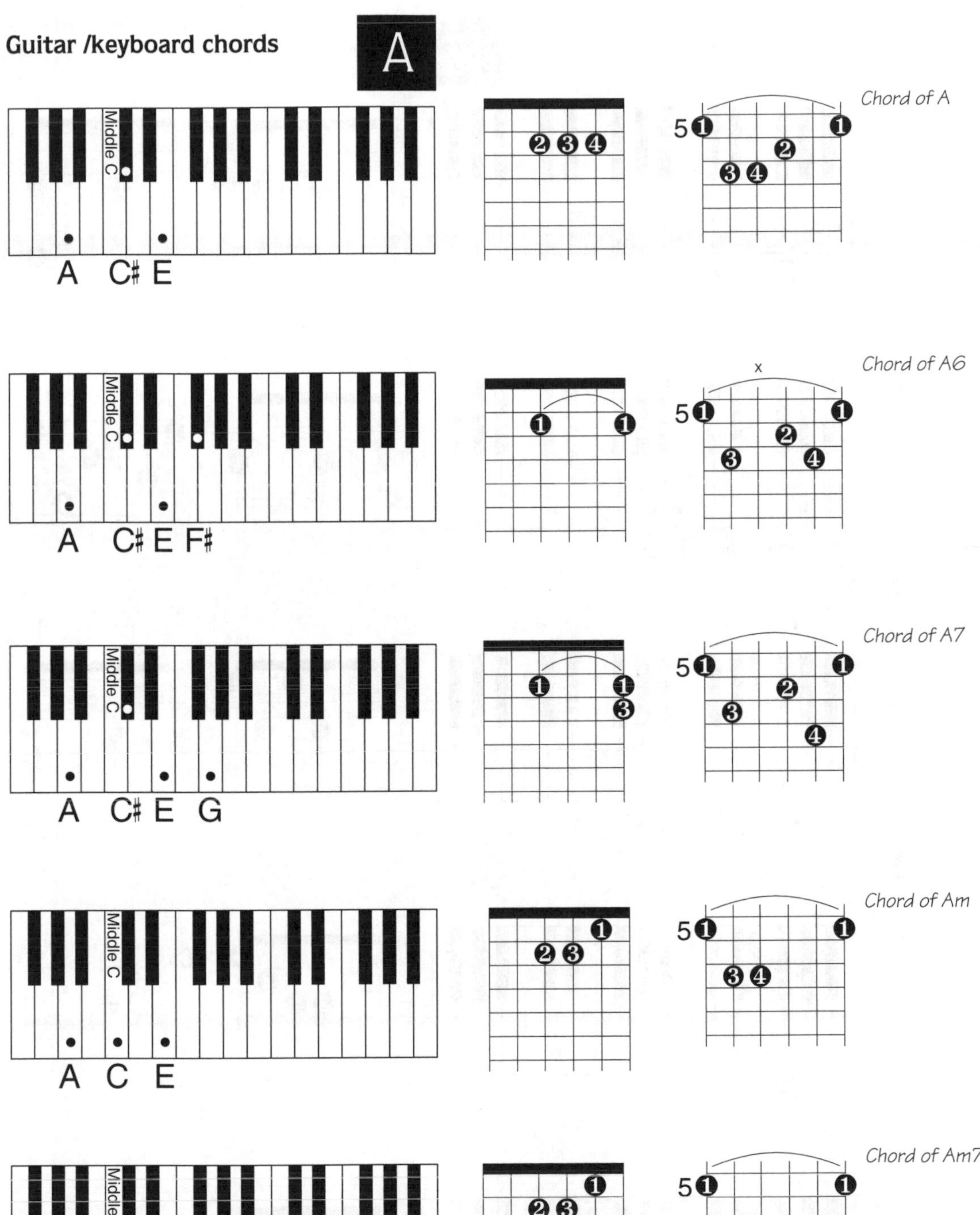

B♭

Chord of B♭

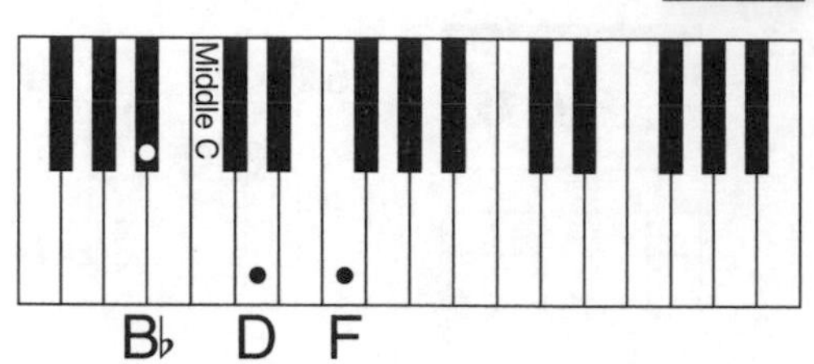

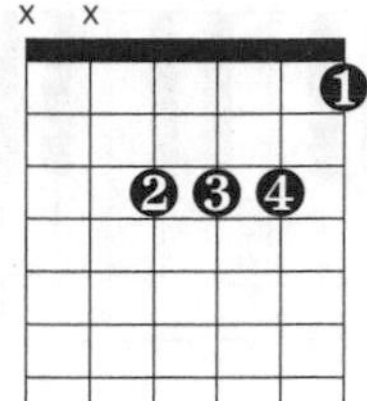

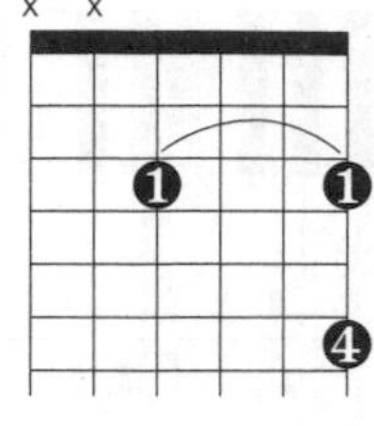

Chord of B♭6

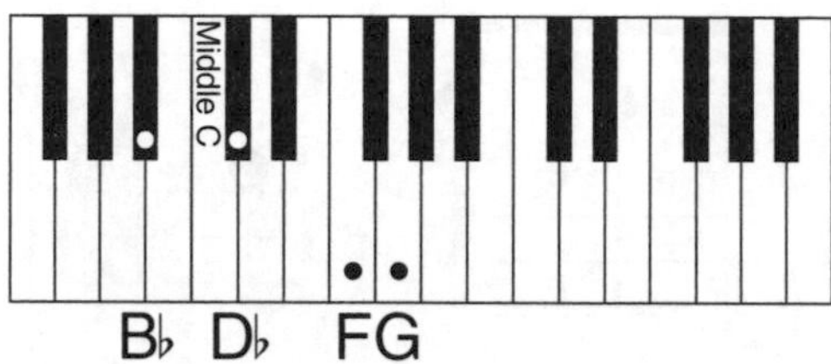

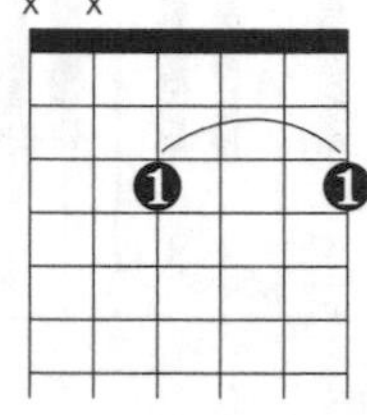

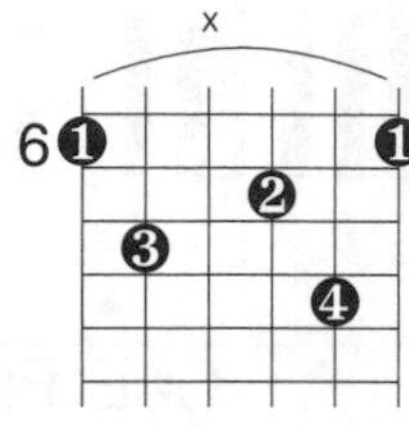

Chord of B♭7

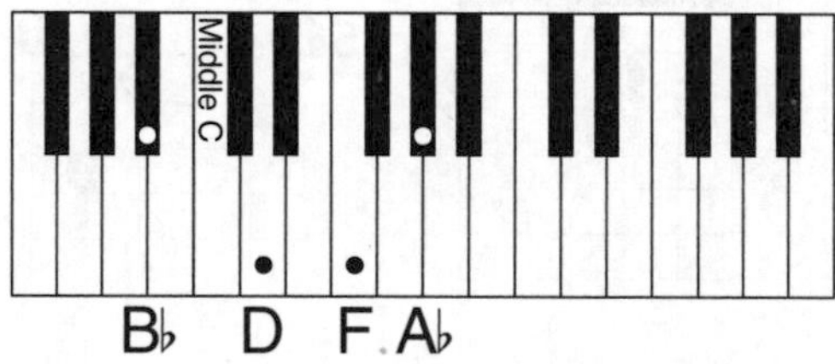

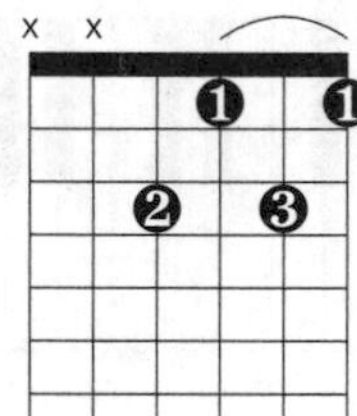

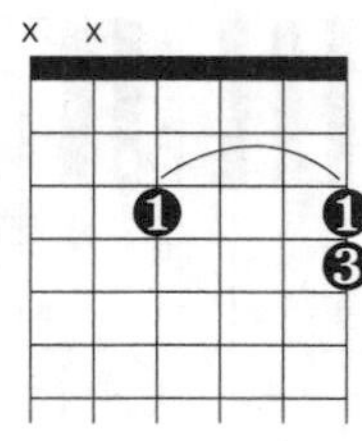

Chord of B♭m

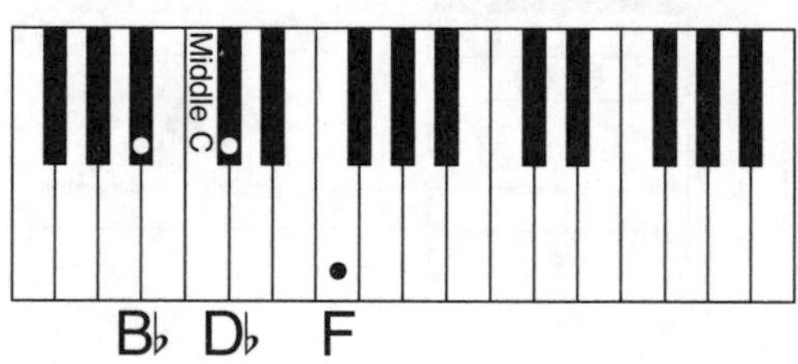

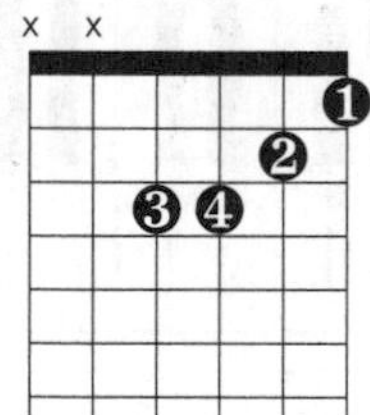

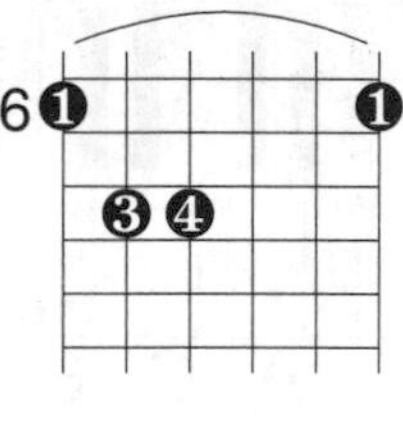

Chord of B♭m7

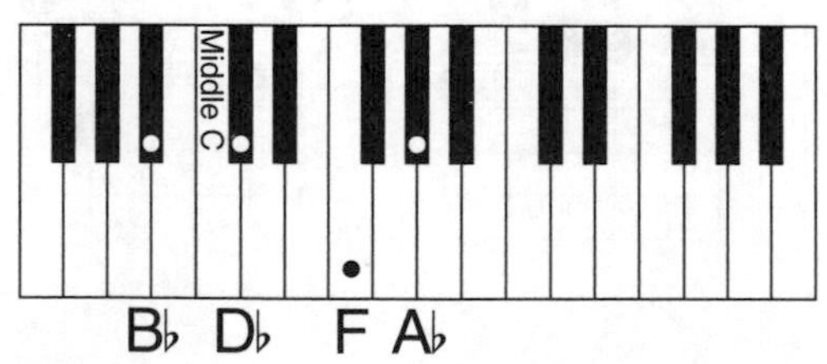

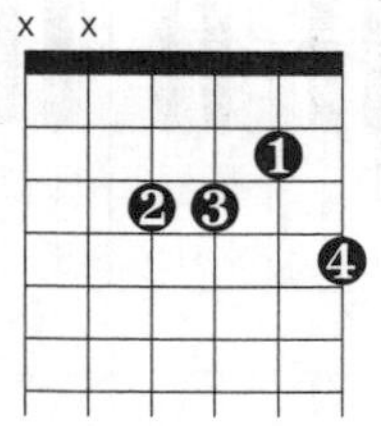

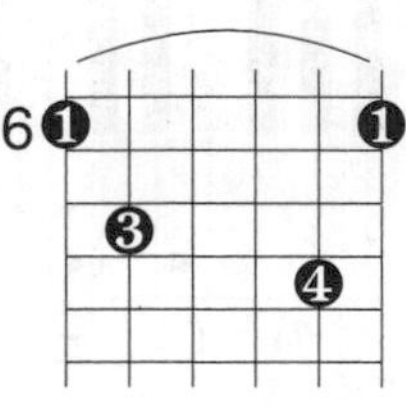

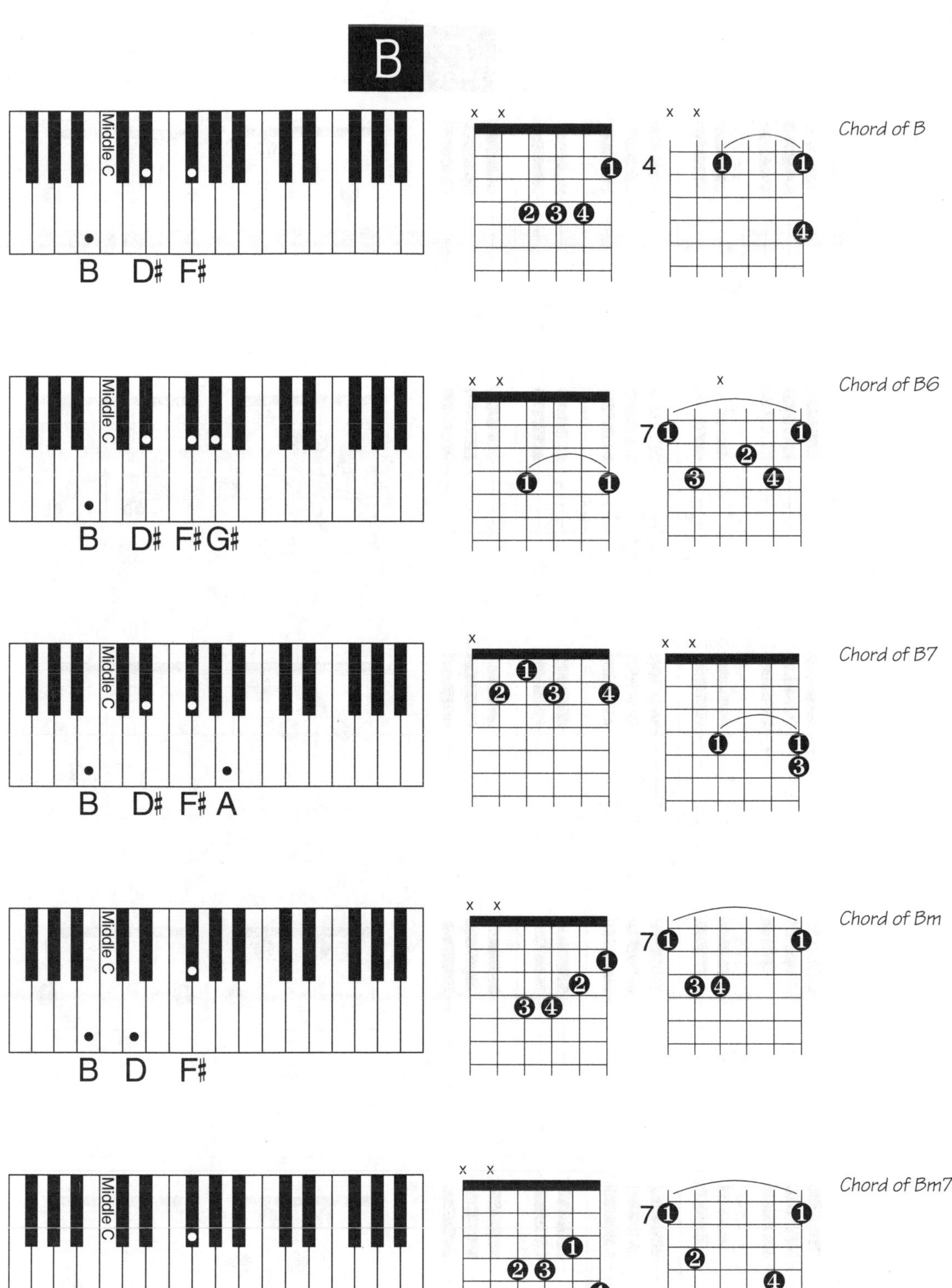

B
Middle C
B D♯ F♯
4
Chord of B
B D♯ F♯G♯
7
Chord of B6
B D♯ F♯ A
Chord of B7
B D F♯
7
Chord of Bm
B D F♯ A
7
Chord of Bm7

Chord of C

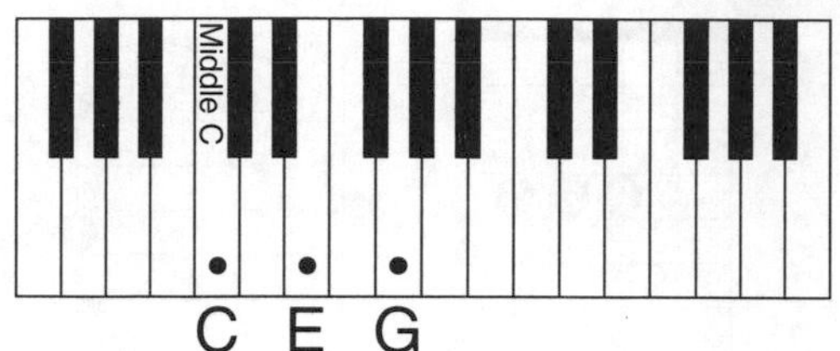

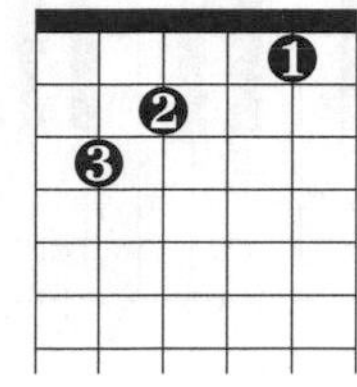

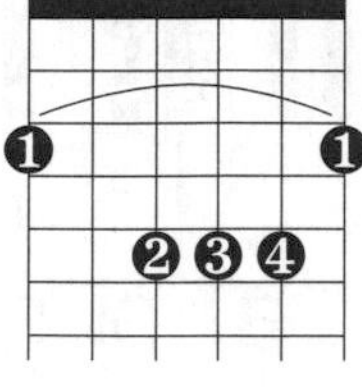

Chord of C6

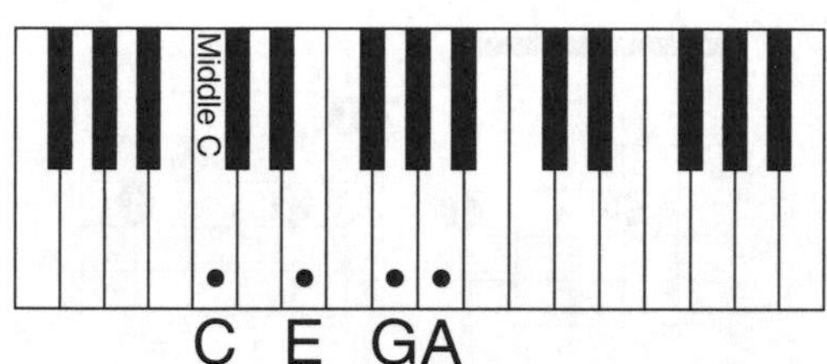

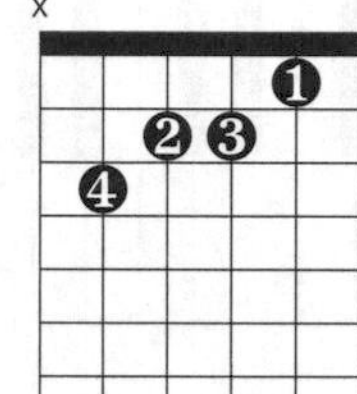

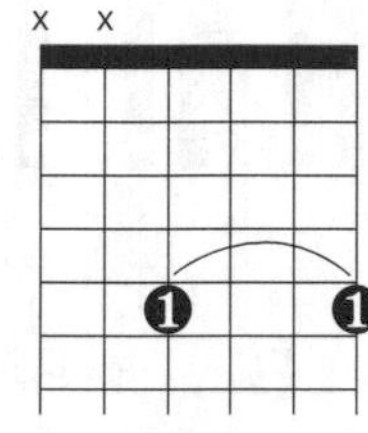

Chord of C7

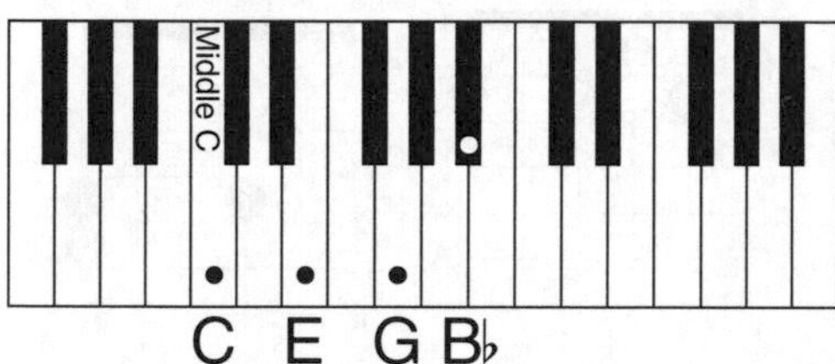

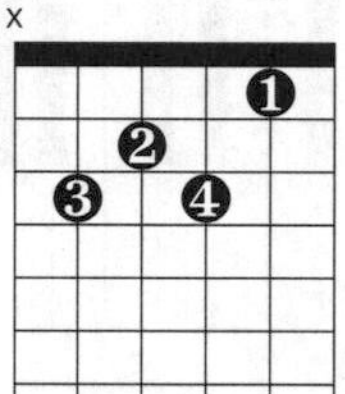

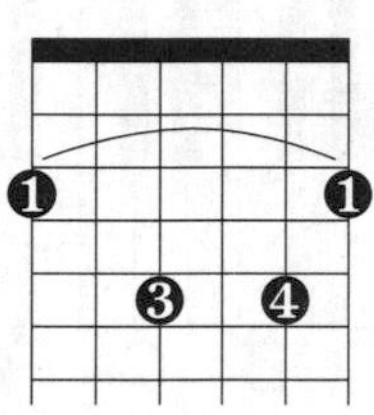

Chord of Cm

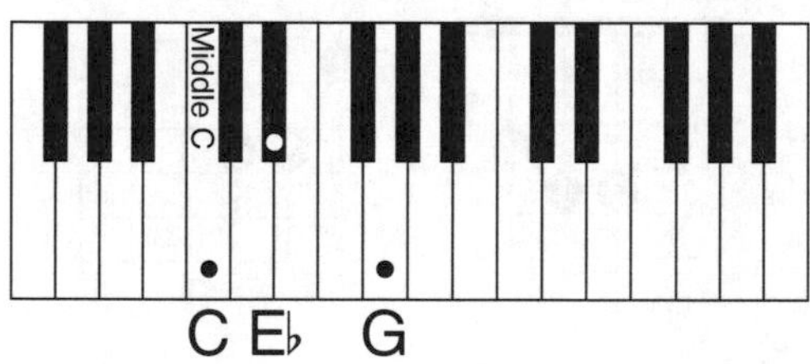

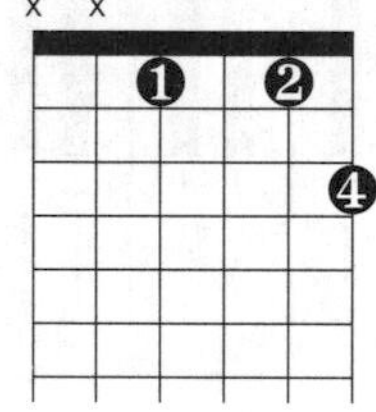

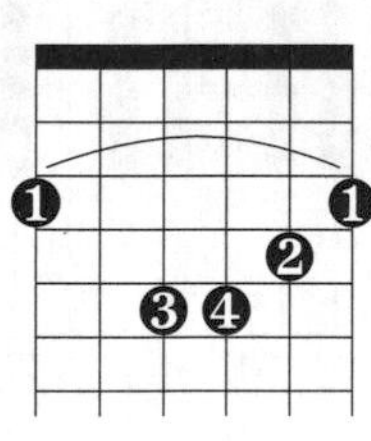

Chord of Cm7

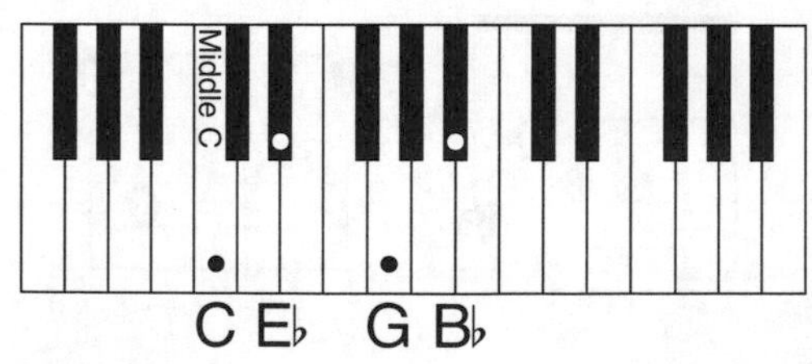

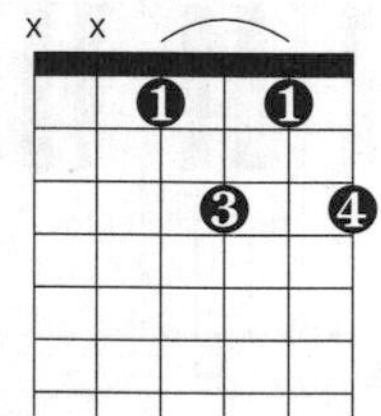

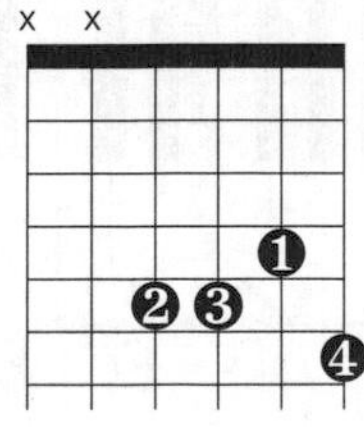

Chord of C♯

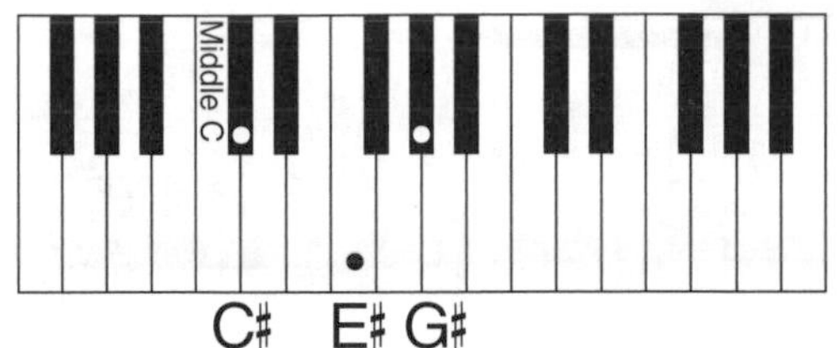

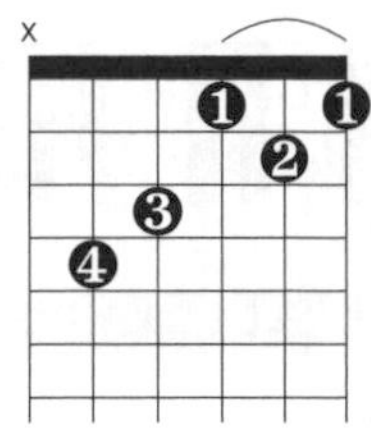

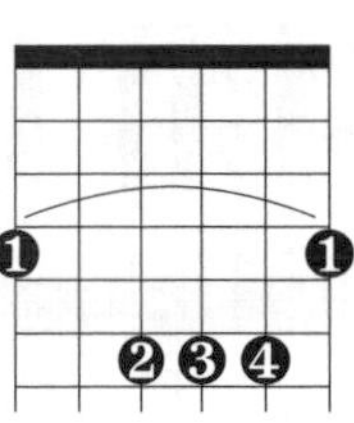

Chord of C♯6

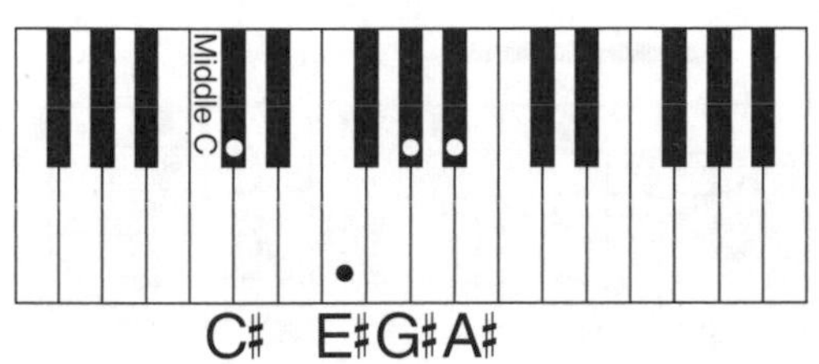

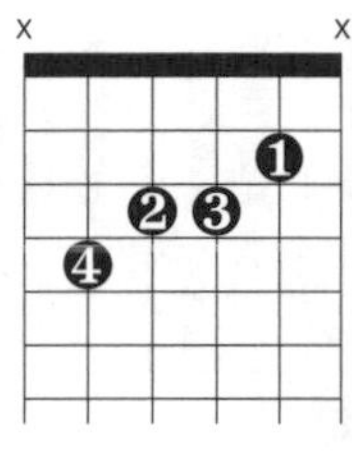

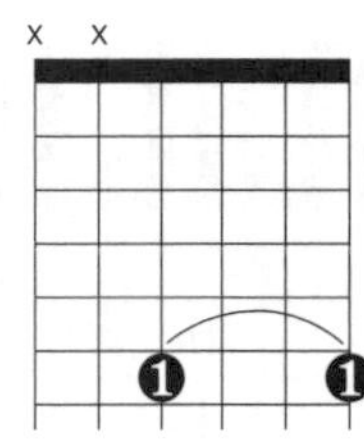

Chord of C♯7

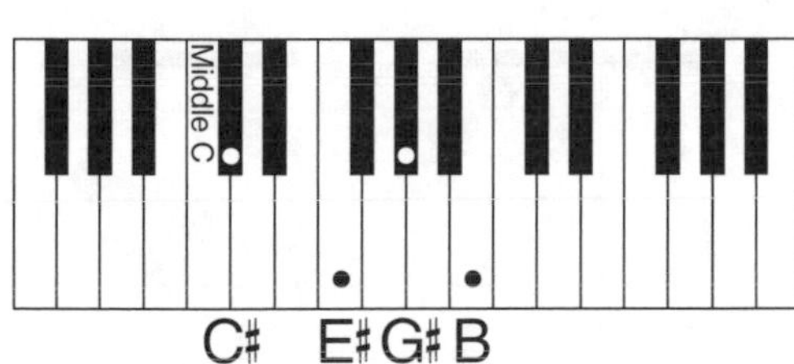

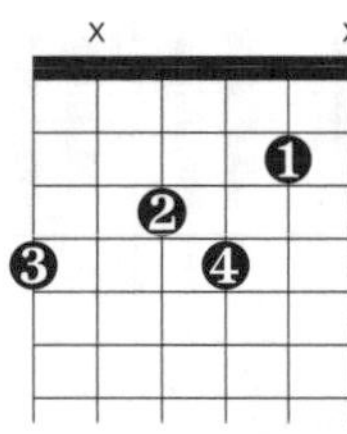

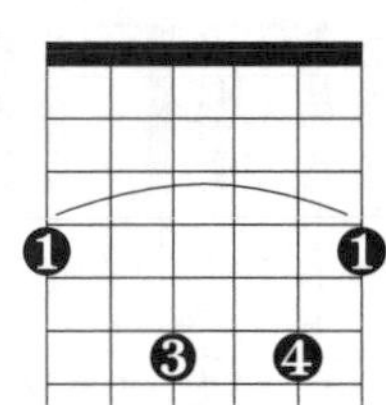

Chord of C♯m

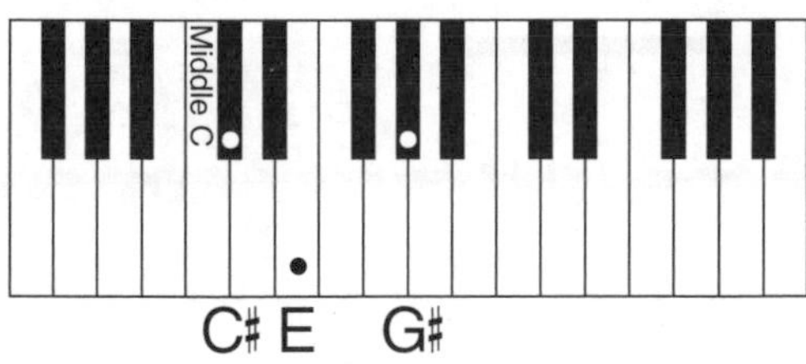

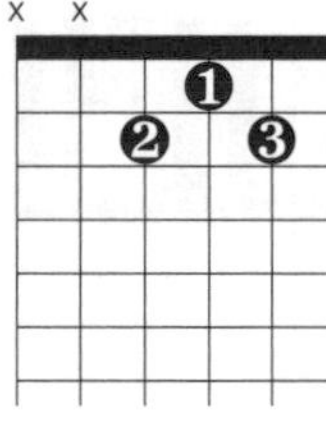

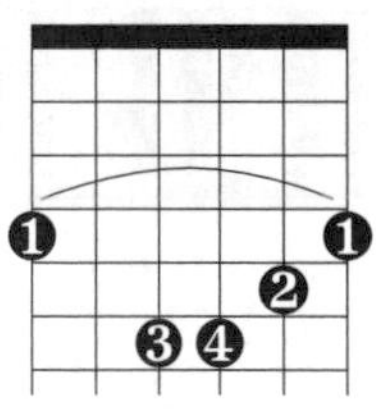

Chord of C♯m7

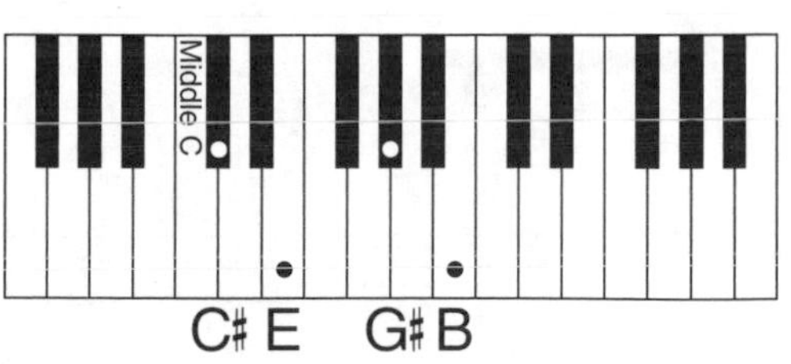

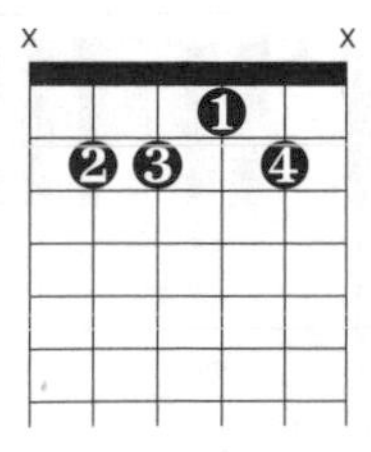

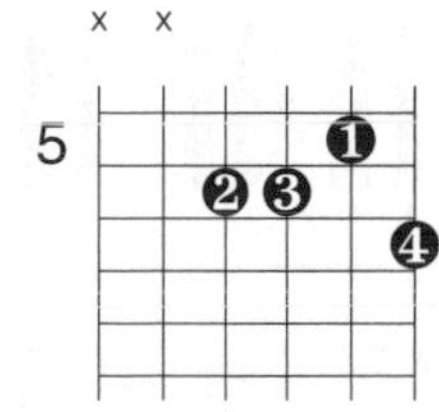

D

Chord of D

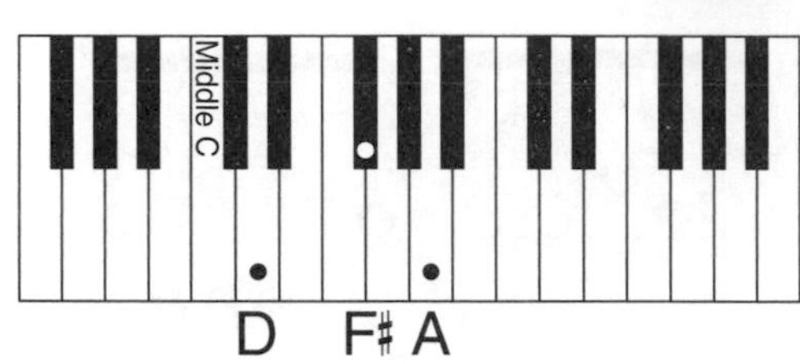

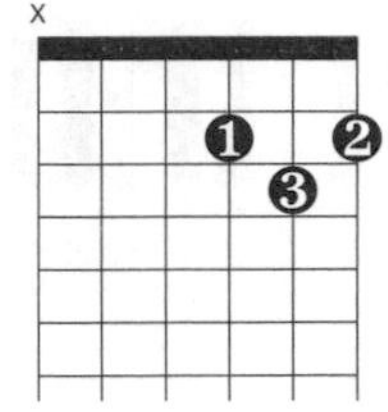

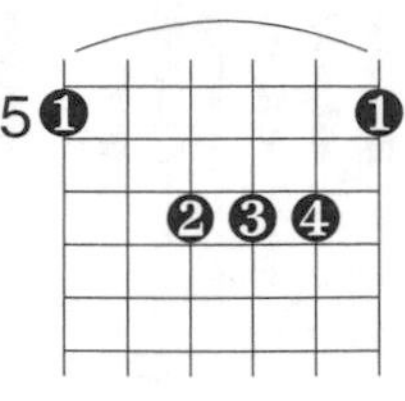

Chord of D6

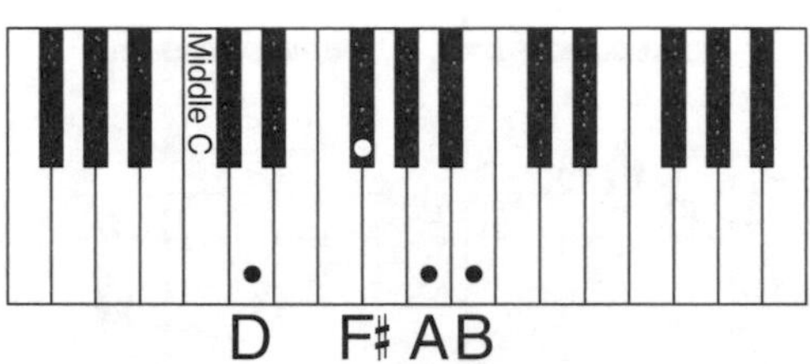

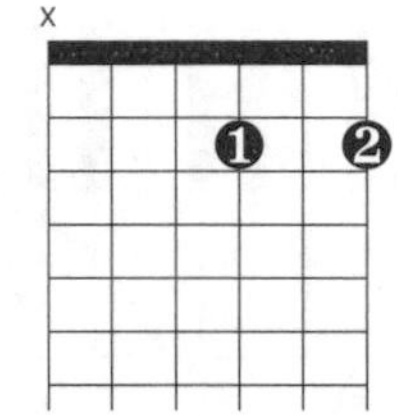

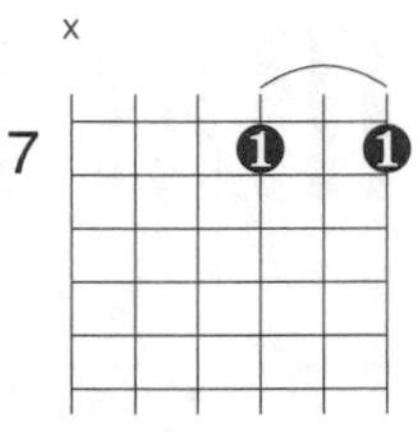

Chord of D7

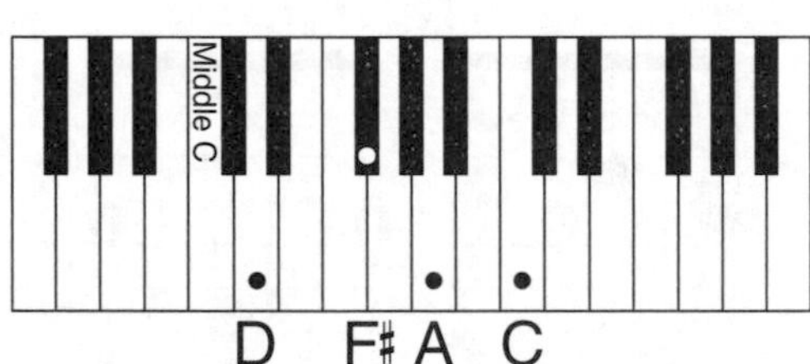

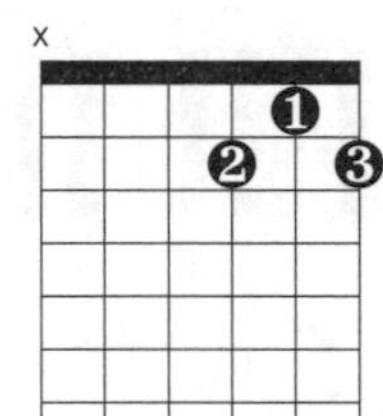

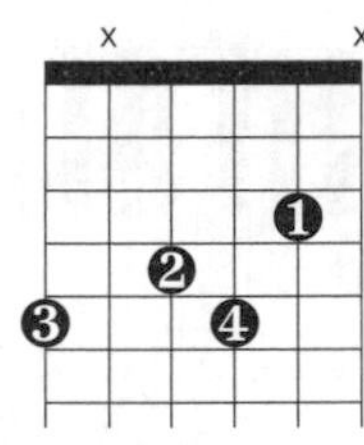

Chord of Dm

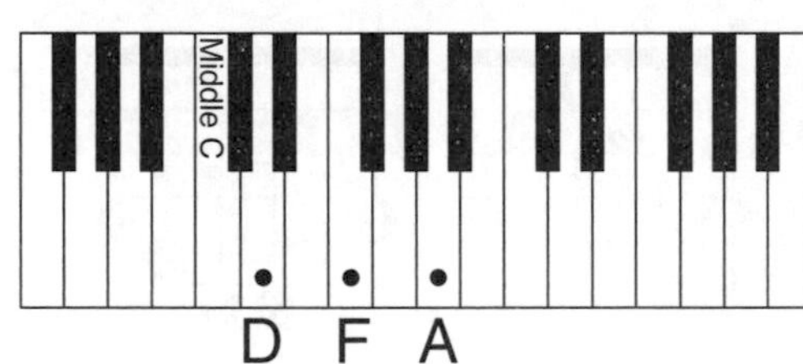

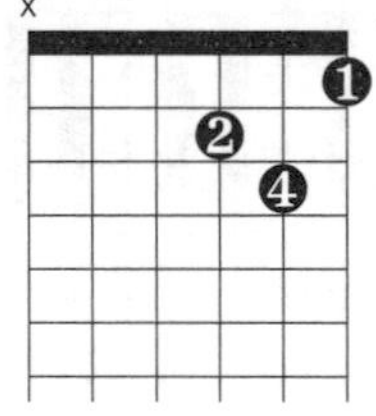

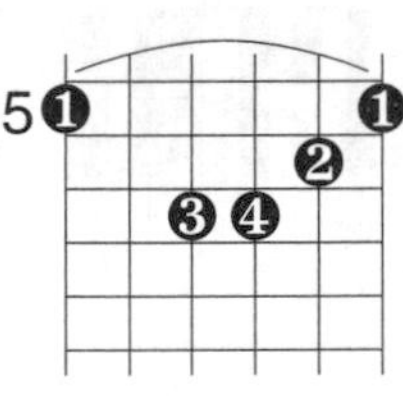

Chord of Dm7

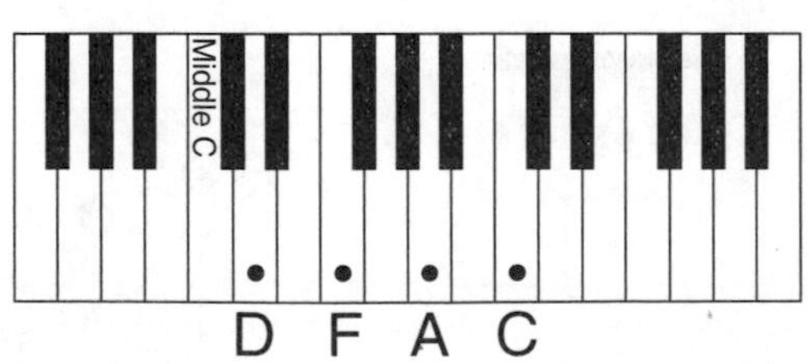

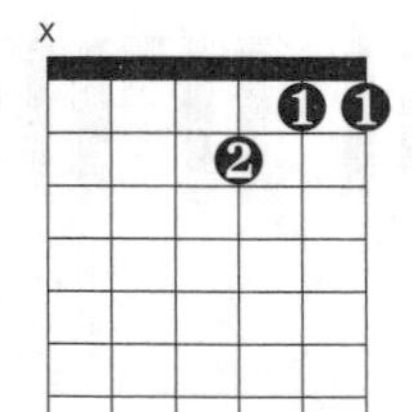

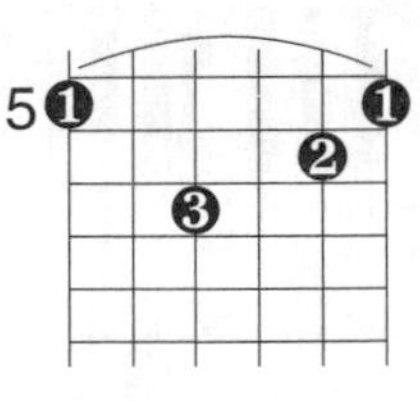

E♭

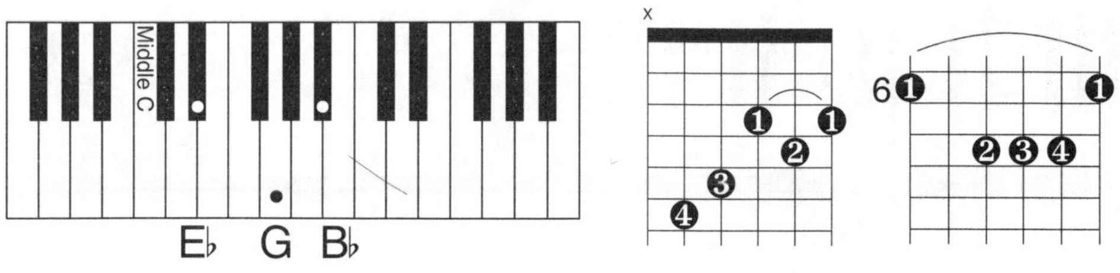

Middle C

E♭ G B♭

x

6

Chord of E♭

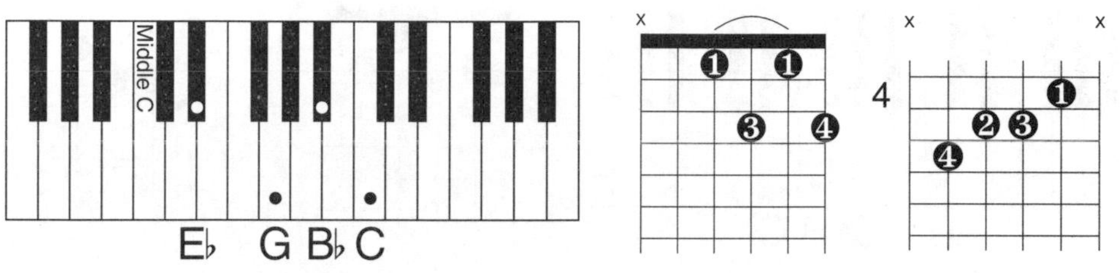

Middle C

E♭ G B♭ C

x

x x

4

Chord of E♭6

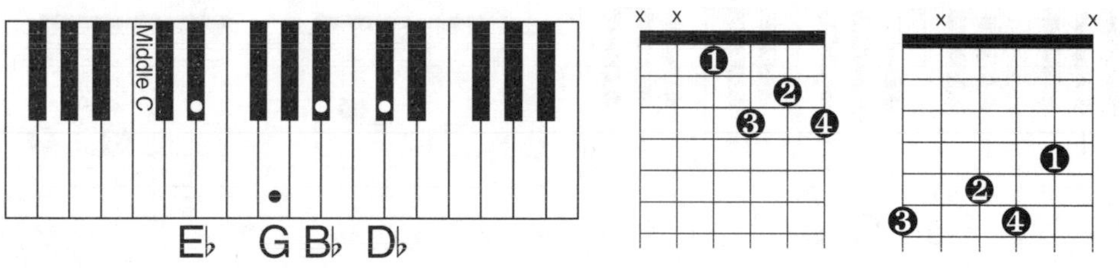

Middle C

E♭ G B♭ D♭

x x

x x

Chord of E♭7

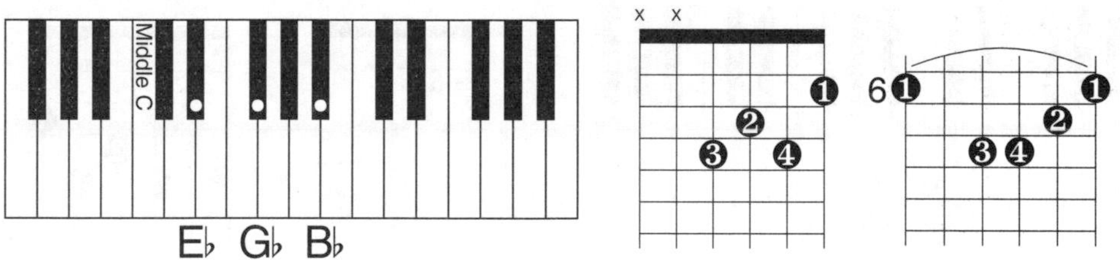

Middle C

E♭ G♭ B♭

x x

6

Chord of E♭m

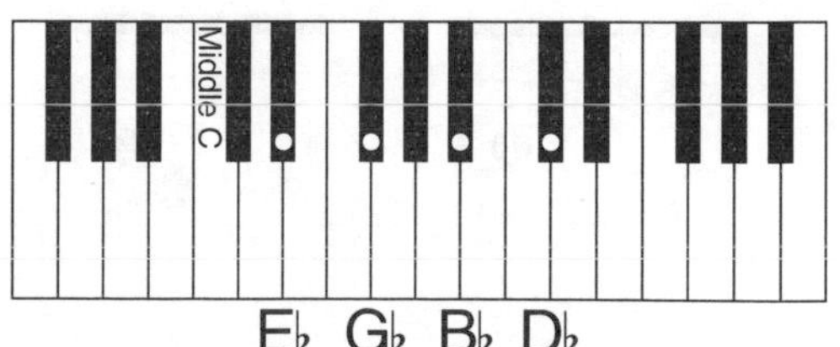

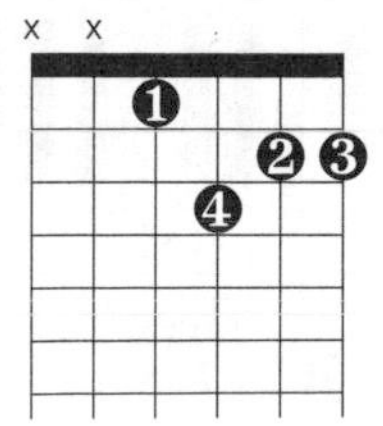

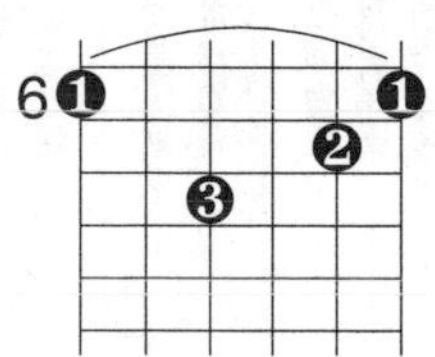

Chord of E♭m7

E

Chord of E

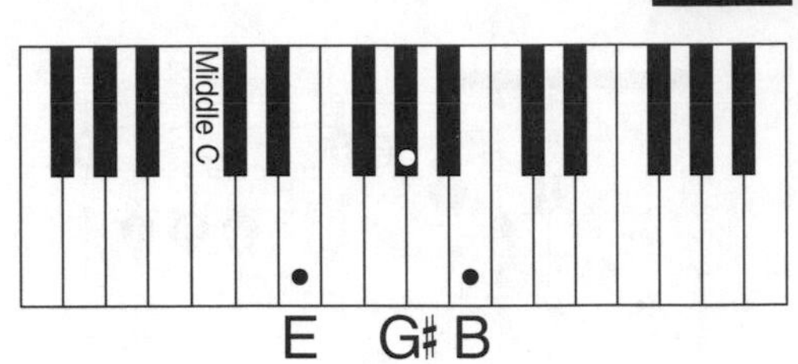

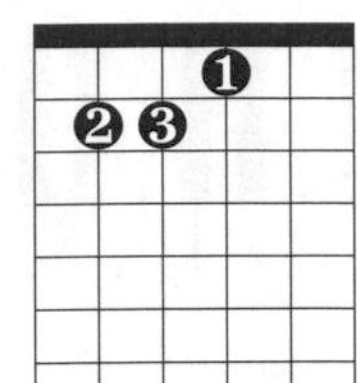

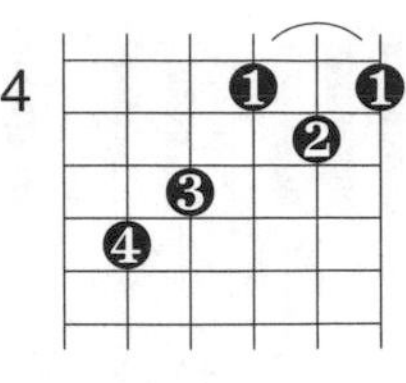

Chord of E6

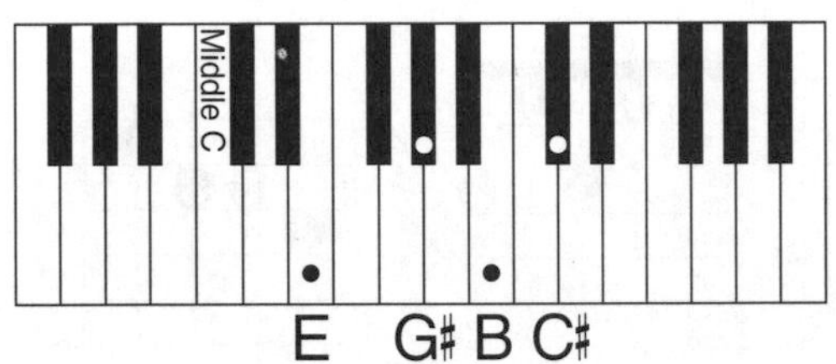

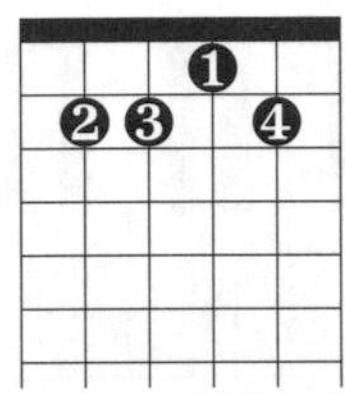

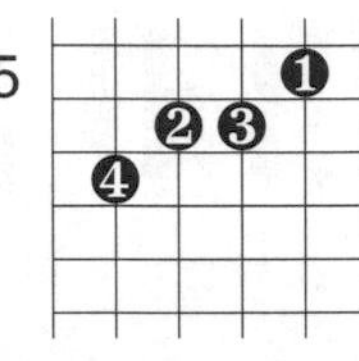

Chord of E7

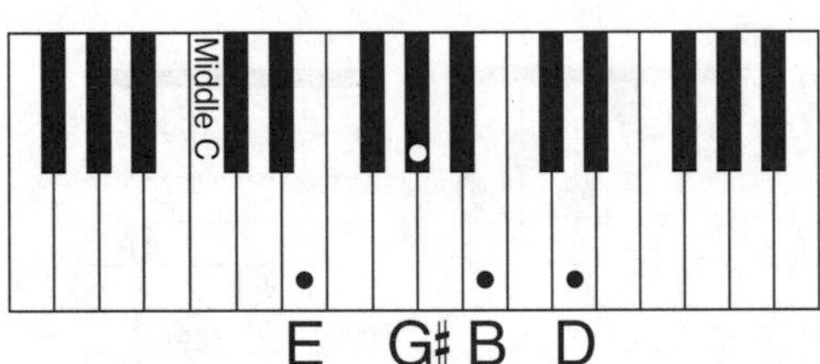

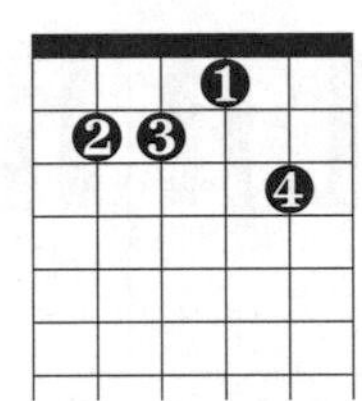

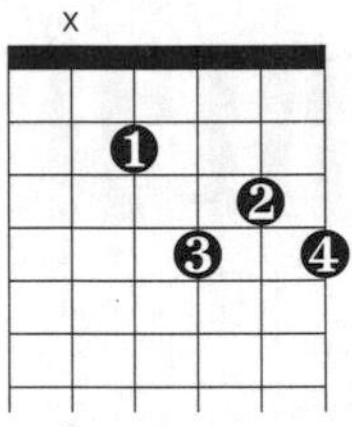

Chord of Em

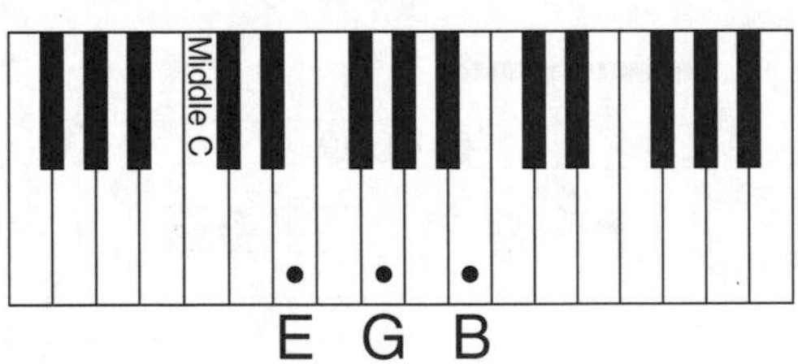

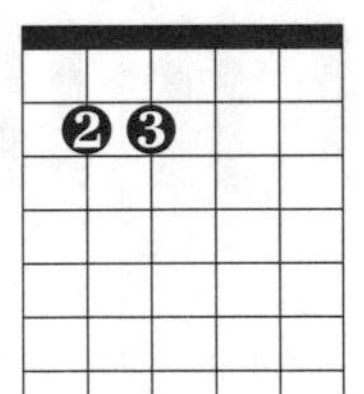

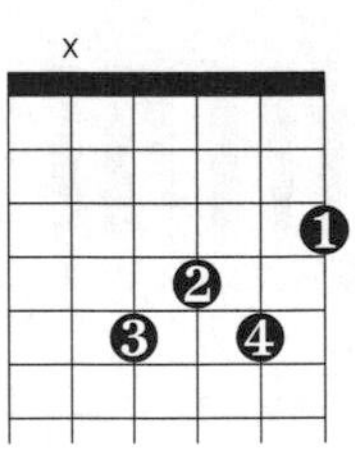

Chord of Em7

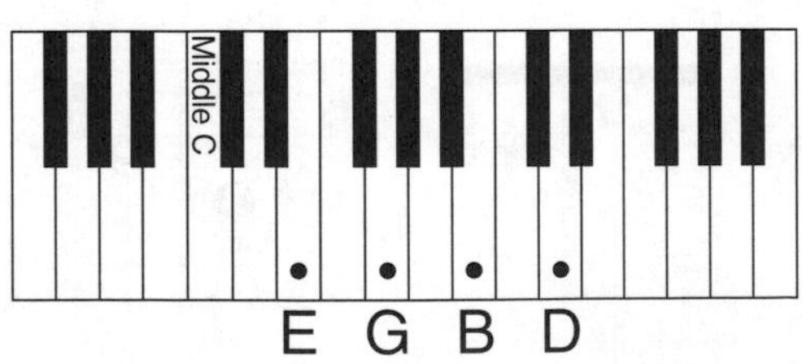

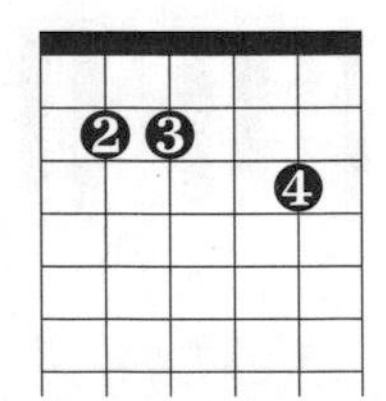

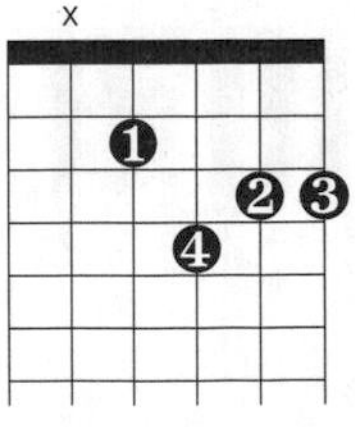

F

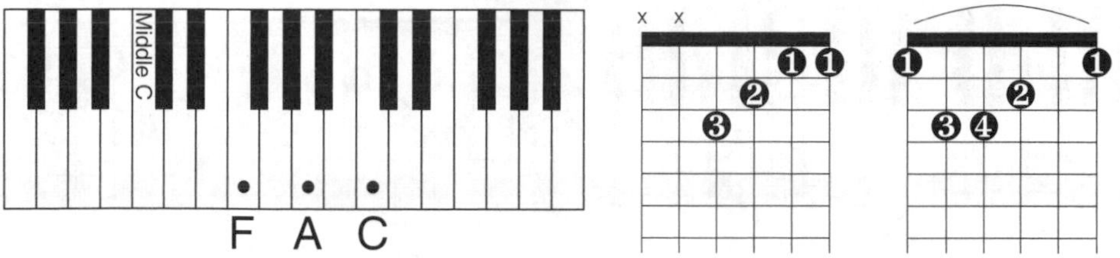

Chord of F

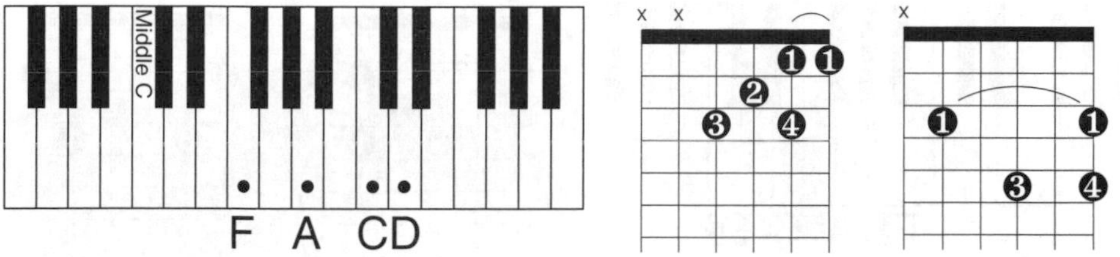

Middle C

F A C

Chord of F6

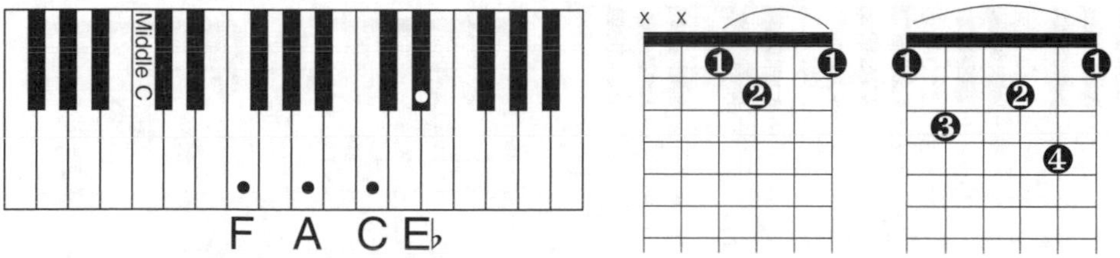

Middle C

F A CD

Chord of F7

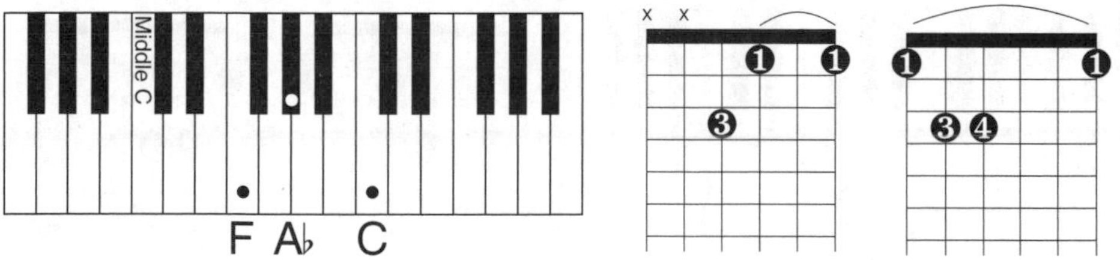

Middle C

F A C E♭

Chord of Fm

Middle C

F A♭ C

Chord of Fm7

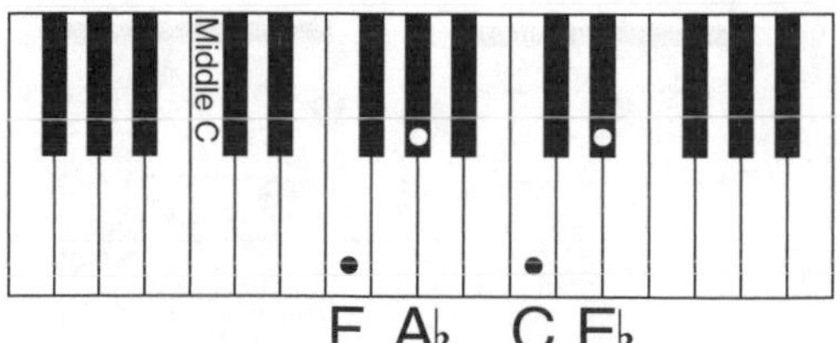

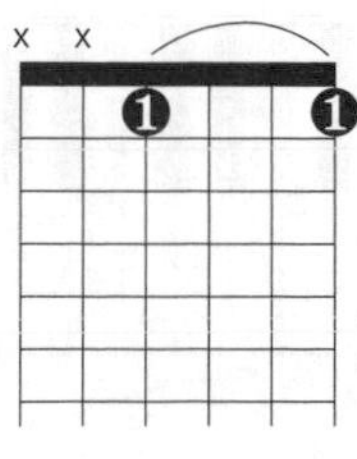

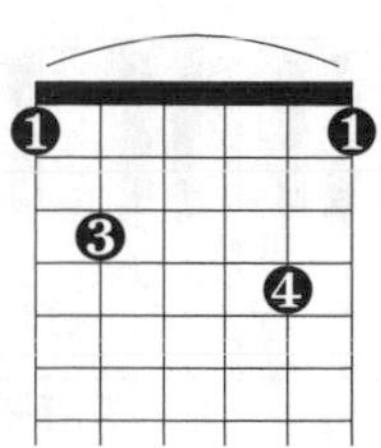

F♯

Chord of F♯

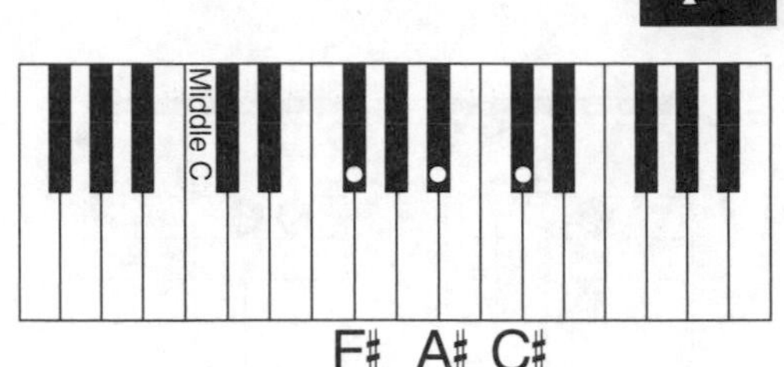

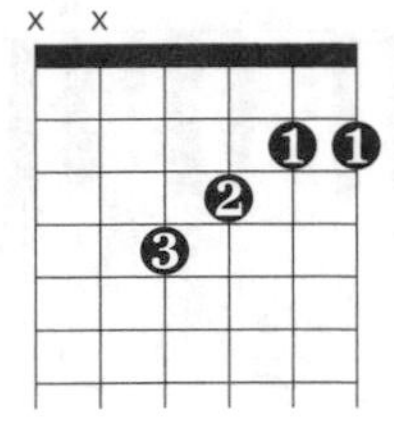

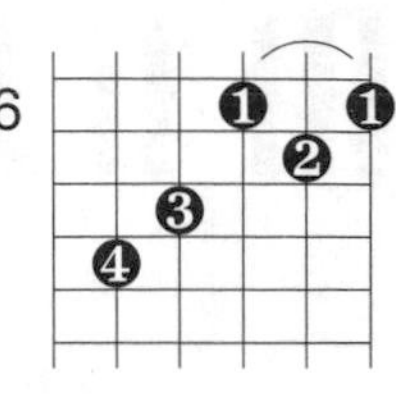

Chord of F♯6

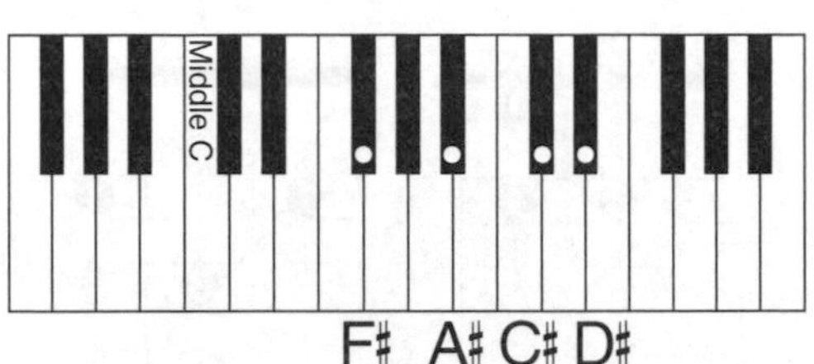

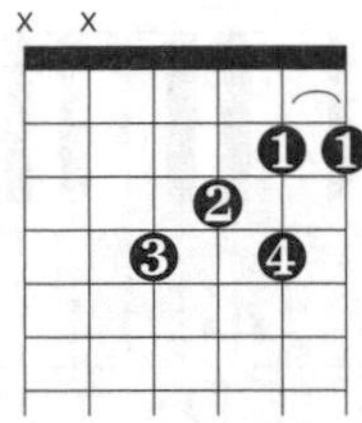

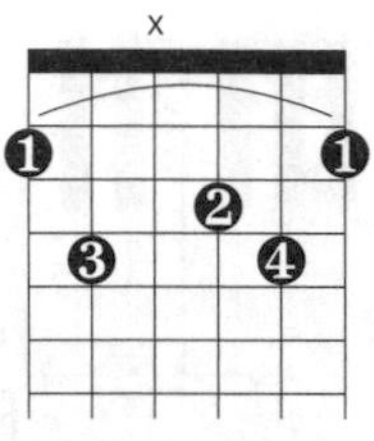

Chord of F♯7

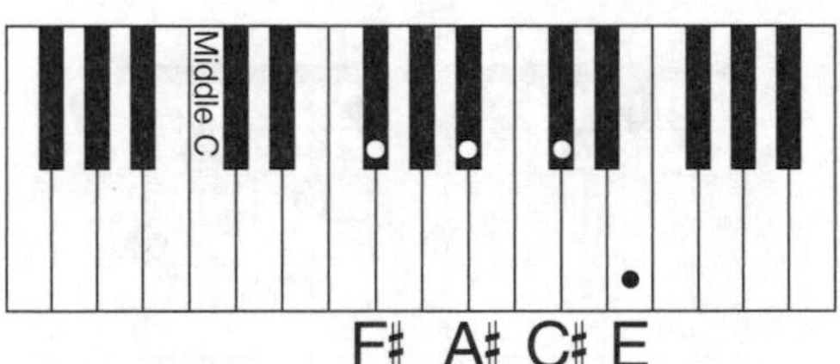

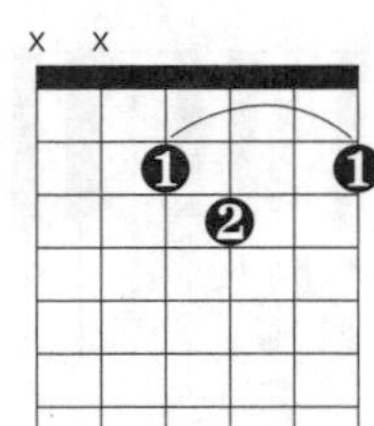

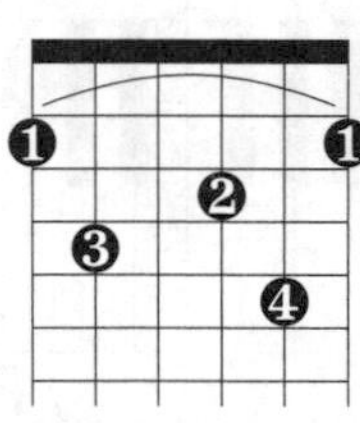

Chord of F♯m

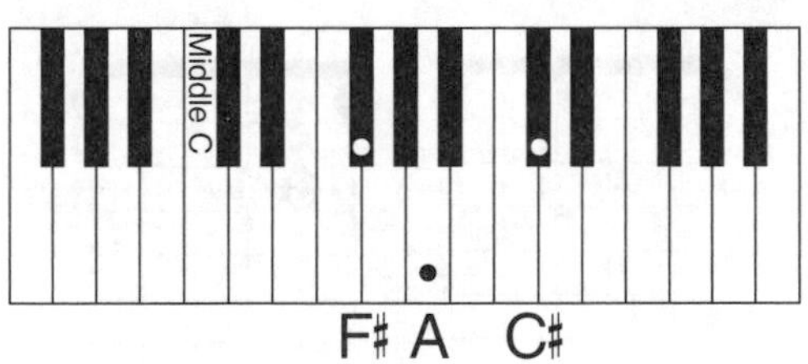

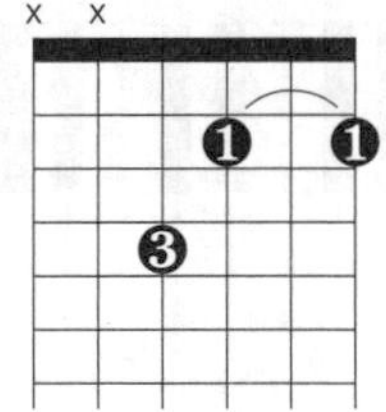

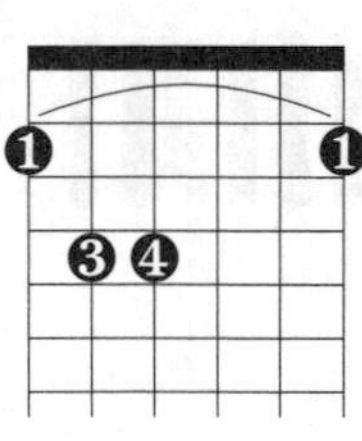

Chord of F♯m7

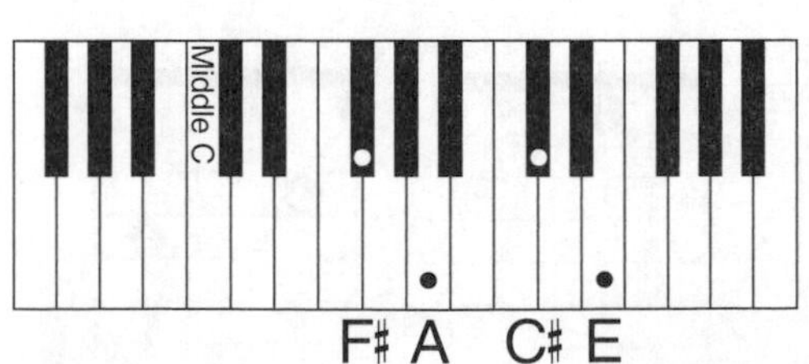

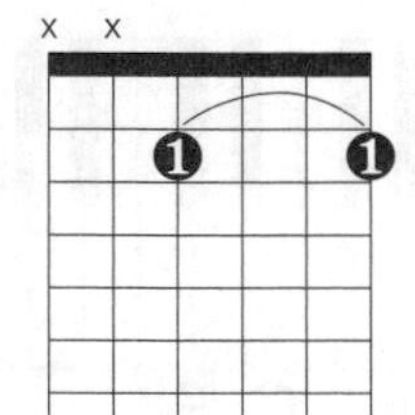

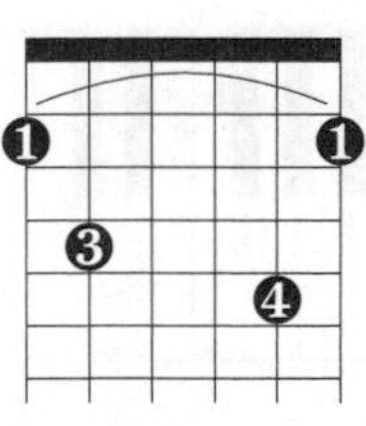

G

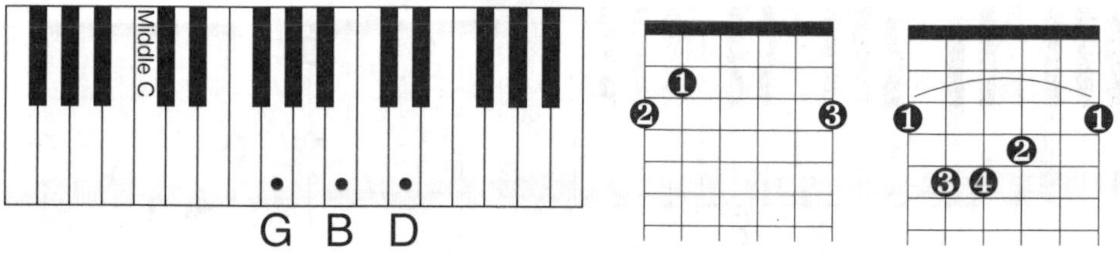

Middle C

G B D

Chord of G

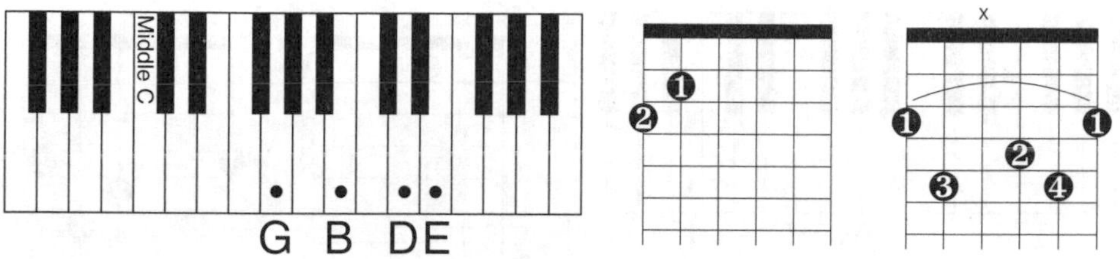

Middle C

G B DE

Chord of G6

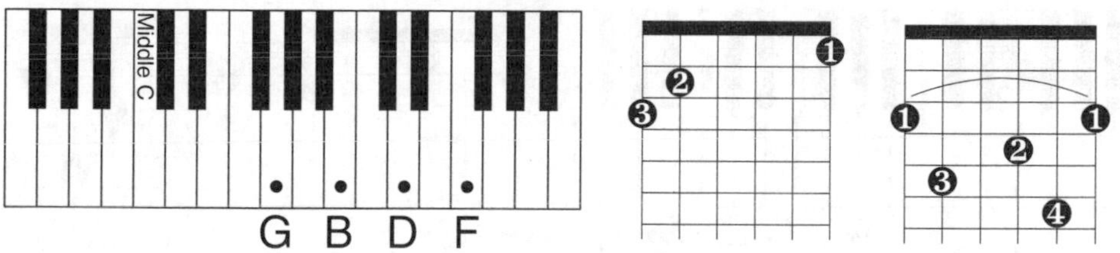

Middle C

G B D F

Chord of G7

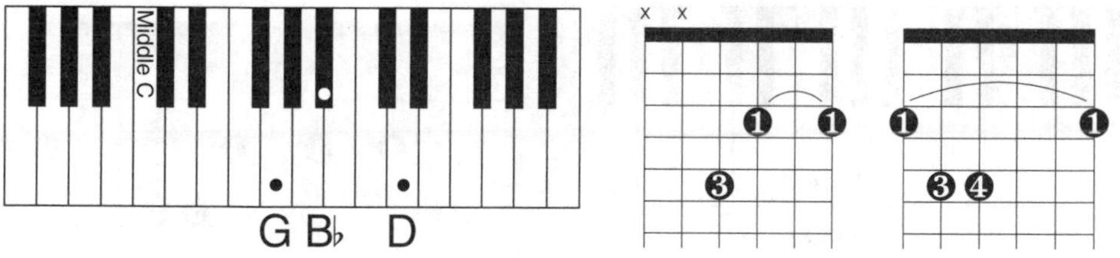

Middle C

G B♭ D

Chord of Gm

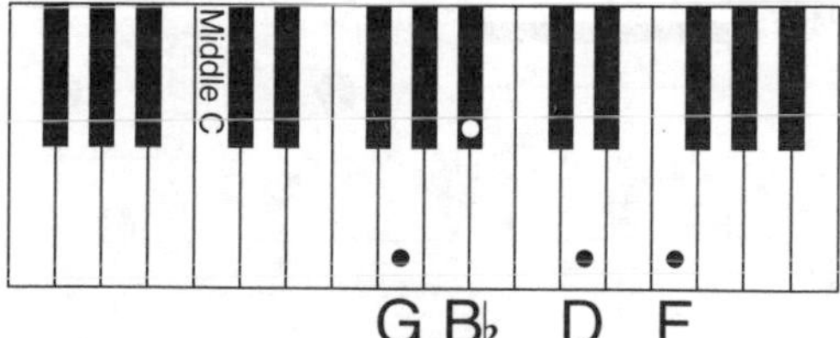

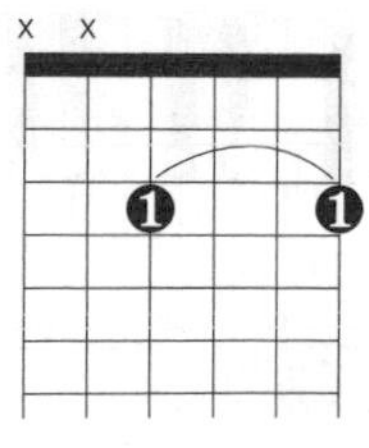

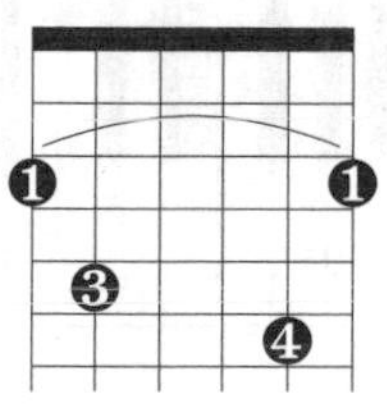

Chord of Gm7

A♭

Chord of A♭

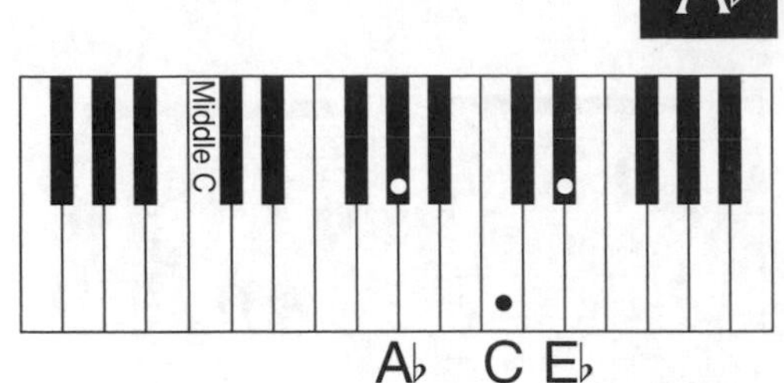

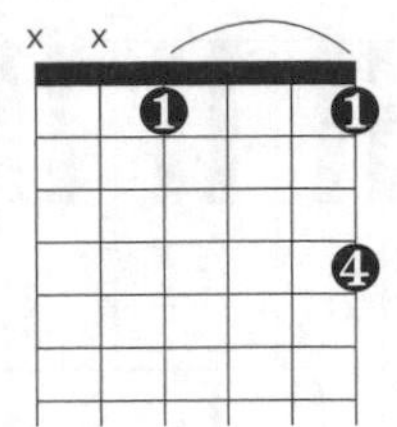

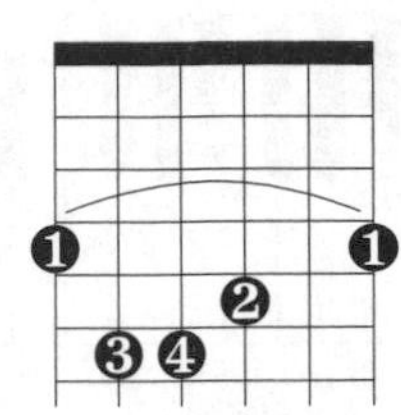

Chord of A♭6

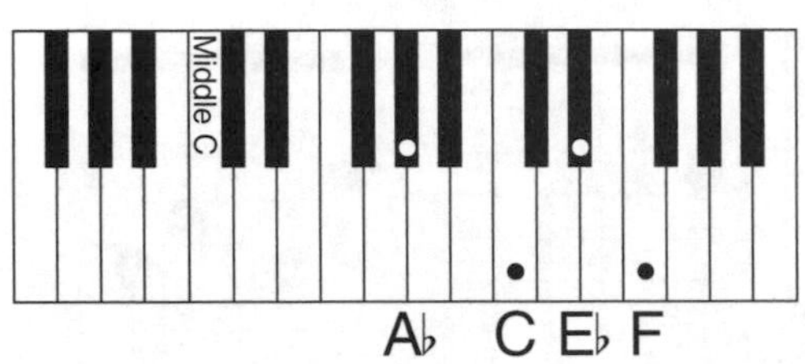

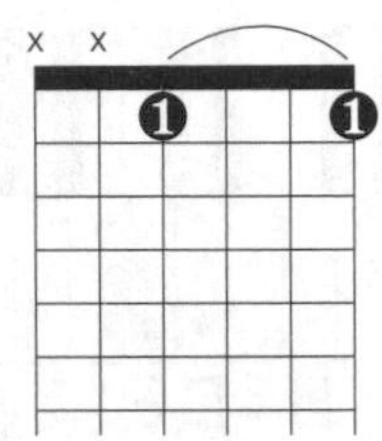

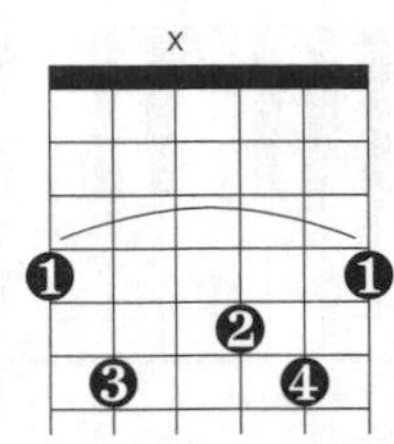

Chord of A♭7

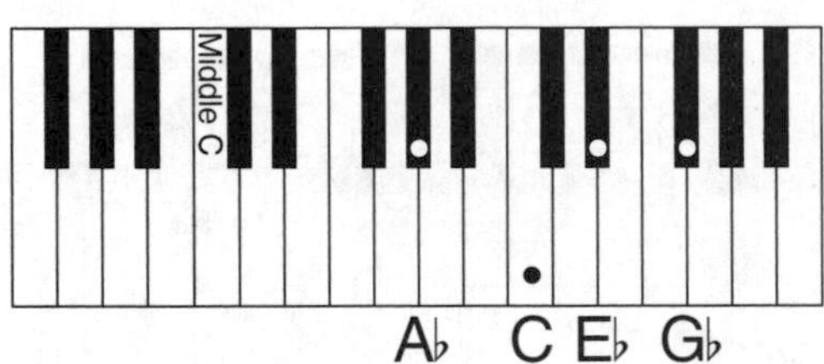

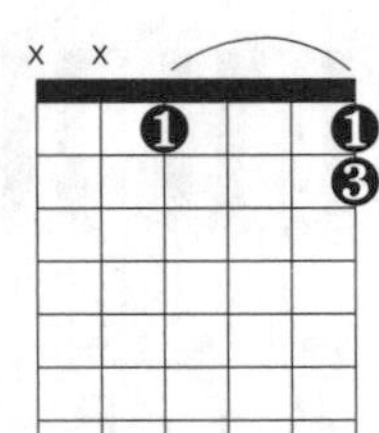

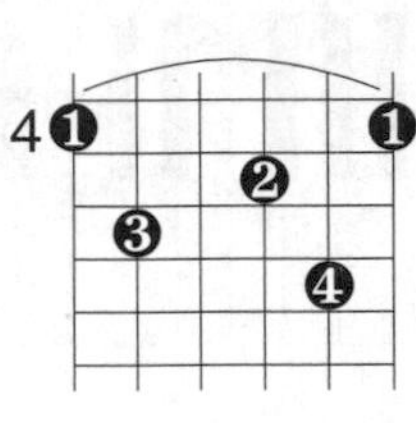

Chord of A♭m

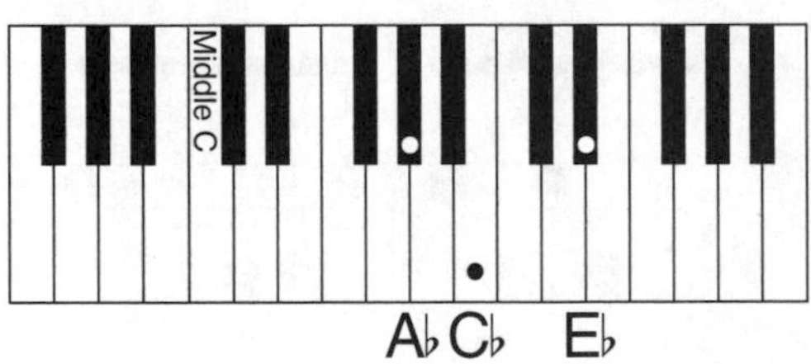

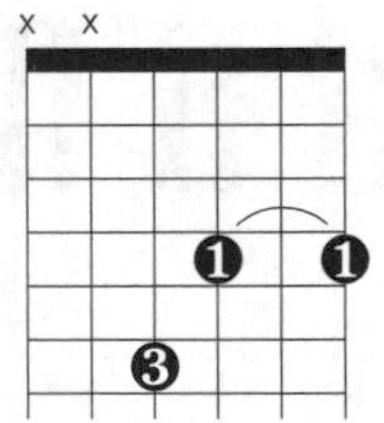

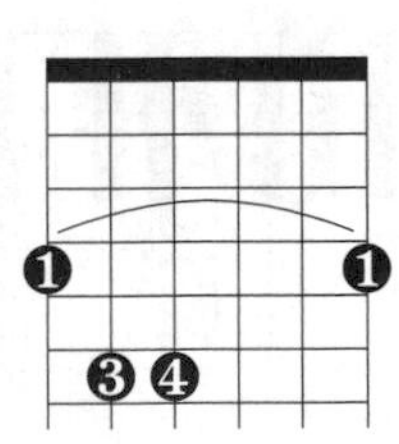

Chord of A♭m7

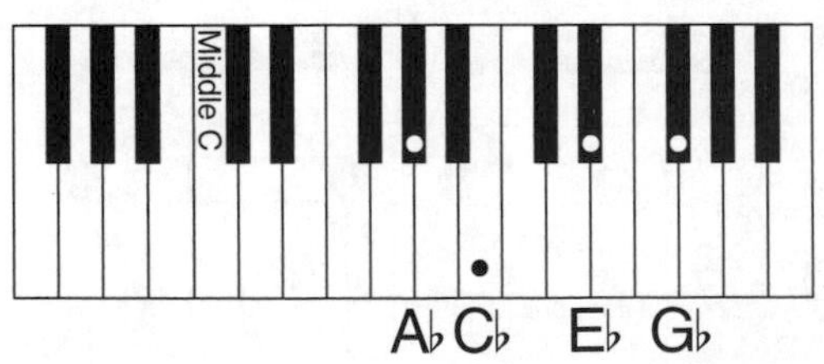

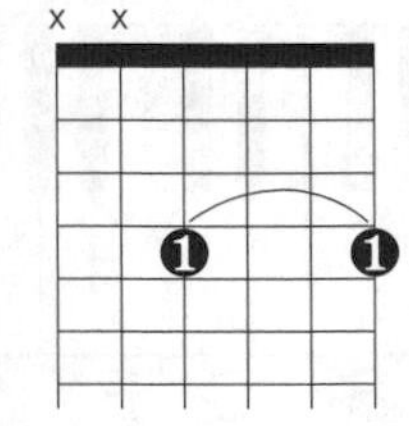

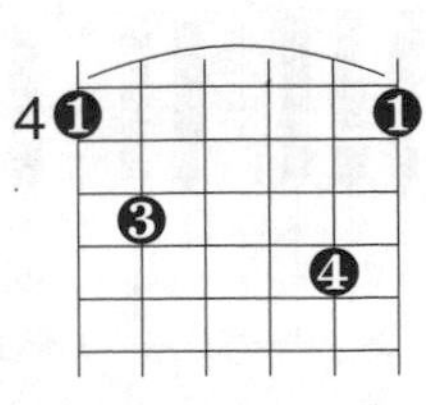

Scales

Music is made up of sounds pitched at relative intervals. The spacing of these intervals makes a scale. The scale largely influences the mood of a piece, as well as the notes that can be used in that piece. However, a piece may change key/scale at any point. A scale comprises of up to twelve notes out of the possible twelve (in equal temperament).

Scale name	*Intervals*	*Example*
major (Ionian)	T T S T T T S	C D E F G A B C
natural minor	T S T T S T T	C D E♭ F G A♭ B♭ C
ascending melodic minor	T S T T T T S	C D E♭ F G A B C
descending melodic minor	T T S T T S T	C B♭ A♭ G F E♭ D C
harmonic minor	T S T T S (T+S) S	C D E♭ F G A♭ B C
jazz minor	T S T T T T S	C D E♭ F G A B C
whole tone	T T T T T T	C D E F♯ G♯ A♯ C
Dorian	T S T T T S T	C D E♭ F G A B♭ C
Phrygian	S T T T S T T	C D♭ E♭ F G A♭ B♭ C
Lydian	T T T S T T S	C D E F♯ G A B C
Mixolydian	T T S T T S T	C D E F G A B♭ C
Aeolian	T S T T S T T	C D E♭ F A♭ B♭ C
Locrian	S T T S T T T	C D♭ E♭ F G♭ A♭ B♭ C
diminished	T S T S T S T S	C D E♭ F G♭ A♭ A B C
blues	(T+S) T S S (T+S) T	C E♭ F G♭ G B♭ C
pentatonic	T T (T+S) T	C D E G A
augmented (symmetrical)	(T+S) S (T+S) S (T+S) S	C D♯ E G A♭ B C
Lydian/dominant 7	T T T S T S T	C D E F♯ G A B♭ C
Hindu	T T S T S T T	C D E F G A♭ B♭ C
oriental	S (T+S) S S (T+S) S T	C D♭ E F G♭ A B♭ C
Hungarian minor	T S (T+S) S S (T+S) S	C D E♭ F♯ G A♭ B C
Chromatic	S S S S S S S S S S S S	C C♯ D D♯ E F F♯ G G♯ A A♯ B C

The scales can be viewed in different ways. The following may help you to remember them:

Scale name	*View*
descending melodic	as ascending but sixth and seventh degrees are lowered a half step.
Dorian	tones are major scale, one step below the root
Phrygian	pure minor with a lowered second degree
Lydian	major scale with a raise fourth tone
Mixolydian	tones are a major scale fifth below root
Aeolian	tones are a minor third above root
Locrian	tones are a major scale, half step above root

A melody can be formed in a chosen scale and, over that, a chord structure evolved that complements the melody, usually by containing some notes from the melody. (Alternatively a chord sequence can be formed and the melody found from that.) Further orchestration/arrangement can then be derived by taking notes from the chord and orchestrating them with different octaves and sounds to create new textures.

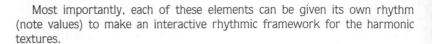

Most importantly, each of these elements can be given its own rhythm (note values) to make an interactive rhythmic framework for the harmonic textures.

Scores

Notes, rests and staves

Fraction name	*Proper name*	*Symbol*	*Rest*	*Value*	*Number per 4/4 bar*
whole note	semibreve	𝅝	𝄻	4 beats	1
half note	minim	𝅗𝅥	𝄼	2 beats	2
quarter note	crotchet	♩	𝄽	1 beat	4
eighth note	quaver	♪	𝄾	1/2 beat	8
sixteenth note	semiquaver	𝅘𝅥𝅯	𝄿	1/4 beat	16
thirty-second note	demisemiquaver	𝅘𝅥𝅰	𝅀	1/8 beat	32

Notes

- A dotted note (.) means add half that note duration – for instance, a dotted crotchet lasts for 1.5 beats.
- A triplet note (^{3}) means three notes played in the time of two.

Instruments, staffs and scoring

The stave is a graphical way of representing note values. The height position on the stave indicates pitch, the symbol used the duration, and the order shown is the order for playing. Note symbols directly above each other represent a chord.

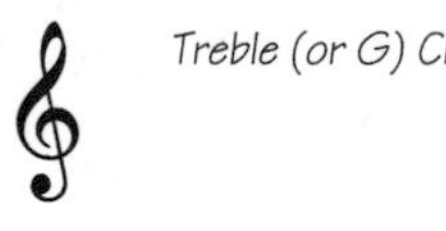

Treble (or G) Clef

There are a number of types of stave employed to aid readability, identified by the stave symbol. The starting points of the clef symbol shows the relevant clef/stave pitch as shown.

Bass (or F) Clef

Alto (or C) Clef

Rhythms

Rhythm is a very important element in music, arguably more important than pitch which can't really exist on its own. As well as the normal rhythmic foundations of drums and bass backline, there is also the rhythmic feel between instruments and parts. Some example drum rhythms follow on pages 84 – 87.

Tempo to style

Style	BPM
Pop	100-125
Techno/Euro	128-138
70s Funk	93-117
House/Garage	118-128
Hip Hop/Rap	93-115
New Jack Swing/US Dance	98-113
Street Soul	92-111
Rave/Hardcore	128-140

Rhythms needn't be based on the normal 4/4 time signature – 7/8 and 5/4 are also quite popular for certain styles of music. While it is possible to count these in more regular timings (like 5/4 = 3/4 + 2/4) this defeats the point. Interesting effects can be achieved by cross running different time signatures for different instruments. Literally thousands of poly-rhythms occur within them.

- Interesting effects and new ideas can be born from imposing the rhythm of one part on another. This could range from playing the kick drum part on a cowbell to playing the hi-hat part with a bass synth sound.
- Adding a delay line effect to percussion can create very rich poly-rhythmical textures, especially if they are slightly out of time.
- See page 111 for details on how to match delay time to tempo.

Sample drum patterns

Rock

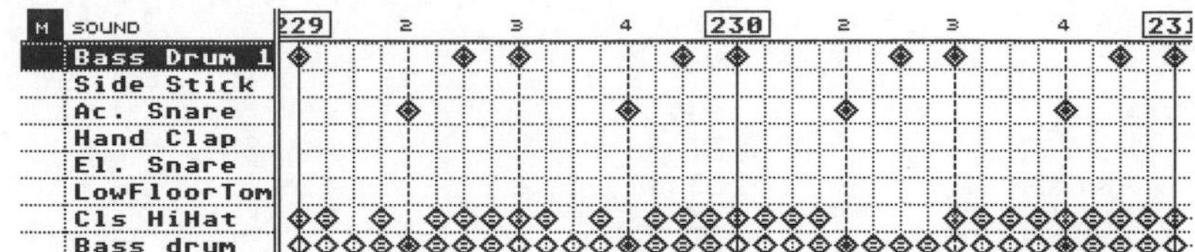

Blues

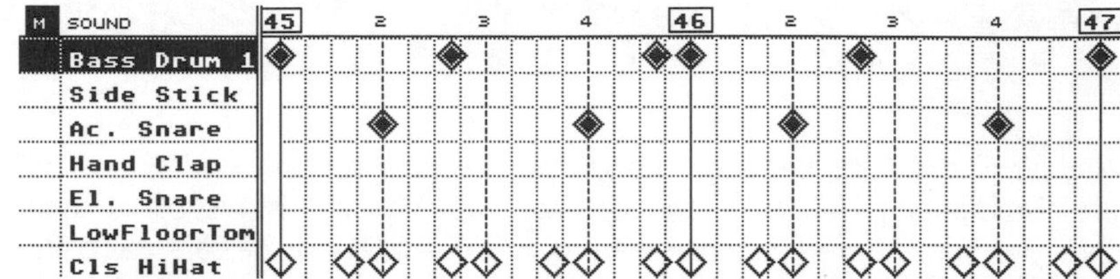

Soul

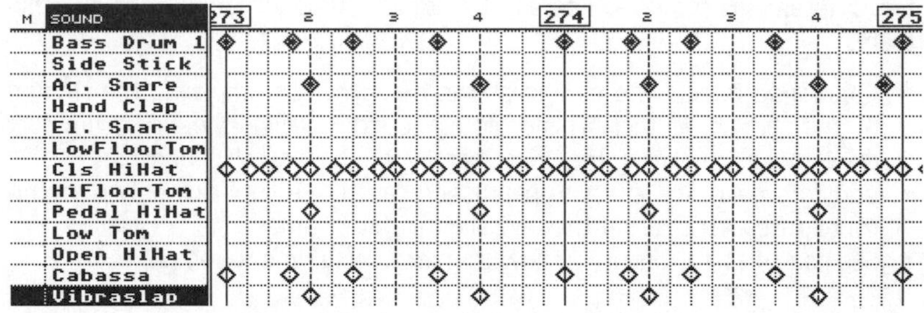

Funky

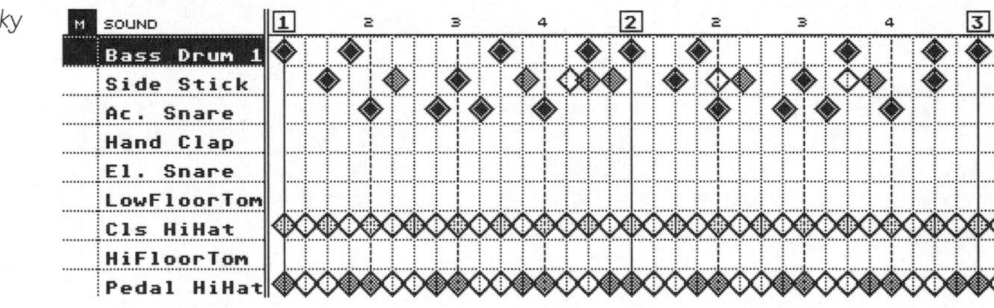

House

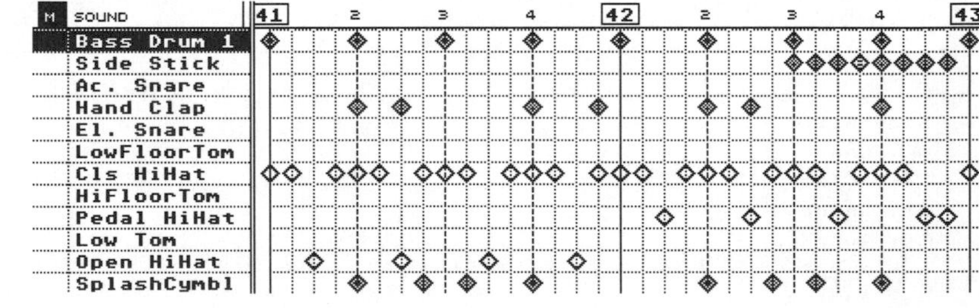

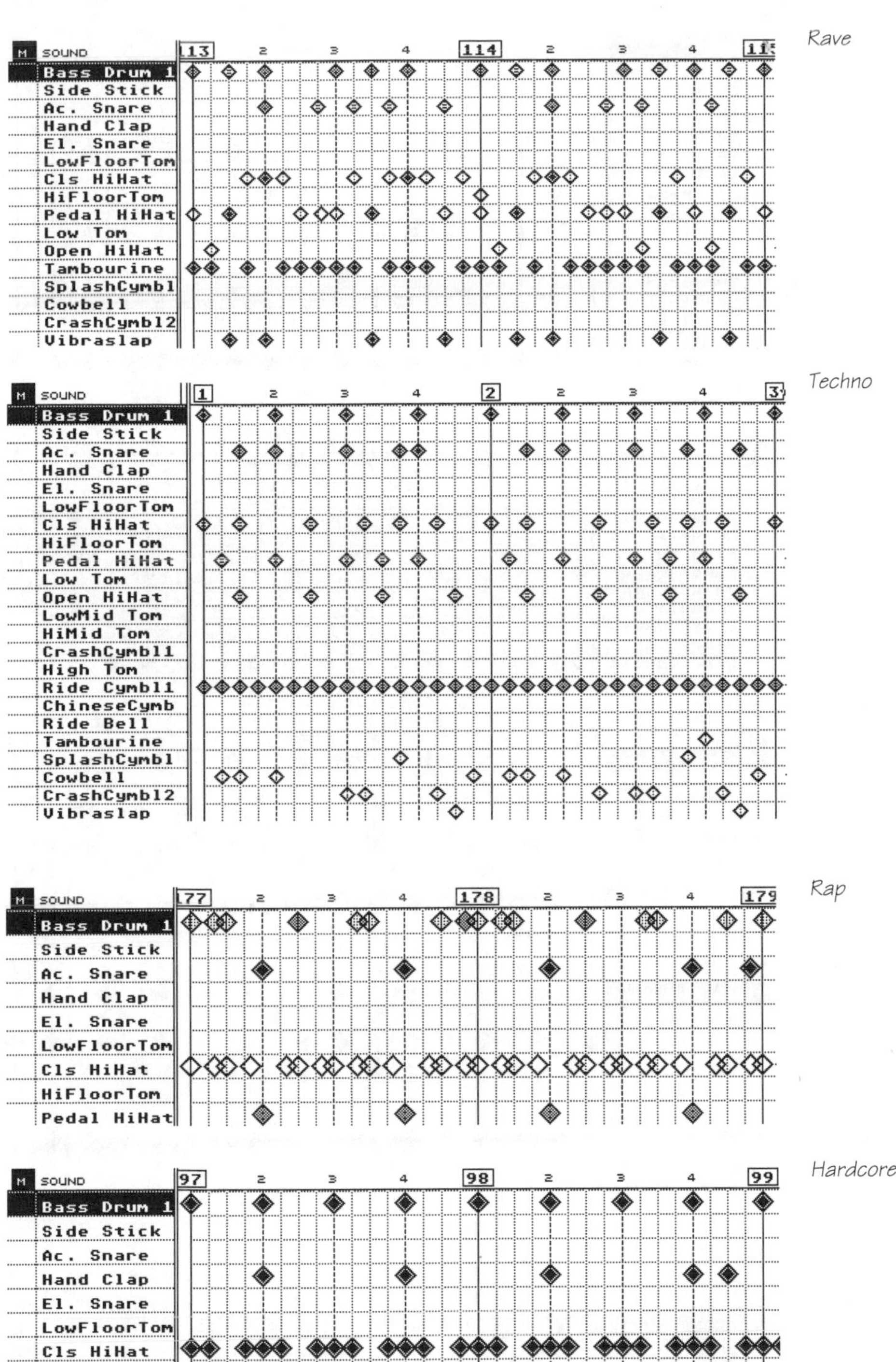
Rave
M SOUND
113 2 3 4 114 2 3 4 115
Bass Drum 1
Side Stick
Ac. Snare
Hand Clap
El. Snare
LowFloorTom
Cls HiHat
HiFloorTom
Pedal HiHat
Low Tom
Open HiHat
Tambourine
SplashCymbl
Cowbell
CrashCymbl2
Vibraslap
Techno
M SOUND
1 2 3 4 2 2 3 4 3
Bass Drum 1
Side Stick
Ac. Snare
Hand Clap
El. Snare
LowFloorTom
Cls HiHat
HiFloorTom
Pedal HiHat
Low Tom
Open HiHat
LowMid Tom
HiMid Tom
CrashCymbl1
High Tom
Ride Cymbl1
ChineseCymb
Ride Bell
Tambourine
SplashCymbl
Cowbell
CrashCymbl2
Vibraslap
Rap
M SOUND
177 2 3 4 178 2 3 4 179
Bass Drum 1
Side Stick
Ac. Snare
Hand Clap
El. Snare
LowFloorTom
Cls HiHat
HiFloorTom
Pedal HiHat
Hardcore
M SOUND
97 2 3 4 98 2 3 4 99
Bass Drum 1
Side Stick
Ac. Snare
Hand Clap
El. Snare
LowFloorTom
Cls HiHat
HiFloorTom
Pedal HiHat
Low Tom
Open HiHat

Jackswing

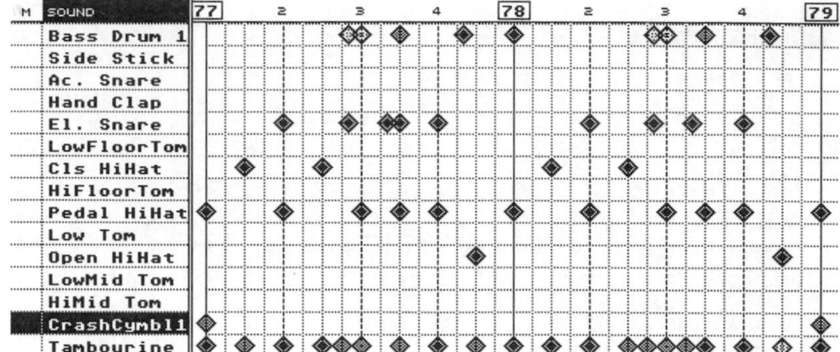

Hiphop

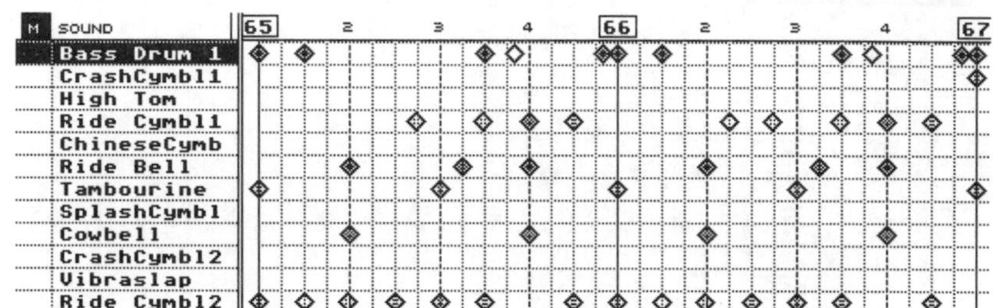

Gospel

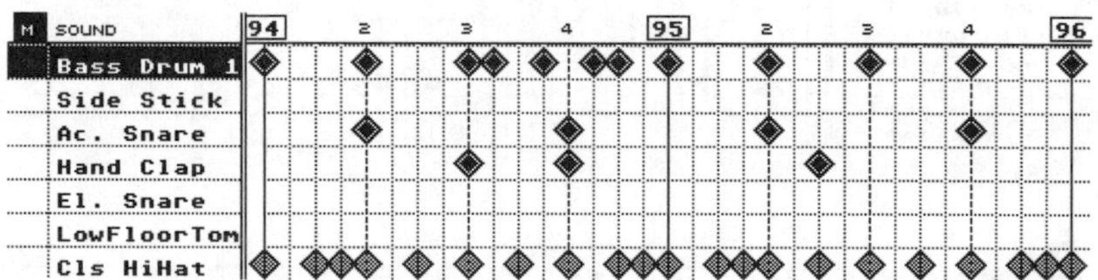

Raga

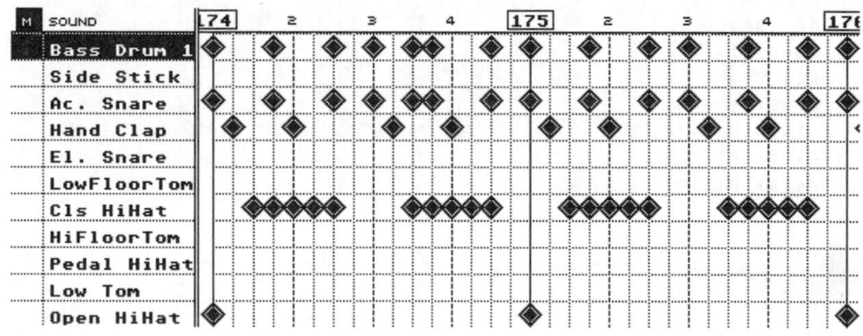

Swingbeat

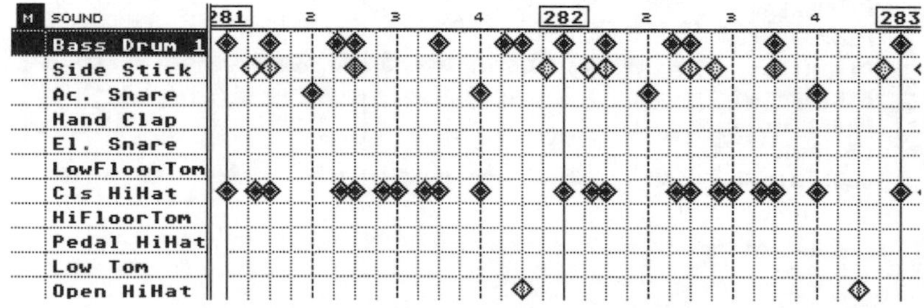

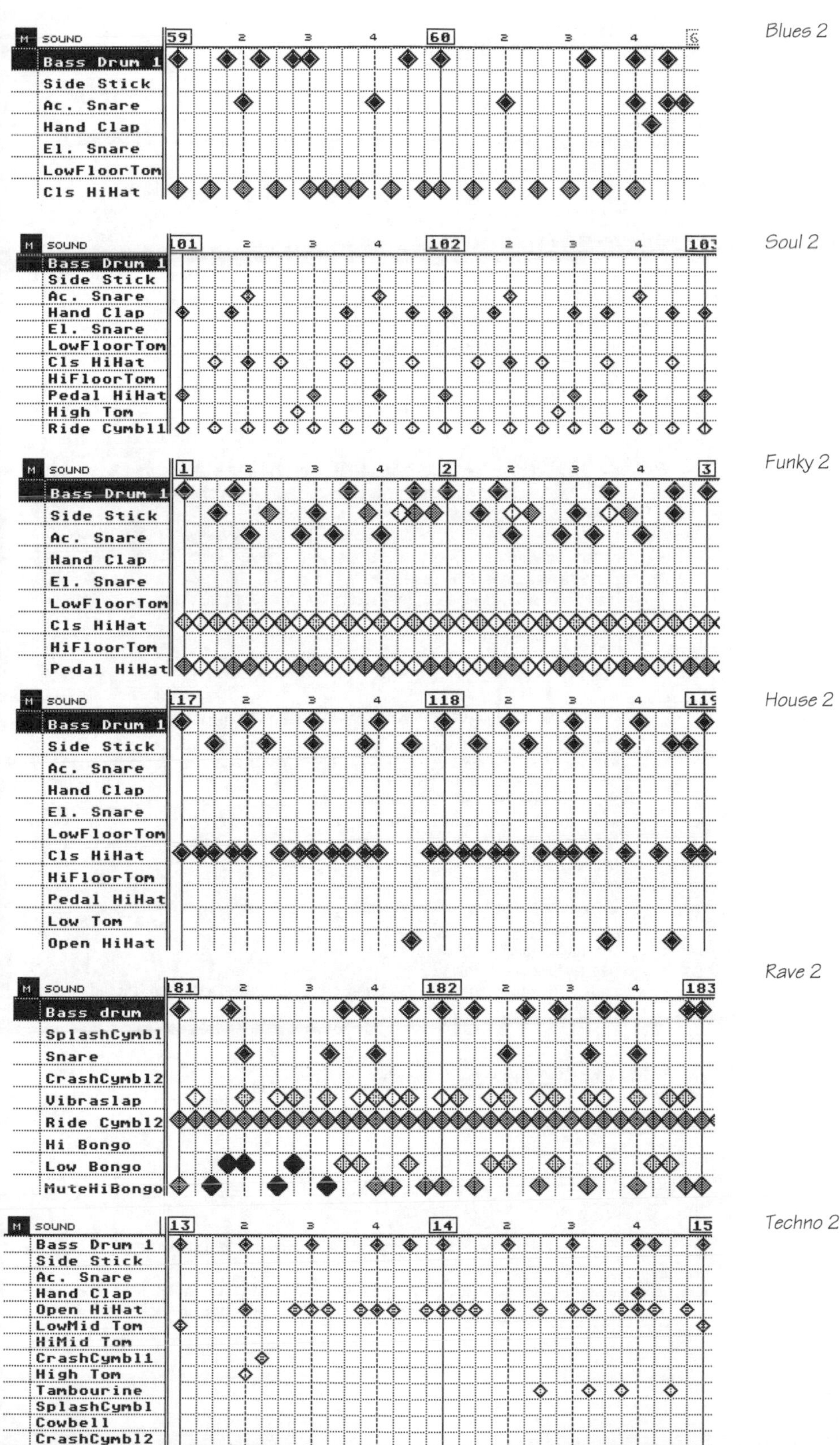

Blues 2

Soul 2

Funky 2

House 2

Rave 2

Techno 2

Lyrics (phonetic rhyming dictionary)

Sound	*Words*
A	
ayy	bay, broadway, clay, day, fate, faraway, fete, gay, hay, jay, kay, knay, lay, may, mockinjay, nay, pay, play, quay, ray, say, stay, tray, way, x-ray, yesterday
arr	arr, bar, bizarre, car, char, dare, far, ha, jar, ma, pa, ya
all	all, ball, call, crawl, drawl, fall, shawl, traul, mall, maul, wall
ack	black, hack, knack, lack, mac, pack, quack, rack, sack, tact
app	bap, chap, clap, crap, flap, lap, slap, trap
att	bat, cat, fat, flat, knat, mat, pat, rat, sat, vat, what, yaught
art	art, cart, chart, dart, heart, mart, part, tart, what
B	(see eee)
C	(see eee)
D	(see eee)
E	
eee	be, cheat, clicky, dee, dicky, dizzy, easy, fee, flea, gee, he, heat, izzy, key, knee, lead, lizzy, lovely, me, pea, picky, plead, please, sea, see, simply, sticky, suddenly, tea, tree, tricky, whizzy, zee
err	air, another, bare, bear, beaver, bother, burr, care, cleaver, clever, clover, cover, dare, err, ever, forever, fur, leave her, lever, lover, murr, never, purr, sir, smother, stair, summer
ear	clear, dear, ear, fear, gear, hear, jeer, lear, mere, near, pear, queer, rear, steer, tear, veer, we're
Sound	Words
eam	beam, cream, dean, dream, keen, lean, mean, queen, ream, seam, seem, team, ween
een	been, dean, green, keen, knee, lean, mean, queen, ream, rean, seen, teen, wean
ell	bell, cell, feel, fell, girl, hell, sell, tell
eet	beat, cheat, eat, feet, heat, meet, meat, neat, pleat, seat, treat
eal	deal, feel, girl, heal, keel, kneel, leal, meal, seal
eev	believe, eve', grieve, heave, leave, sleeve, weave
emm	hem, them, trem, mem, nem, when
enn	ben, children, den, end, gen, happen, hen, men, pen, ten, vixen, when, zenn
est	best, nest, quest, zest, rest
east	beast, cease, east, feast
edd	bed, cred, dead, fed, head, held, jed, lead, ned, red, said, shed, thread, tread, wed, zed
ess,	bess, best, chess, desk, guess, jest, less, mess, press, quest, rest, wrest, yes, zest
exx,	guest, jest, necks, pecks, perplex, sex
eff,	jeff, left, zeff
eez	bees, chinese, ease, please, seize, sleeve, sleeze, trees
F	(see eff)
G	(see eee)
H	
aitch	ache, bake, break, cake, fake, lake, make, quake, rake, sake, take, wake
I	
igh	buy, by, chi, die, eye, fly, guy, hi, I, lie, my, nigh, night, pie, rye, sigh, sight, sly, try, why
ick	flick, trick, sick, brick, chick, dick, lick, kick, nick, pick, quick, tick, wick
ile	smile, while, beguile, trial, style, file, dial, beguile, mile, nile, pile, tile, vile, exile

Sound	Words
ill	will, bill, still, trill, kill, chill, fill, hill, mill, nil, pill, till, will, eel
ite	white, night, tonight, knight, sight, fight, right, light, kite, bite, shite, might, mite, flight, slight, tight
J	(see ay)
K	(see ay)
L	(see ell)
M	(see emm)
N	(see enn)
O	
ode	toad, road, snowed, abode, ode, crossroads, rode, mode, node
ooo	blue, boo, you, true, sue, do, oooh, few, new, knew, flew, queue, due, dew, glue, hue, jew, loo, leu, moo, pooh, rue, shoe, true, view, zoo, two, to, cruise, lose, choose, noose, crews, fuse, use, fews, flews, ooze, boose, clues, hues, jews, queues, loos, moos, news, pues, pubes, woos, does, cue, viewsue, do, chew, few, jew, queue, loo, moo, new, knew, pew, rue, to, too, you, view, woo, zoo, boo, you, view, do, true, sue, glue, knew, new, few, clue, hu, jew, queue, loo, moo, new, knew, pew, queue, rue, chew, woo, zoo, blue, who
ohh	oh, show, so, wow, bow, doe, foe, go, low, no, oh, quo, row, tow, toe, sow, fellow, yellow, dow, snow, hoe, mow, row, so, toe, yo, bellow, flow, wow, flow, dough
oom	doom, tomb, room, noon, dune, tune, soon, june, balloon, fume, loom, moon, croon, prune
ogg	dog, fog, bog, trog, agog, frog
opp	drop, plop, flop, chop, cop, hop, mop, pop, top
ound	found, sound, pound, round, around
own	flown, own, moan, loan, own, down, town, noun, clown, found, foam, roam, dome, home
odd	odd, god, pod, sod, plod, knod, trod, clod
ous	mouse, house, nouse, louse
oil	oil, boil, soil, foil, royal, goal, girl, dole, sole, pole, soul
P	(see eee)
Q	(see ooo)
R	(see arr)
S	(see ess)
T	(see eee)
U	(see ooo)
uvv	love, above, guv, shove, dove
unn	won, one, fun, ton, bun, none, done, tongue, some, sum
V	(see eee)
W	(see ooo)
X	(see exx)
Y	(see ii)
Z	(see ee or ed)

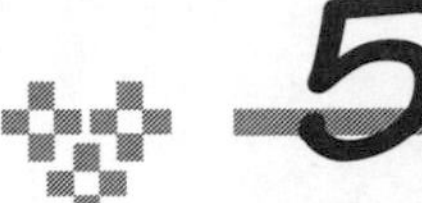

5

Recording and production

Microphones

Construction

The basic principle behind any microphone is that of a membrane vibrating in sympathy with sound. The acoustic energy is then converted into an analogous electrical signal.

Factor	*Construction* *Moving coil*	*Ribbon*	*Capacitor**
normal polar response	cardioid	figure of 8	cardioid/switchable
robustness	high	low/average	average
cost	low	average	high
examples	Shure SM58 (£110) Electrovoice RE20 (£300)	Beyer M88 (£240)	AKG C451 (£250) Neumann U87 (£1200)
transient/high freq response	good	very good	excellent
diaphragm weight	high	low	average
output level	average	low	high
sensitivity/efficiency	average	low	high
application	general purpose vocal, brass combos, kick drums	strings, vocal overheads	instruments – piano, kit vocals with pop shield snare, hi-hats
side effects	average sound	handling and rumble slightly fragile	crackle when wet need phantom power
characteristic	solid	smooth	crisp

* Some types also referred to as electret or condenser

Pressure zone

A pressure zone microphone usually uses a capacitor construction, but its uniqueness comes from the fact that the microphone is housed in a hood, suspended around 1/10th of an inch above a solid plate or boundary. Anything that the plate is attached to also becomes part of the boundary and helps to pick up the sound.

It features a hemi-spherical (180°) polar response and is excellent for group or ambient mic'ing but very bad at rejecting unwanted signals. The Tandy Realistic PZM offers surprisingly good results at £35 but is a little insensitive and hence noisy. Amcron invented the principle: its mics range from £120 to £500.

Piezo and contact

Although these types of microphone can offer excellent isolation and feedback rejection, they do not normally sound as good as a conventional type. They are often used for triggering the side chain of a gate or to trigger a sample or MIDI device.

Famous microphones

Microphone	*Cost*	*Use*	*Notes*
AKG C414	£800	Instruments, stereo pair and vocals (with a shield)	Switchable polar response.
AKG D12		Square microphone mainly used for deep kick drum sounds	
Beyer M201	£160	Excellent for guitar and instruments	Needs popshield for vocals
AKG C451/CK1	£250	Excellent for acoustic guitar and snare	
Beyer M201	£240	Instrument mic, especially acoustic guitar and snare	
Crown PCC160	£220	Phase coherent cardioid PZM-type	Popular in theatres
Crown PZM30F	£268	PZM-type	
Electrovoice RE20	£400	Excellent for vocals and clickier kick drums	
Neumann U87	£1,200	Vocals and instruments	Switchable polar response
Realistic PZM	£35	The famous Tandy PZM	
Sennheiser MD421	£210	Square shaver-shape mic used for clicky kick	Can withstand high SPLs such as gunshots drum sounds, toms and vocals
Black Rogue			
Sennheiser MD441		Excellent for snare, guitar, overheads and vocals (if used with care)	A capacitor mic sound from a moving coil mic
Sennheiser MKH series	From £525	Clean sound for stereo microphone techniques, instruments and vocals	Uses RF technology for less noise
Shure SM58	£110	Famous stage vocal microphone	There are better alternatives...
STC 4038		Excellent for strings, orchestra and as an overhead	Very BBC

Polar responses

A microphone is a bit like an eye: it has a field of vision before it needs to turn its head. The area that it can "see" is called the *polar response*.

Unidirectional polar responses

Cardioid: a heart-shaped response that picks up sound mainly from the front, a little from the sides and almost nothing from the rear.
Hypercardioid: also like the cardioid, but has a very narrow pick-up pattern at the front. A side effect of this narrow response is that it exhibits a slight lobe-shaped response at the rear as well. The off-axis spill that these mics pick up tends to be very coloured and filtered.
Supercardioid: like the cardioid but has a narrower front.
Figure of 8: picks up equally well from the front and back, but very little from the sides. Useful in between two singers or used sideways on tom drums.
Hemispherical: a 180° (half globe) pick up pattern, usually found in PZM-type microphones. Very good for group or ambient uses, but poor at rejecting other sounds. Quite often used in theatres and for conferences.
Rifle: the rifle, or shotgun, mic is an ultra-directional microphone. It has a very narrow pick up beam (a bit like a spotlight) and is used mainly for long distance work such as video or broadcast.
Parabolic: a microphone mounted in a concave dish and pointing towards it.

The dish acts as a collector and tends to focus the sound onto the microphone. Used extensively for long distance ambient work such as nature recordings.

Polar patterns: Top to bottom: Cardioid, hypercardioid, omnidirectional and figure of eight

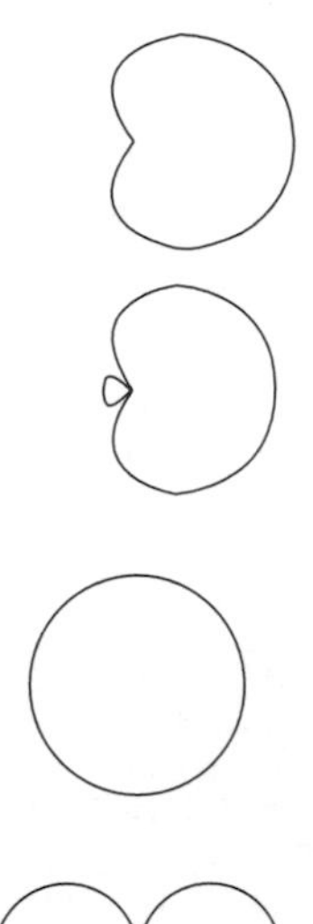

Omnidirectional polar responses

An omnidirectional microphone picks up sound equally from all directions. It tends to give a very natural, well-balanced sound and suffers less from handling noise and blasting. It is not very good at rejecting unwanted noises, relying purely on the proximity to the source to reduce spill.

Switchable polar patterns

Some microphones, such as the Neumann U87 and AKG C414, have switchable polar patterns. This is achieved by using two capsules and combining them in different ways. For example, by using two cardioid capsules the following can be achieved

Cardioid A	*Cardioid B*	*Result*
in phase	in phase	omnidirectional
in phase	not used	cardioid
in phase	out of phase	figure of eight

Note: By using different proportions of level from each capsule, in-between responses can be achieved such as hypercardioid and wide cardioid.

Similar results can be achieved by using a figure of eight and an omnidirectional capsule. As no rear porting is used to achieve a cardioid response initially, in theory a better sounding microphone could be achieved.

By switching a figure of eight and an omnidirectional capsule in and out of phase, the various combined polar responses can be achieved

Omni A	*Figure of 8*	*Result*
in phase	not used	omni
not used	in phase	figure of 8
in phase	in phase	cardioid
in phase	out of phase	reverse cardioid

Microphone considerations

Frequency response and coloration

In theory, a microphone should have a full range frequency response and introduce no coloration (emphasis of certain frequencies). In practice, although most microphones do extend over the full frequency range, due to coloration and transient response, some microphones are certainly better at some jobs than others. So all microphones have some effect on sound character and, despite any written specifications, can only be judged aurally.

Off-axis response and spill

A microphone should have a perfect polar response and not pick up any sound beyond its response pattern. In practice this is impossible, especially with bass frequencies whose wavelength, in comparison to the size of the microphone, negates its polar response.

The main problem with microphone technique is not normally the fact that there is spill, but that the spill is highly coloured and affects the main sound as well. So considerations of the quality of the spill must also be taken and acoustic methods such as orientation, distance and the use of acoustic screens may need to be varied. Microphones that are less directional will tend to have a better quality spill, so omnidirectional or wider cardioid types should be tested.

Working range

Owing to the laws of sound, which make the sound pressure from a source drop by 3dB every time the distance is doubled, and the counter effect that the level of indirect sound (such as reflections and reverberation) do not, all microphones have a working range.

A directional microphone tends to exhibit a boosting of the bass frequencies when used close up (less than 6 inches) – the *proximity effect.* Some performers make use of this effect for artistic reasons. Often these microphones are fitted with a bass roll-off filter switch to counteract this effect if desired.

If a microphone is used too close (less than 3 inches), popping and sibilance may become a problem. Popping is caused by the intense pressure of air causing a blasting sound, usually heard on "p" sounds. Sibilance is an unnatural emphasis of the high frequencies which causes a ringing distortion of "s" sounds.

Dynamics and transient response

As all microphones rely on some form of free-moving diaphragm, there will be a physical distance through which this can move before distortion results from restrained vibration.

The more responsive the diaphragm can be to the incoming sound, the better. It needs to respond as quickly and as accurately as possible or it will have a severe effect on the sound.

The rigidity of the diaphragm plays a part in the microphones response, with a harder (and hence heavier) diaphragm introducing less modulation distortion caused by the diaphragm's reflections.

The size of the diaphragm is also related to its weight but conversely affects the available low frequency response.

Sensitivity

For a given sound pressure level, a microphone produces a certain amount of electrical signal – referred to as the microphone's *sensitivity*. The more sensitive a microphone, the less amplification (from the mixer) is required and the less resulting noise.

The British Standard uses a reference of 1 pascal (10 microbars). Comparing this with the threshold of hearing for a frequency of 1kHz (which is 20 x 10^4 pascals) gives a reference SPL dB measurement of 94dB.

Another measurement used to determine the self noise of a microphone is to state the SPL required to produce the same noise from a theoretically ideal, noise-free microphone. The difference between this noise figure and the level attainable before distortion gives the usable dynamic range of the microphone.

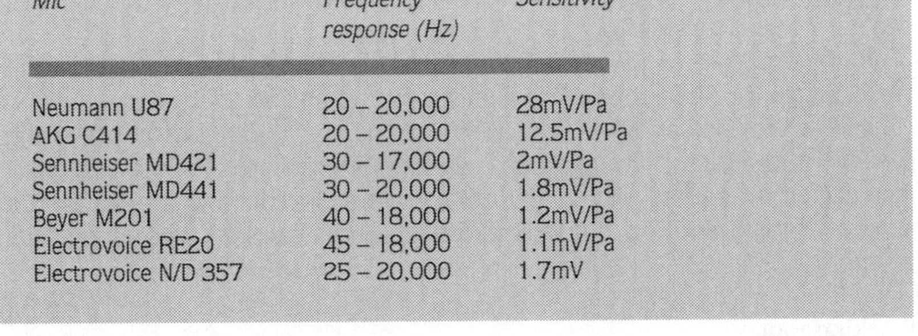

Mic	*Frequency response (Hz)*	*Sensitivity*
Neumann U87	20 – 20,000	28mV/Pa
AKG C414	20 – 20,000	12.5mV/Pa
Sennheiser MD421	30 – 17,000	2mV/Pa
Sennheiser MD441	30 – 20,000	1.8mV/Pa
Beyer M201	40 – 18,000	1.2mV/Pa
Electrovoice RE20	45 – 18,000	1.1mV/Pa
Electrovoice N/D 357	25 – 20,000	1.7mV

Studio microphone placement

The following pictures show mic positionings for live work, which often differ from those used in the studio

Vocals Working range 6 inches to 24 inches (15 – 60 cm). Will give a very close effect if less than 2 inches (5 cm) but may also introduce popping and sibilance. A windshield is recommended, the most popular being a stocking on a coat hanger frame!

Singer: typically 0 – 3 inches (0-8cm)

Vocal group A microphone suspended 6 feet (180 cm) above the air, or use a PZM mounted on a minimum 3 foot (90 cm) boundary surface, 6 feet (180 cm) away.

A stereo coincident pair could also be appropriate. Spot mics will give the most flexibility but will remove much of the natural balance and acoustic environment.

Backing: typically 14 – 48 inches (35-120cm)

Grand piano Best recorded in stereo, with a microphone for treble and bass ranges. Each mic should be placed 3 inches (8 cm) from the first and third sound hole from the player's left.

In high spill environments, a PZM can be taped to the closed lid and should be placed favouring the weaker treble range.

Piano: lid closed, mic over soundhole

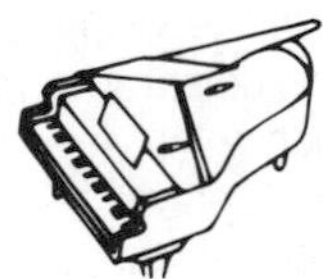

Piano: natural sound, open lid (20cm apart)

All microphone placement pictures are used by kind permission of HW International/Shure Brothers

Upright piano Either place microphones at the rear soundboard, or via the open top flap. The microphones should favour the weaker treble end of the piano.

For maximum stereo effect, point the microphones away from each other. The further away they are from the piano, the more natural it will sound.

Guitar: improved bass, no feedback 3 inches (8cm) from soundhole

Acoustic guitar The sound hole produces the most volume, but also sounds boomy. Either side of the sound hole, towards the bridge of the neck, will produce different results. It is well worth experimenting with the mic positions and recording in stereo if you can.

Guitar: natural sound 6 inches (15cm)

Cello/fiddle Over the bridge for a brighter sound, or near the "f" holes for a more mellow sound. A distant approach is preferred.

Violin/viola Best several feet from the instrument, or close mic'd near the "f" holes for a scratchier sound.

Violin/viola: full tone 4 – 12 inches (10–28cm)

Violin/viola: natural sound 4 – 12 inches(10-28cm)

Kick drum: inside 3 – 14 inches (8-35cm) from head

Kick drum The nearer to the beater, the more click you will get. The further out from the drum, the fuller the low frequency tone. Inside the shell will give the best isolation from spill and room resonance, but the further out of the drum, the better the fuller the sound. If spill permits, 4 inches (10 cm) from the rear head is a good starting point. The mic will collect more tone, the more off-centre it is.

Snare/toms: typically 1 – 3 inches (2-8cm)

Snare Deep snare drums may also need a bottom snare mic for sufficient snap. The top mic should be pointed down to the head at an angle of 45° about 2 inches (5 cm) from the surface.

More tone will result from placing the mic nearer to the rim rather than the centre. If using an underside snare mic, phase reverse it to avoid bass cancellation.

Toms Close to the head and off-centre gives best results. For less spill, the bottom head can be removed and the mic placed inside although it will reduce the tone of the drum. A figure of 8 mic can also be used sideways to pick up two toms.

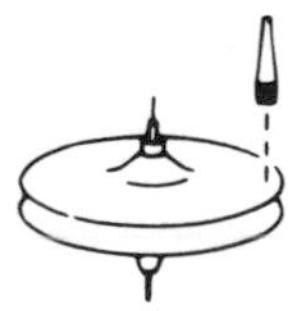

Hi-hat: typically 3 – 6 inches (8-15cm)

Hi-hats Placed nearer to the bell of the hat will produce a tighter sound. One inch away from the open position and pointing away from the snare is a good starting position. Sideways on can also sound good but care must then be taken with open hi-hat sounds. You may find it hard to stop hi-hat spill on the snare mic.

Cymbals If placed too close to the surface, some strange ringing and filtering sounds will be achieved. Cymbals are best mic'd from a minimum distance of 8 inches (20 cm) to allow the full sound to be heard.

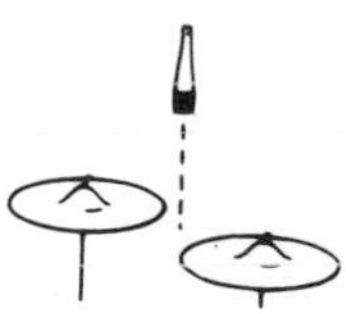

Cymbals: typically 14 – 28 inches (35-70cm)

Overheads An overhead tends to maintain the natural balance of the drummer and the kit. They are best placed 90 cm (3 feet) above the kit and in some form of stereo arrangement. In addition to a kick and snare mic, the overheads may be sufficient for many applications.

Ambients Much greater depth can be achieved with a drum sound by using additional mics many feet away from the kit. It is not unusual for them to be very high in the air or facing in the opposite direction or towards a hard reflective surface. When combined with the closer mics, a much fuller sound is achieved. In cases of difficulty with spill, sampling and then triggering with contact or close mics is certainly an option.

Brass/saxophone Most volume comes from the bell of the instrument, but so does most of the wind noise. Mic'ing from a distance between 6 and 24 inches (15 and 60 cm) is one option, but mic'ing closer and at an angle to the rear of the bell gives a softer sound. Sometimes a better sound can be achieved from the perspective of the mouthpiece or valves, but experimentation is necessary. A combination of close and ambient mics also works very well. The more on-line with the bell, the raspier and more brash the tone.

Reed instrument: full tone without feedback 3 – 8 inches (8-20cm)

Brass: full tone 3 – 14 inches (8-35cm)

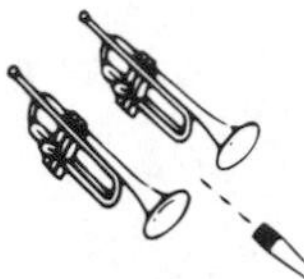

Brass: natural sound 8 – 28 inches (20-70cm)

Flute: with sibilance 3 inches (8cm)

Clarinet/flute Most of the tone comes from the mouthpiece, but care should be taken to avoid breath and key noise. A distant approach usually works best if possible. Some people favour mic'ing more towards the keys. For a fuller sound, the mic should be placed near the rear of the bell of the clarinet.

Amplifier combos Most vocal microphones will work well with combos. The mic should be place off-centre of the speaker for a fuller tone, or nearer the centre for a brighter sound. Start at a distance of 5 inches (13 cm). An ambient mic can add a lot to even a little amp.

Amplifier: central 1 – 4 inches (3-10cm) for full tone

Amplifier: off-centre 1 – 4 inches (3-10cm) for selected tone

Harmonica The AKG D190 is often used hand-held. Alternatively, a stand-mounted vocal mic could be used. Conventionally used very close up.

Percussion Capacitor mics are very popular for percussion as they respond well to the transients; 2 to 6 feet (60 – 180 cm) is a recommended distance.

Stereo mic'ing

XY (coincident) Two directional microphones with capsules in vertical line with each other. Advantages include good phase stability offering mono compatibility. Disadvantages are a slightly diluted stereo image with a poorer centre stage image.

Spaced XY By separating the two directional microphones, a greater stereo effect can be achieved but at the cost of mono compatibility. The combined mono signal may suffer from comb filtering effects (like flanging or phasing). The distance between them will change the results. Spacing less than 12 inches (30 cm) is recommended.

Spaced omni (AB) By using omnidirectional microphones, spaced several feet apart, a good stereo effect can be achieved that doesn't suffer from filtering when combined to mono. However a hole-in-the-middle effect may result, requiring a third central microphone. Care should be taken to avoid any phase cancellation effects from the microphones.

MS A figure of eight and a cardioid (or omnidirectional) microphone. The figure of eight microphone points left and right while the other picks up the centre image. To decode the sound, three mixer channels are used. The directional mic is panned centrally, while the figure of eight mic is split to two channels, each panned hard opposite, one with the phase reverse button pushed.

The level of the two outside channels must be equal, which can be tested by panning centrally and adjusting for minimum level (as they are out of phase, they cancel). Advantages include excellent mono compatibility and a stable centre image.

Soundfield The Calrec Soundfield (£2,500) is a special microphone that allows switchable polar responses after the event. It comes with an electronic device to achieve this.

- It can save a lot of time if you monitor the microphone placement through headphones so that you can hear the effect of any changes live.
- The nearer a microphone is to a source, the greater the direct to reflected sound will be. Conversely, the less the natural the balance of the instrument (or player) will be.
- It is much better to try different microphone positioning, or indeed types of microphone, rather than relying on equalisation. It should also be noted that it is easy to remove factors with EQ, but much harder to try and boost characteristics that aren't there in the first place.
- The true sound of an instrument cannot be achieved from a single spot source, as this true sound is the sum and interaction of its many emanating parts. Also, the listening perspective and the sound of the environment play a major role.
- Any device that can convert one form of energy into another is called a *transducer.*
- You can use a pair of headphones as a microphone. A speaker could also be used except that as it has such a large cone that it needs a lot of energy to get it moving.
- Very few microphones have used a multiple capsule design, as has been used in loudspeakers for years. The AKG D202 used two capsules, one dedicated for treble and one for bass. In principle, some sort of crossover would be required to get the most from each capsule, as is the principle with crossover and speaker design. Microphones like the Neumann U87 use multiple capsules to get their switchable polar responses, but are aimed equally at the whole frequency range.

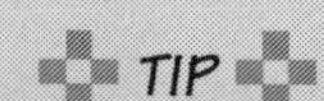

Performers can monitor on speakers if they use the following technique: the mono monitor signal is fed to two speakers, wired out of phase with each other. By positioning the microphone equidistant from the speakers, the monitor mix cancels as far as the microphone concerns, leaving negligible spill. As the performer has two ears, the cancellation effect is not a problem.

Tapping the cone of a woofer speaker can provide a good sample source for a kick drum. Simply mic it up as normal. Be very careful not to damage the speaker cone – don't use any other than one finger to hit it.

Guide To EQ

Instrument	Effect of boost	Effect of cut	Comments
voice	hot at 8 or 12kHz clarity above 3kHz body between 200-400Hz	scratchy at 2kHz nasal at 1kHz pops below 80Hz	when combining voices, make each thinner
horns/strings	hot at 8 or 12kHz clarity above 2kHz lush between 300-400Hz	scratchy at 2K honky at 1kHz muddy below 125Hz	
piano	presence at 5kHz bass at 125Hz	tinny at 1-2kHz boomy at 320Hz	avoid too much bass when mixing with rhythm tracks
electric guitar	clarity at 3.2kHz bass at 125Hz	muddy below 80Hz	mic off centre of speaker for more harmonics
acoustic guitar	sparkle above 5kHz full at 125Hz	tinny at 2-3kHz boomy at 200Hz	
double bass	slap at 3-5kHz bass below 125Hz	hollow at 600Hz boomy at 200Hz	
electric bass	growl at 600Hz bass below 80Hz	tinny at 1kHz boomy at 125Hz	
cymbals/bells	sparkle above 5kHz	jangling at 1kHz	
toms	slap at 3-5kHz bass at 80-200Hz	boomy at 300Hz	
snare	crisp above 2kHz full at 125Hz	peaky at 1kHz deep at 80Hz	
kick	slap at 3-5kHz bass between 80-125Hz	floppy at 600Hz boomy below 80Hz	

Stereo perspectives

Stereo allows us to recreate the aural effect of space: direction and distance. A number of factors give directional information:

- Level difference between the ears.
- Time delay or phase relationship between sounds reaching the left and right ear.
- High frequency content reaching each ear.

These attributes can be simulated by the following methods:

- The pan pot or using two channels one panned left, the other right.
- Using a delay line with a short delay (<40ms) or a reverb with a simulated stereo response.
- Using EQ or filtering to achieve this effect.

Ideally, some combination of all of the above would be used.

The easiest way to create stereo is to retain the stereo effect of the original source by using two discrete channels (just like the ears on your head), including microphones, mixer channels, tape tracks, amplifier and speakers.

INFORMATION

The word "stereo" comes from the greek word meaning solid.

Working with tape

Tape time chart

Speed ips	cm/s	Time for 7 inch (17 cm) spool 1200 feet min	Time for 7 inch (17 cm) spool LP 1800 feet min	Time for NAB spool 2400 feet min
30	76	8	12	16
15	38	16	24	32
7.5	19	32	48	64
3.75	9.5	64	96	128
1.875	4.76	128	192	256

CONVERSIONS

Inches	mm
2	50.8
1	25.4
0.5	12.7
0.25	6.35
0.125	3.175

Tape widths

Tracks	Historical width (inches)	Next standard (inches)	Modern width (inches)
24	2	1	
16	2	1	1/2
8	1	1/2	1/4
4	1/2	1/4	1/8 (cassette)
2	1/4	1/2	(DAT)

Open reel equalisation curves

Speed in ips	1 7/8	3 3/4	7 1/2	15	30
Speed in cm/s	4.76	9.5	19	38	76
NAB/AES	3180+90	3180+90	3180+50	3180+50	17.5
IEC 1	3180+90	3180+90	70	35	35
IEC 2	3180+90	3180+90	3180+50	3180+50	17.5
CCIR/DIN	280	140	50		

Time constants in microseconds

Equalisation time constant to turnover frequency

µs	Hz
3180	50
280	568
200	796
140	1136
129	1326
100	1592
90	1768
70	2273
50	3183
35	4547

Tape flux levels (in nWb/m)

Europe	USA	Notes
160	150	Cassette
200	185	Dolby/Ampex level
250	230	$3^3/_4$ and $1^7/_8$ ips (9.5 and 4.75 cm/s)
280	260	elevated operating level
320	295	30, 15 and $7^1/_2$ ips (76, 38 and 19 cm/s)
510	470	stereo format

Cassette

Tape type		Equalisation	Record boosted at	Coercivity (in oersteds)
Ferric	Group 1	3180+120µs	1.326kHz	380
Chrome	Group 2	3180+70µs	2.273kHz	650
Ferrochrome	Group 3	3180+70µs	(not very common today)	
Metal	Group 4	3180+70µs		1100 (needs higher bias)

Cassette specifications

Speed – $1^7/_8$ ips (47.625 mm/s)
Track width – 0.6mm, gap 0.3mm
C90 – 135m tape length; C60 – 90m tape length

RIAA record equalisation

In order to assist vinyl record reproduction and to minimise the effect of bass frequencies at high volumes (which require large grooves), the following equalisation curve (RIAA and BS1928:1955) is employed:

RIAA record equalisation curve (record)

Frequency (Hz)	Level adjustment (dB)	Frequency (Hz)	Level adjustment (dB)
20	-18.6	2,000	2.6
30	-17.8	3,000	4.7
50	-17.0	4,000	6.6
60	-16.1	5,000	8.2
80	-14.5	6,000	9.6
100	-13.1	7,000	10.7
150	-10.2	8,000	11.9
200	-8.3	10,000	13.7
400	-3.8	12,000	15.3
500	-2.6	14,000	16.6
700	-1.2	16,000	17.7
1,000	0	18,000	18.7
1,500	1.4	20,000	19.6

A replay curve of 3180, 318 and 75µs will restore the response. Alternatively, plugging a record player directly into a mixer can give rough results as to what mixer equalisation is required to restore normal playback.

24 TRACK PLANNER

Please photocopy and use this planner

Project ______________________ Title ______________________

Artist ______________________ Performers ______________________

Client ______________________ Engineer ______________________

Producer ______________________ Programmer ______________________

Start/end __________ __________ Invoice no. and details ______________________

Tape no. ______________________ Location ______________________

SMPTE (rate ________ fps) Start time and tempo ______________________

Track 1	Track 2	Track 3	Track 4
Track 5	Track 6	Track 7	Track 8
Track 9	Track 10	Track 11	Track 12
Track 13	Track 14	Track 15	Track 16
Track 17	Track 18	Track 19	Track 20
Track 21	Track 22	Track 23	Track 24

24 Track Planner (cont)

Project ______________________________

Song sections/time

Section										
Time										
Bar										

Mix notes (levels, EQ, automation file...)

____

____

____

____

MIDI Notes

	Port A	Port B	Port C	Port D
1				
2				
3				
4				
5				
6				
7				
8				
9				
10				
11				
12				
13				
14				
15				
16				

Project ______________________________

Module and sound bank notes

Storage notes

Song files

Sound files

HDR files

DAT mix

DAT back-up

Other notes

Status Current / Mixed / Complete / Client authority to erase / media blanked

Mixer map

Project ______________________

Project ______________________ Artist ______________________

Title ______________________ Client ______________________

Engineer ______________________ Date started/completed ______________

Producer ______________________ Tape no. ______________________

Programmer ______________________ SMPTE (rate _____ fps)

Invoice no. and detail ______________ Start time and tempo ______________

Location ______________________

Channel	1	2	3	4	5	6
Source						
EQ1						
EQ2						
EQ3						
EQ4						
Level						
Pan						
Aux						
Outboard						

Section notes ______________________

Other notes ______________________

Channel	7	8	9	10	11	12
Source						
EQ1						
EQ2						
EQ3						
EQ4						
Level						
Pan						
Aux						
Outboard						

Section notes ______________________

Other notes ______________________

Mixer map (cont)

Project ______________________

Channel	13	14	15	16	17	18
Source						
EQ1						
EQ2						
EQ3						
EQ4						
Level						
Pan						
Aux						
Outboard						

Section notes ______________________

Other notes ______________________

Channel	19	20	21	22	23	24
Source						
EQ1						
EQ2						
EQ3						
EQ4						
Level						
Pan						
Aux						
Outboard						

Section notes ______________________

Other notes ______________________

Section										
Time										
Bar										

Other notes ______________________

____

Studio user's hints and tips

The following guidelines are well worth following:

- Planning is obviously very important. Your chosen studio could easily be booked for a month in advance and the logistics of getting everyone to turn up together isn't easy.
- Before you book a studio, it is important to visit it and meet the engineer for your session and listen to some existing projects. This will check that you have compatible ideas and confirm the location and presence of any required facilities.
- Buy the multi-track tape in case you need to remix it later, whether for a remix or because of a change of band line-up.
- Record and mix on separate days. This will keep you fresh for the mix and allow you to check how the monitor mix sounds on a known system at home.
- Don't use the studio as a rehearsal room. Be well rehearsed and have a clear idea of the production. It will probably change on the day, but at least you'll be part way there.
- It is best to use a producer or, failing that, elect an impartial band member that you all respect. Otherwise every musician will just want his part louder in the mix!
- Try to be as communicative and supportive to the engineer as possible. He is not a mind reader and any help you can give him as to the song order, or final arrangement, will speed up the process.
- There is no excuse for a poor foldback mix. If you need to hear something differently while you perform, ask for it.
- Don't rely on a "we'll fix it in the mix" philosophy. It is better to get the effect you require at the time. Pre-processing does commit you, but usually offers better results and maximises facilities.
- Don't waste expensive studio time on cassette copying. Get one copy made and duplicate it yourself externally. The studio may have a separate facility for duplicating at a normal rate itself.
- Ensure your instruments are up to scratch before you go in (tuned kit, new strings, a singer without a cold...).
- It might be a good idea to stagger the arrival times of certain band members, to save them getting in the way. For instance, the drum sounds usually take at least an hour to sort out.
- If you need to hire in additional equipment, you may find the studio has preferential rates so check first.
- Remember that in the studio you will have the chance to double instruments and play extra parts. Some tracks will be laid down separately, so you should rehearse this technique as well.
- It may be a good idea to do two mixes, one by the engineer and one with all hands on board. The real solution usually lies somewhere in between...
- Lastly, don't try to record too many songs in one session. It is better to have two well-recorded songs in a day than five bad ones. Unlike a gig, a recording is for life and every tiny mistake will glare at you every time you play it.

Studio user's checklist

- Choose engineer and studio, including pre-visit
- Confirm dates and details, including a map, with all involved
- Studio booked
  - Recording session date
  - Mixing session date
- Hire of special equipment confirmed
- Issue contracts to all parties
- Rehearsals arranged
- Production arranged
- Pre-production finalised
- Transport arranged
- Session equipment checklist
- Purchase multi-track tape
- Payment details
- Copying session arranged
- Copies distributed

Home studio owner's hints and tips

- Creating your own home studio gives you the freedom to create music whenever you want. It could also save you a lot of money in studio fees. However, it is very easy to keep on buying equipment that concentrates on pre-production and track laying rather than mixing equipment. You will then need to use a commercial studio to mix it in. The cost of installation, such as wiring, patchbays and studio furniture can be a significant part of the budget (around 10%) which most people forget about.
- At the end of the day, unless you have the facility and room to create a soundproof, acoustically treated area, which doesn't annoy the neighbours or the wife, you are best to keep your recording habit in check. Fire and structural building regulations and, perhaps, planning permission may have to be considered.
- Egg boxes are *not* a suitable method of soundproofing or acoustic treatment and pose a fire hazard! They will dampen down the high frequency reverb time, but this will probably not help your recording. Proper advice from the material's supplier should be sought – usually free if you are buying from them. You could make some very costly mistakes otherwise.
- Other factors involved include care over the mains and audio installation. Use a star network for the mains and invest in an ELCB breaker.
- Ergonomics of the room are important. Can you cater for one-man operation as well as for working with other artists? Do you have enough areas and tielines available when working with real performers?
- Maintenance and upgrading are an essential part of the environment. Tape heads do wear out (around 600 hours usually till the first re-lap) and then are costly to replace. Interesting new equipment is bound to appear, no matter what you say now.
- No matter how many tracks or mixer channels (or effects) you have, it will never be enough. Welcome to the home studio!

Home studio owner's checklist

- Ergonomic layout
- Sound proofing and acoustics
- Star mains system, patchbay and cabling
- Maintenance and upgrade costs

Commercial studio hints and tips

Setting up a commercial studio is not an easy task. With modern technology making high-quality self-recording a reality, a studio needs to specialise to survive.

- There are a few unique things that studios have to provide:
- A sound-proof, acoustically treated area that is large enough to perform in, without disturbance to (or from) the neighbours.
- Experienced staff and a creative environment.
- A greater range, choice, quality or quantity of equipment including outboard, microphones, tracks or even instruments (old synths, a fabulous grand piano or drum kit, classic/custom guitar selection...). The importance of a good sound library should not be neglected here, including CD-ROMs, and a working knowledge of where they are and how to use them.
- Specialising in a particular area is an important reason why people will choose you – for your experience in the equipment, sound, production, contacts and the process (record pressing).
- The image and atmosphere of the place and people will be a final factor. Your potential clients will choose a place that they can get on with.
- The premises need to be a long-term entity: you don't want to have to move once you're set up. The location and access of the premises are a major factor for attracting clients.
- Easy access, parking and loading are considerations, as well as the options for residential and recreational facilities.
- It is very important to target your customer and meet their needs. How will they get to know of your existence and how can you make them choose you instead of someone else?
- You will need a business-like approach to getting paid on time, and good budgeting and cash flow skills to cope with expansion and upgrading.
- Meeting all of the regulations can be a nightmare, including fire regulations, planning permission, noise control and access/loading facilities.

Markets available to a studio

- Band recording for demos or masters. The type of music is important (classical, jazz, rock...).

    Track laying (favourable/unusual acoustics)
    Re-mixing
    Pre-production
    Long-term projects
    Solo composers
    Theatre and voice-over studio
    Video and TV post-production
    Radio commercial or play production
    Sound effects specialists (for cartoons, sci-fi...)

Music for multimedia
Music for dance specialists
Music for corporate events and entertainment outlets (in-flight, games arenas...)

- Some form of packaging might also work, e.g. CD or cassette manufacture.
- Maintenance and upgrade costs must be carefully considered. A breakdown will mean you are losing money and your customers will be very upset. You also need to make sure that your terms of business protect you from being sued for loss of earnings and breach of contact.
- Insurance for equipment, premises and public liability are essential, as is a good security system. You might also want to consider health insurance and loss of earnings too.
- Cashflow is a headache for any business, so keep a slush fund for emergencies, such as if you get no clients that week and still want to eat!
- You need to have a stock of tape etc, or you won't be able to work.
- Although it's hard to accept, professional advice from accountants and equipment/acoustic installers could save money and hassle in the long run.
- Realise that you won't be able to do all the sessions yourself: a good team of staff are vital. All studios are much the same – it's the people who make the difference.
- A good working relationship with session musicians, freelance engineers and producers, and your local tradesmen (including music shop and pro audio supplier) will serve you well.

Commercial studio checklist

- Rates and planning permission on a property with a long-term lease.
- Soundproofing, acoustics, access and loading need careful consideration.
- Fire regulations, planning permission and insurance are not optional extras.
- Specialising in a particular market will probably earn you regular customers.
- Budgeting for maintenance and expansion is just as important as the initial opening.
- Staying ahead and keeping a regular client base are essential.
- Studios are about people – never forget that.

Patchbay design/layouts

A patchbay is nothing magical: it simply provides all of the important connectors in the studio in one central place with a common connector, so that using and connecting equipment is as easy and efficient as possible. Who wants to crawl on the floor to find a cable, just because someone wants to try de-essing the vocals?

With this in mind, designing a patchbay layout is not that hard. Good labelling is important as it might not always be you trying to find a particular hole. Don't mix incompatible items on a patchbay. For instance, use a separate patchbay and connector type for the microphone (and loudspeaker) connections. Following is a list of the order of the most important things to include on your patchbay:

> **INFORMATION**
>
> *There are two systems for normalising: half and full. With half normalising, inserting the top jack acts as a "listen" and allows the normalising to continue. Only when the bottom row is inserted too will the connection be broken with whatever is in the path of the leads. This is the normal system. With full normalising, a plug must be inserted in both sockets for the path to be broken. This complicates patching in most systems.*

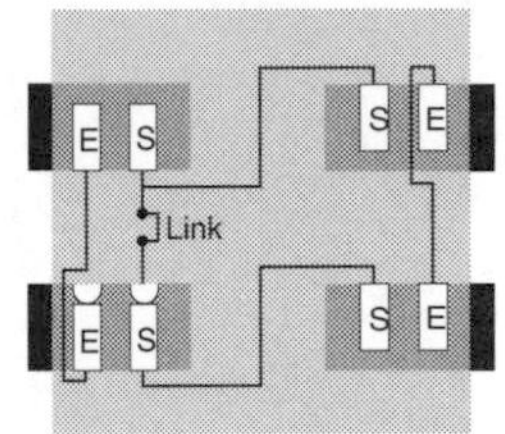

Typical four-socket patchbay card showing the normalising link.

- Insert points (normalised) and serial effects (not normalised).
- Auxiliary sends and returns (not normalised to each other but to parallel effects).
- Tape, cassette and CD machines and mixer stereo out and stereo tape returns, normalised as required.
- Line inputs and instrument outputs – normalised.
- Multi-track tape ins and mixer group outputs (for direct recording without groups or to use group outs as an extra type of auxiliary send) – normalised.
- Multi-track tape outs and mixer returns (for inserting serial effects or swapping channels on mixdown…) – normalised.
- It is very useful to have some rows of parallel sockets.
- By convention, outputs are on the upper row and inputs on the lower row.

Normalising

Normalising is a system whereby a number of sockets are automatically joined when no lead is inserted in them. This is useful for insert points and normal connections (such as instruments to particular channels, effects to auxiliaries). This saves a lot of patch-chord spaghetti and means you can remove all of the patch chords to make your system work normally, rather than have to trace them all.

Notes

- Auxiliary sends would be hard wired to parallel effects sends and returns.
- Serial effects are in-line, such as equalisers, graphics, flangers and phasers, chorus units, compressors and gates. This can include delay units if being used on one instrument only.
- Parallel effects include reverb and delay effects to be used on more than one instrument simultaneously.

Patchbay design

Ideally all the connections in the studio should be brought up on the patchbays (except microphones). Outputs are usually on the top row and inputs on the bottom row. Each two vertical sockets we shall refer to as a pair. A 16 track, five patchbay system is described below (all normalised unless stated).

Patchbay 1 – Insert patchbay

Pairs 1–16	Channel insert sends and returns

Patchbay 2 – Effects patchbay

Pairs 1–16	Serial effects units o/ps and i/ps (not normalised) and group insert send and returns

Patchbay 3 – Instrument/line patchbay

Pairs 1–16 top row	Instrument outputs
Pairs 1–16 bottom row	Channel line inputs

Patchbay 4 – Tape and monitor patchbay

Pairs 1–16 top row	Multitrack tape machine outputs
Pairs 1–16 bottom row	Mixer tape returns and and/or monitor returns

Patchbay 5 – Auxiliary patchbay

Pairs 1– 8	Auxiliary sends and returns (normalised to parallel effects)
Pairs 9 –12	Mastering and cassette tape machine o/ps and i/ps and stereo tape return
Pairs 13 –16 top row	Stereo mixer outputs and studio sends/foldback auxiliaries
Pairs 13 –16 bottom row	Monitor amplifier and foldback amplifier inputs

Synchronisation concepts

SMPTE frame formats and resolution

SMPTE is used to synchronise tape machines (ATR and VTR), tape-to-MIDI sequencers, tapeless (hard disk) recorders and even cue list-triggered devices such as samplers, lighting and mechanical devices. In essence, it acts like an electronic conductor which tells the time to any listening devices. The devices then interpret this time to their internal tempo maps or cue lists and decide where they should be or what they should be doing at that time.

In concept, SMPTE is a Manchester bi-phase encoded tone that represents the time in hours, minutes, seconds and frames. Owing to original mains and television broadcast standards, a number of formats of SMPTE frame exist:

Frame rate	*Usage*	*One frame duration (ms)*
30 drop frame (29.97)	USA colour video	33.366ms
30	USA b/w video	33.333ms
25	EBU video	40.000ms
24	film	41.666ms

INFORMATION

SMPTE (Society of Motion Picture and Television Engineers, the body that finalised the format) is a system used to synchronise systems together. Originally developed owing to the adoption of video tape without sprocket holes. SMPTE provided an electronic sprocket hole.

SMPTE calculator

The following formula can be used to determine the corresponding value:

Tempo x duration = beats x 60

Note that duration is in seconds, and beats are relative to time signature with a crotchet (4) base. With formula manipulation it can be seen that:

For time fit tempo = beats x 60/duration

For time length calculation duration = beats x 60/tempo

For bar length calculation beats = tempo x duration/60

To calculate bars, divide beats by the crotchet base (4).

Film hit list calculation

To fit music to picture, it is normal to take the best average feel tempo that matches most elements of the action. Extra accents or textures can be added to highlight any extra action points. Alternatively, by timing the section a time-fit tempo can be calculated to fit that duration. Computer programs are available to calculate the average tempo that best fits the cue list actions.

Tempo/delay calculator (tempo to delay in ms)

BPM	*4/4 bar*	*1/4 note*	*1/8*	*1/16*	*1/32*
60	4000	1000	500	250	125
65	3692.30	923.07	461.53	230.76	115.38
70	3428.57	857.14	427.57	214.28	107.14
75	3200	800	400	200	100
80	3000	750	375	187.5	93.75

BPM	4/4 bar	1/4 note	1/8	1/16	1/32
85	2823.52	705.88	352.94	176.47	88.23
90	2666.66	666.66	333.33	166.66	83.33
95	2526.31	631.57	315.78	157.89	78.94
96	2500	625	312.50	156.25	78.12
97	2474.22	618.56	309.28	154.64	77.32
98	2448.98	612.24	306.12	153.06	76.53
99	2424.24	606.06	303.03	151.51	75.75
100	2400	600	300	150	75
101	2376.23	594.06	297.03	148.51	74.25
102	2352.94	588.23	294.12	147.06	73.53
103	2330.09	582.52	291.26	145.63	72.82
104	2307.69	576.92	288.46	144.23	72.11
105	2285.71	571.43	285.71	142.86	71.43
106	2264.15	566.04	283.02	141.51	70.75
107	2242.99	560.75	280.37	140.19	70.09
108	2222.22	555.55	277.77	138.88	69.44
109	2201.83	550.46	275.23	137.61	68.81
110	2181.81	545.45	272.72	136.36	68.18
111	2162.16	540.54	270.27	135.13	67.56
112	2142.86	535.71	267.85	133.93	66.96
113	2123.89	530.97	265.48	132.74	66.37
114	2105.26	526.32	263.16	131.58	65.79
115	2086.96	521.74	260.87	130.43	65.22
116	2068.96	517.24	258.62	129.31	64.65
117	2051.28	512.82	256.41	128.21	64.10
118	2033.89	508.47	254.24	127.12	63.56
119	2016.81	504.20	252.10	126.05	63.02
120	2000	500	250	125	62.50
121	1983.47	495.87	247.93	123.97	61.98
122	1967.21	491.80	245.90	122.95	61.47
123	1951.22	487.80	243.90	121.95	60.97
124	1935.48	483.87	241.93	120.97	60.48
125	1920	480	240	120	60
126	1904.76	476.19	238.09	119.05	59.52
127	1889.76	472.44	236.22	118.11	59.05
128	1875	468.75	234.38	117.19	58.59
129	1860.46	465.11	232.56	116.28	58.14
130	1846.15	461.54	230.77	115.38	57.69
131	1832.06	458.01	229	114.50	57.25
132	1818.18	454.54	227.27	113.63	56.82
133	1804.51	451.13	225.56	112.78	56.39
134	1791.04	447.76	223.88	111.94	55.97
135	1777	444.44	222.22	111.11	55.55
136	1764.71	441.18	220.59	110.29	55.15
137	1751.82	437.96	218.98	109.49	54.74
138	1739.13	434.78	217.39	108.69	54.35
139	1726.62	431.65	215.83	107.91	53.95
140	1714.28	428.57	214.28	107.14	53.57
145	1655.17	413.79	206.89	103.45	51.72
150	1600	400	200	100	50
155	1548.38	387.09	193.55	96.77	48.39
160	1500	375	187.50	93.75	46.88
165	1454.54	363.63	181.81	90.91	45.45
170	1411.76	352.94	176.47	88.23	44.12
175	1371.43	342.86	171.43	85.71	42.86
180	1333.33	333.33	166.66	83.33	41.66
185	1297.29	324.32	162.16	81.08	40.54
190	1263.15	315.79	157.89	78.95	39.47
195	1230.77	307.69	153.85	76.92	38.46
200	1200	300	150	75	37.50

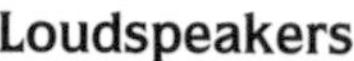

Loudspeakers

Amplifier/speaker efficiency for an amplifier rated into 4 ohms

Speaker load	*Efficiency*
4	100%
8	70%
16	50%

Safe monitoring conditions

Level in dB	*Safe period in minutes per day*
96	120
99	60
102	30
105	15
108	7.5
111	3.75
114	1.875
117	0.94
120	0.47 (under half a second!)

(As defined by the British Occupational Hygiene Society)

Tape editing

Tape editing is the process of physically cutting and joining sections of tape. The element should be marked at its beginning with a chinagraph pencil on the current playback head. The destination is marked in the same manner. The two marks are then cut and joined.

Marking the beginning of the element (word or music beat) is important to maintain a natural flow to the material, otherwise double breaths, gaps or beats may be introduced. It is best to mark strong consonants (such as "B" or "T" sounds but not "S") for speech, or a bass drum or strong pulsed instrument for music. The edited sections should be kept in case they need to be rejoined due to an error. After marking the tape, it is wise to play it from each mark from pause to check the point.

The speed of rotation affects the intelligibility during marking. Find the approximate mark at higher speed, and then rock the section back and forth at slower speeds until the exact point is found.

Leader colour	*Usage*
red	end of tape
green	beginning of tape
yellow/blue/white	section marker

Editing cut angle	*Application*
90°	leader join
60°	stereo material edit
45°	mono material edit

Production

Currently there are two types of producer: the performing type and the directing type.

A *performer producer* will have his own musical skills, songwriting and arranging style and impose this on the project. Record companies can find this a safe bet as the record will be like one of the producer's own, but with different artists (in name at least). He will also probably have strong engineering, programming and technical skills, often performing these roles himself.

A *directing producer* is more like the traditional concept of producer. He will not be so obsessed with making a version of one of his own records. In contrast, his job will be to get the best from the original performers and engineer but working around a commercial, palatable framework that helps to ensure acceptance by the listening public. He will have good people skills and ideas in terms of sound, arrangement and performance, but will not necessarily be able to perform these himself. He will use the available talent to do this to the best possible standard. He may bring in external talent to perform certain tasks, but the end result will certainly be one of the original artists' records. He will try and mould the project but will be open to suggestions from all parties. At the end of the day, his job is to deliver a finished master on time and within budget, which the record company will think the public will accept.

Producers usually work on a points system, that is a percentage of royalties from sales. Re-mixers often work for a fixed fee, and so may not reap the benefit from massive sales – other than to be booked again for another project.

Production techniques

Owing to the large number of variables and distractions when using a recording studio, it is often wise to write down your ideas, so that you can refer back to them should the project move off at a tangent.

In terms of production it may be worth bearing in mind the expression *FASA*. This stands for Frequency, Amplitude, Spectrum and Ambience, the basic criteria that can be changed in sonic terms. Here are some of the possibilities:

- *Frequency* – Pitch, transposing parts, chord inversions, layering with other octaves.
- *Amplitude* – Level, use of dynamic range (drop and build sections) and relative volumes between parts.
- *Spectrum* – Textures and the range of frequencies present, layering sounds with others, introducing new textures from other parts, changing the sounds for a part (like playing a percussion line as a bass part), the contrast in frequency and textures used.
- *Ambience* – Space, reverb and position information such as panning, depth, height, forward or recessed, for each part playing.

Contrast is another important point in production. A poem might be very interesting, but if spoken in a monotone it will be wearing on the listener. Music is a similar entity and a balance between keeping an expected flow (like keeping the beat so it can still be danced to) has to be balanced against listener fatigue and boredom. Also, if a song tells a story with a beginning, middle and end, and a point with climaxes and release, then each section/point merits its own unique handling. All of this happens against a backdrop of the repetitive/cyclic nature of music.

Production options and contrasts (for each part or section of a song)

build	drop
increase tempo	decrease tempo
advance part	retard part
quantise part	free, shuffle or groove quantise
more effects	less effects
wide pan	narrow pan
increase level	decrease level
bring forward	recess
introduce more instruments	drop instruments
layer, ADT or chorus parts	focus parts
change instrumentation	keep instrumentation
key change	no key change
octave shift parts	keep octaves
invert chords	split notes to textures
increase rhythmic element	increase harmonic element

Mixing tips

When mixing we suggest you try the following:

• Pre-processing sounds during recording tends to produce better results although you have to be careful as you cannot undo any treatment you have recorded. Remember, when combining sounds during the mix, reverb and effects reduce in effect and bass becomes more prominent.

• Listen to each sound in isolation first to determine the contents and treatment needed.

• Start to mix, using your loudest sound (e.g. main vocal) as the first reference. You can mute it once you have determined the level if desired. Then treat the accumulative sound as desired.

• Sub grouping sections of the mix, or mixing in sections and then tape editing it together later, can help considerably.

• You should mix at a moderate level. Listening at too high a level will not give you the expected mix at normal levels, due to the non-linear response of the human ear.

• To test the mix, listen at high and low levels and even listen to the mix from outside the room. This will accentuate any problems with the mix.

• Listen on a variety of systems (including in-car). Mixing on headphones is not recommended as the results from speakers will be markedly different.

• You should consider the intended listener's environment when mixing. Wide stereo is pointless for a mobile or off-centre audience, and a widely dynamic mix is problematic in noisy arenas such as in-car.

• If your monitoring system is coloured in any way, your recorded mix will have the opposite effect unless you allow for it. For instance, bass heavy monitors provide a bass light mix on tape. You should listen to pre-recorded music you know well on the studio system.

• Try to give sounds room to breathe by not letting sounds compete against each other in the same spectrum.

• When equalising a sound you will find it easier to boost the frequency by a large amount to find the frequency and then back off to the amount required. Also if you wish to reduce a frequency, it is easier to accentuate it first by boosting to find it, and then once found to cut it. With equalisation you will often find that cutting can be just as effective as boosting — try it.

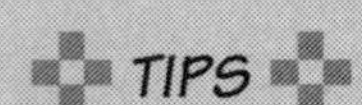

• When mixing "less is more".

• Contrast is essential for clarity and effect.

• Using no effect on one sound can be as effective as using an effect.

PRODUCTION MAP

Please photocopy and use this map

Music Technology Reference Book

Section	*Timing*	*Cue*	*Mood*	*Achieved by*	*Musical and mix notes (Chords/pan/reverb/EQ)*
(eg):					
verse	*1'00"-1'30"*	*"Don't turn back"*	*Dark*	*Low rumble/reverb/arpeg*	*A min, A-F-G melody*

Locator positions

Section										
Time										
Bar										

Other notes (SMPTE, Tempo, sequencer files, Sound banks/samples, FX and EQ settings...)

Audio for video

Matching audio with vision is becoming an increasing necessity, for film, TV, video, multimedia, and computer games. As sound is a linear thing, it is best if the vision is cut to the sound, or at least with some musical rhythm in mind.

In any case, the job of the composer is to find the best fit of musical events with visual action, while retaining the musical mood of the piece. It may be that not all of the cues can fit on a musical division but the key is to make the feel of the music and visual action fit. Accents, sound effects and new textures can be added if necessary.

Changing the tempo to fit each section does not usually work and other techniques such as free tempo or a-tempo techniques can be used (like a sustained chord or non-related rhythmic part). When working to picture, it is often best to mark the cues with a sonic event and label each section of time. Then the music can be built to these cues, without having to refer continuously to the picture. This will also reduce the need to wait for synchronisation and tape shuttling.

When the soundtrack is finished, it will usually be laid back on to video by the video house. Suitable formats include centre time code DAT or open reel, or with free running audio which includes 30 seconds of original video sound (perhaps dialogue) cut five seconds before the music starts.

Video editing techniques

It might be helpful to realise how video editing works. Video editing uses a process of accurately copying a section of one tape to another. This is called *insert editing* and can be video, audio 1, audio 2 or any combination. This allows the pictures to be cut to an already laid soundtrack – essential for pop video work.

A video, however, uses a fourth track called the control track, which is used to synchronise the video head with each video frame of information and to locate sections of the tape. This control track is recorded during assemble edit recording, which records all four tracks at once. This is usually done before the tape is first used, and is called *blacking* the tape. It is important to use a very stable source of video sync when doing this, to ensure trouble-free editing in the future.

During insert editing, the control track also helps to ensure a clean edit at the video frame point. A control track is a simple repetitive pulse and can drop count slightly, so checking with the preview function before each edit is essential. This simulates the effect of the edit on-screen, without actually recording onto tape. SMPTE can also be used in conjunction with the control track, but must be recorded while jammed to the control track/video frame sync.

For advance editing techniques, like using fades between scenes rather than straight cuts, a three-machine edit suite is required so that the vision can be mixed between them while being recorded onto the third master machine.

Each edit is recorded as a series of time and action cues that form an EDL (edit decision list). This EDL is stored and can be re-used or changed at a later date, making repeating or changing any edits a fairly automatic process. This also allows for a process called *off-line editing*, where the producer can use a lower cost facility to decide on his EDL which can then later be "conformed" (realised) on-line in the full blown edit suite.

When creating a video, it is essential to do two things: create a storyboard plan to shoot to, which will help reveal any special shooting requirements (such as camera angles for continuity); log all of the tapes and shots so that they can be found easily later.

The storyboard planner

The storyboard planner is like a cartoon, in that a number of boxes are used, each containing the essence of each shot. A template follows:

STORYBOARD PLANNER

Please photocopy and use this planner

Music Technology Reference Book

SHOOT LOG

Please photocopy and use this log

Project ______________________

Date ______________________

Film reels ______________________

	Time (start/end/duration)	*Scene*	*Shot details*	*Cue*	*Notes*
1					
2					
3					
4					
5					
6					
7					
8					
9					
10					
11					
12					
13					
14					
15					
16					
17					
18					
19					
20					
21					
22					
23					
24					
25					

Audio for video hints and tips

Using audio in a video environment requires some special precautions:

- Microphone cables should use star quad cable (two twisted pairs, screened) to minimise induction from lighting equipment.
- Lighting and vision cables should be laid first so that sound cables can be routed away from them, or crossing at 90° to minimise interference.
- Special equipment is used to synchronise the vision and sound equipment together, such as the 50Hz pilot tone, a common SMPTE feed (also to the audio on the video recorders) or a common sound source such as the clapper board.
- For pop video work it is normal to record the backing tape first and then get the performers to mime to it a number of times, in order to get enough visual angles, zooms and cuts, Normally one wide angle shot is taken in its entirety and the other shots cut into it.
- It is quite hard to get high-quality location sound, which is why it is common to add sounds after the shoot and editing, during a stage called *post-production*. The sound can also be used to help make the vision cuts appear more natural because, unlike the vision, an audience expects the sound to be continuous and logical. It is often necessary to over-emphasise elements of the sound for impact, such as footsteps which, unless you had your ear on their boot, wouldn't naturally be that loud!

APRS tape label system

The APRS (Association of Professional Recording Studios) decided on a standard for tape labelling using particular colour labels as follows:

Type	*Colour*	*Details*
Session tape	blue	A multi-track or two-track work tape that may contain out-takes.
Original master	red	The first generation of the final stereo product. Not necessarily suitable for production purposes.
Production master	green	All necessary EQ and treatment has been applied to the programme (vinyl, cassette, CD, DAT) material for the format indicated. A CD master would need further PQ-encoding for the pressing process.
Production master copy	orange	If source and duplicate are digital, then the tape is a (vinyl, cassette, CD, DAT) clone. If the duplicate is analogue, the tape is a copy and should not be duplicated further without the producers' consent.
CD tape master PQ-encoded	grey	Fully prepared and PQ-encoded tape for glass mastering. (original, digital clone). Any clones generated must include re-generated timecode and re-laid PQ-encoding information.
Safety copy	pink	Strictly for safety. Only to be used with producer's permission.
Not for production	yellow	Identifies a tape that is not currently suitable for production.
Media version include	yellow	Supplied for a specific medium and not for general production. May also include timecode as detailed on the box.

Note: A clone is digital and a copy is analogue.

Printed versions of these labels are available from the APRS or via some pro audio suppliers.

Master tapes should be leadered and include a section of line-up tones as follows:

20"	1kHz at 0vu (0db)	(maximum level check)
20"	1kHz at -10db	(to signify the -10 mark)
20"	10kHz at -10dB	(for azimuth line-up check)
20"	100Hz at -10dB	(for EQ alignment).

The tape should state the speed, equalization curve (NAB or IEC) and carry full program details of the tone and program, including durations and running order. A note should also be made of the peak level used above 0VU, in case level elevation is required.

Music technology – historical overview

Date	*Relevance*
Before 1900	Live performances only, right back to the cave men!
1896-1906	Thaddeus Cahill builds an electronic instrument weighing 200 tons, called the Dynamophone or Telharmonium. Alternators are driven by electric motors to produce pitched sounds.
1904-1915	The invention of the radio valve (or diode) enables the valve oscillator to produce pitched sounds.
1919-1924	Leon Theremin invents the Theremin, a device producing "wailing" sounds played by moving your hands around two antennas to manipulate pitch and loudness.
1928-1950	The Ondes Martenot, based on the Theremin, uses a sliding finger ring on a ribbon to alter pitch. Messiaen and Boulez compose for it.
1928-1930	The Trautonium is produced in Germany by Trautwein. A wire pressed against a metal rail triggers an oscillator. A foot pedal controls volume and early filters provide coloration.
1935-1960	Laurenns Hammond introduces the tone-wheel organ. Timbres are created by stacking sine waves using draw bars.
1939	Hammond brings out the Novachord, the first polyphonic electronic organ. The monophonic Solovox follows which offers timbre and pitch control.
1948	Pierre Schaeffer tapes some trains and creates music concrete by editing and tape manipulation. He lays the foundation for Stockhausen and others.
1954	The monophonic RCA music synthesiser uses perforated tape to control oscillators, filters and mixers.
1955	Stockhausen composes *Gesang der Junglinge*, which combines a choir boy singing with electronic sounds.
1963	Herb Deutsch meets Robert Moog and discusses using a voltage-controlled synthesiser inspired by the Theremin and RCA machine.
1965	Robert Moog unveils his first voltage-controlled synthesiser.
1968	Walter Carlos records *Switched-on-Bach* played entirely on a Moog synthesiser.
1969	EMS produces the VCS3, nicknamed the Putney.
1978	Polyphonic synths such as the Yamaha CS80 and Sequential Circuits Prophet V appear.
1979	The Fairlight CMI is introduced, incorporating sampling and synthesis techniques.
1982	Various Japanese and American manufacturers agree on the idea of the MIDI standard. The first MIDI synths, the Prophet 600 and Roland Jupiter 6, appear.
1983	The Yamaha DX7 comes on the scene, replacing many Rhodes pianos for gigging due to weight considerations.
1987	Roland introduces LA synthesis and the concept of sample plus synthesis evolves.
The Future	Interactive Hi-Fi and re-synthesis under computer control are likely...

6 Audio

Formulae

The decibel

The decibel (abbreviation: dB) is a convenient way of looking at a value in terms of a ratio. As it is just a ratio, it provides for very easy comparison but ideally the reference should also be known. It is also easier to work out the gain of a system by working with the dB ratios (that is, just adding to work out the gain of a number of stages).

The reference or standard to which a value is compared depends on the application. The *dBv* is referenced to 1 volt, while the *dBm* (the more common standard) references to 1mW into 600 ohms giving 0.775 volts. Meanwhile sound pressure is measured in dBs referenced to 20 $\mu N/m^2$.

dB formulae

Electrical power (and sound power) ratio:

For dBm, pr = 1mW into 600 ohms
dB = 10 log (p/pr)

Electrical voltage (or current) and sound pressure ratio:

For dBv, vr = 1.0V
For dBm, vr = 0.775V
dB = 20 log (v/vr)

You need to double the power of an amplifier to get a 3dB increase in level. This is one reason why using an efficient speaker system of the correct impedance will help to save buying a bigger amplifier (see speaker efficiency section).

Sound pressure ratio

By international agreement, the reference (pr) is:

0.0002 dyne/cm^2 = 20µPa = 0.0002 microbar = 20 µnewton/m^2.
SPL dB = 20 log (p/pr) where p is the pressure to be quantified.

Sound power

SWL dB = 10 log (w/wr) where wr=10^{-12}W and w is the total radiated power in watts.

- In sound terms, the smallest detectable change by the human ear is 1dB. The figure of 3dB is a more realistic detectable change.
- In air, sound reduces in level by 3dB every time the distance it has travelled doubles. 96dB at 1 metre reduces to 93dB at 2 metres.
- Japanese manufacturers tend to use the dBv as their reference instead of dBm. So a figure of -10dBv actually equates to 316.2mV (-7.79 dBm).

dB table

dB Value	Power ratio (10 log p1/p2)	Voltage ratio (20 log v1/v2)	dBm Ref 0.775V	dBv Ref 1.0V
+30	1000 (10^3)	31.62	24.94V	31.62V
+28	630.96	25.12	19.46V	25.12V
+26	398.1	19.95	15.46V	19.95V
+24	251.2	15.85	12.28V	15.85V
+22	158.5	12.59	9.752V	12.59V
+20	100.0 (10^2)	10.00	7.746V	10.00V
+18	63.10	7.943	6.153V	7.943V
+16	39.81	6.310	4.887V	6.310V
+14	25.12	5.012	3.882V	5.012V
+12	15.85	3.981	3.084V	3.981V
+10	10.0	3.162	2.449V	3.162V
+9	7.943	2.818	2.183V	2.818V
+8	6.310	2.512	1.946V	2.512V
+7	5.012	2.239	1.734V	2.239V
+6	3.981	1.995*	1.546V	1.995V
+5	3.162	1.778	1.377V	1.778V
+4	2.512	1.585	1.228V	1.585V
+3	1.995*	1.413	1.094V	1.413V
+2	1.585	1.259	975.3mV	1.259V
+1	1.259	1.122	868.1mV	1.122V
0	1.000	1.000	774.6mV	1.000V
-1	0.7943	0.8913	690.4mV	891.3mV
-2	0.6310	0.7943	615.3mV	794.3mV
-3	0.5012*	0.7079	548.4mV	707.9mV
-4	0.3981	0.6310	488.7mV	631.0mV
-5	0.3162	0.5623	435.6mV	562.3mV
-6	0.2512	0.5012*	388.2mV	501.2mV
-7	0.1995	0.4467	346.0mV	446.7mV
-8	0.1585	0.3981	308.4mV	398.1mV
-9	0.1229	0.3548	274.8mV	354.8mV
-10	0.1000 (10^{-1})	0.3162	244.9mV	316.2mV
-15	0.03162	0.1778	137.7mV	177.8mV
-20	0.0100 (10^{-2})	0.1000 (10^{-1})	77.46mV	100.0mV
-25	0.003162	0.05623	43.56mV	56.2mV
-30	0.0010 (10^{-3})	0.03162	24.49mV	31.62mV
-35	0.0003162	0.01778	13.77mV	17.78mV
-40	0.0001 (10^{-4})	0.0100 (10^{-2})	7.746mV	10.00mV
-45	0.00003162	0.005623	4.356mV	5.623mV
-50	0.00001 (10^{-5})	0.003162	2.450mV	3.162mV
-55	0.000003162	0.001778	1.377mV	1.778mV
-60	0.000001 (10^{-6})	0.0010 (10^{-3})	774.6µV	1.000mV
-70	10^{-7}	0.0003162	244.9µV	316.2µV
-80	10^{-8}	0.0001 (10^{-4})	77.46µV	100.0µV
-90	10^{-9}	0.00003162	24.49µV	31.62µV
-100	10^{-10}	0.00001 (10^{-5})	7.746µV	10.00µV
-110	10^{-11}	0.3162 x 10^{-6}	2.449µV	3.162µV
-120	10^{-12}	10^{-6}	0.7746µV	1.00µV

*Important dB reference points of half and double power and voltage.

To determine a voltage from a dB value using a known reference requires simple formula transposition and substitution. dB = 20 log (v/vr) and so V = antilog(dB/20)Vr.

For example, -96.3dB as a voltage referenced to 0.775V is:

V = antilog(-96.3/20) x 0.775V = 0.0000118V = 11.8µV.

> **INFORMATION**
>
> *The dB: decibel (one-tenth of a bel). A measurement of a ratio between a value and a known reference.*

Adding dBs

If two signals of a random nature, such as noise, are added together, the effect is not the same as simply adding the two levels. The formula is:

$y = (10 \log(1+\log^{-1}x/10)) - x$

where y is the dB value to be added to the greater figure and x is the dB difference between the two values. In practice if the values are the same then the increase is 3dB. If the values are different by up to 2dB then 2dB is added. If the values are different by up to 6dB then 1dB is added. If the difference is greater than 6dB then less than 0.5dB is added.

Sound

Speed (velocity) of sound:

c = square root of (yp/d)

where y = ratio of specific heats (1.4 for air)
p = pressure (normally 10^6 dynes, 10^5 newtons/m^2)
d = density (normally 1.2kg/m^3 for air)

Speed of sound at sea level at 20 degrees C is 344 metres/second or 1,130 feet/second.

Velocity, wavelength and frequency

Velocity is also related to wavelength and frequency:

c = w x f

where c = velocity of sound
w = wavelength
f = frequency

To find the wavelength of a frequency, formula transposition gives w = c/f. This gives one of the most useful factors in microphone and speaker placement and listening room size as the following table indicates. An understanding of wavelength can help in a number of audio factors such as when investigating standing waves and room response:

Wavelength/frequency table

Frequency (Hz)	Wavelength feet/inches	metres/cm
20	50'	16.5 m
50	20'	6.6 m
100	10'	3.3 m
250	4'	1.32 m
500	2'	66 cm
1000	1'	33 cm
2000	6"	16.5 cm
5000	2.4"	6.6 cm
10,000	1.2"	3.3 cm
15,000	0.8"	2.2 cm
20,000	0.5"	1.65 cm

(assuming C = 1,000 feet/second or 330 metres/second.)

Tips

- As you can see from the wavelength/frequency table, in terms of high frequencies, moving a microphone by less than 1inch (2.4cm) is significant in terms of the high frequency's wavelength and could change the response as the microphone travels through each frequency's peaks and dips. In terms of mic placement, moving the microphone less than an inch radically changes the sound.
- To get a true bass response, a quarter wavelength should be used. In other words, the bass response heard in the control room at 6 feet (2m) from the speakers will be less than the bass response heard at 20 feet (6m).
- For convenience, sound is depicted (usually in diagrams of sine waves) as being a transverse wave, in that the oscillation is perpendicular to the direction of the wave. In reality, sound actually travels as a longitudinal waveform – the oscillations are parallel to the direction of the wave. This means that the air compresses and expands just like the air in a piston. So from any fixed point, the air pressure will change through the whole cycle of the waveform – no matter where you stand along the waveform's path, you will hear the sound. This should make the above two statements impossible! However in practice, due to the complex interaction of the sound source and reflections, the effect is true.
- Regarding a mixing console's fader, it has been mentioned that the wavelength of the sound and the position of the fader knob has a relevance to the way sounds mix, with the assumption that moving the fader knob by a small amount changes the phase relationship to the other faders. In reality this cannot be true, as the electrical signal representing the sound also travels longitudinally. However, for some mysterious reason, there is a practical truth to this concept which is hard to explain...

Sound pressure

The normal atmospheric pressure of air is 10^6 dynes/cm^2, 10^5 pascals, 0.0002 µbar. Sound causes pressure changes ranging from 20 µPa (for the threshold of hearing) to 60 Pa, 600 µbar (for the threshold of pain).

Sound power

The power in a sound can be determined by:

$$W = pu$$

where W = the power (in joule/m^2 or watts/m^2)
p = RMS gas pressure (in Pa)
u = RMS gas/particle velocity (m/s)

The radiation impedance (z) is given by:

$$z = pc \text{ or } w = zu^2 \text{ or } w = p^2/z$$

where c = the velocity of propagation (in m/s)
u = the RMS particle velocity
p = the gas density (in Pa)
w = power (in joules/m^2)
z = radiation impedance (in c.g.s. ohms)

z is often given the value of 40.7 c.g.s. units (407 acoustical ohms in SI units).

Sound decay

Power falls = 1/distance ^{2}

Pressure falls = 1/distance

Hearing response

The human ear does not exhibit a linear response to all frequencies at all volumes. The following table illustrates this response. In specification measurements, this factor is often included to give a weighted response which simulates the effect of the human ear.

A-weighted sound pressure levels in dB (0.0002 dynes/cm²)

SPL	*Examples*
160	Inside a kick drum
150	Snare drum at 1inch
140	Loud battlefield (World War 2).
	Operatic voice at 1 inch
130	Threshold of pain.
	Symphony orchestra at 30 feet (triple forte)
120	Loud parts of a rock concert.
	Trumpets at 5 feet
110	Club disco sound system.
	Guitar amp at 6 inches
105	Piano at 4 feet
100	Very loud classical music
95	Average speech at 1inch
90	Roaring drunk.
	Duo in small club.
	Acoustic guitar played with pick
80	Classical music.
	Inside a sports car at 55mph.
	Acoustic guitar played with fingers
70	Speech at 6 feet
60	Background music
55	Home in city, with background noise and traffic
50	Average residence ambience.
	Light traffic at 100 feet.
	Frog pond at dusk
45	Home in city at night
40	Quiet battlefield
20	Record studio ambience
15	Open field at night, no wind – just crickets!
0	Threshold of hearing in young children

Sound proofing

Absorption coefficients

All materials exhibit a degree of sound absorption and reflection at certain frequencies. See the following table for examples:

Material	*Frequency (Hz)*					
	125	*250*	*500*	*1,000*	*2,000*	*4,000*
Acoustic panels	0.15	0.3	0.75	0.85	0.75	0.4
Brick	0.024	0.024	0.03	0.04	0.05	0.07
Carpet	0.05	0.1	0.2	0.25	0.3	0.35
Concrete	0.01	0.01	0.02	0.02	0.02	0.03
Curtains	0.05	0.12	0.15	0.27	0.37	0.5
4 inch fibreglass	0.38	0.89	0.96	0.98	0.81	0.87
Wood floor (joists)	0.15	0.2	0.1	0.1	0.1	0.05
Glass	0.03	0.03	0.03	0.03	0.02	0.02
Seated person	0.18	0.4	0.46	0.46	0.5	0.46
Plasterboard	0.3	0.3	0.1	0.1	0.04	0.02
Plywood on 2 inch batten	0.35	0.25	0.2	0.15	0.05	0.05
0.75 inch wood	0.1	0.11	0.1	0.08	0.08	0.11

Note: A coefficient of 1.0 means 100% absorption (like an open window) while 0 means 100% reflection. A high coefficient means high absorption, hence less reverb at these frequencies. All figures are per square metre of material.

The reverb time can be calculated as follows:

R = 0.161Vm/A

where R = reverb time in seconds
Vm = volume in cubic metres
A = total absorption (square metres x absorption coefficient)

Panel absorbers

Panel absorbers work best between 1/4 and 3/4 of the wavelength. They should be away from any solid surface, the gap perhaps filled with damping material, although this may reduce the efficiency of the absorber.

The resonant frequency of a panel can be found from:

f = 6000/square root of (md)

where f = resonant frequency in hertz
m = mass in kg/m^2
d = distance from wall in metres

Helmholtz resonators

A cylinder with an open top neck that will damp at the following frequency:

$f = (340/2\pi)(s/lv)$

where f = resonant frequency in hertz
s = the cross section area of the neck in m^2
l = length of neck in m
v = volume of chamber in m^3

Filling any absorber or helmholtz resonator gaps will increase the range of frequencies affected, but also reduce the efficiency of the system.

Room resonance

Excluding contents, the half wavelength of the resonant frequency due to air of each surface in a room can be calculated as follows:

$f = v/2d$

where f = the resonant frequency in hertz
v = velocity of sound in m/s
d = room dimension in m

Note that this occurs at a fundamental frequency and at harmonics of this.

Room dimensions

The ideal dimensions of a room to counteract standing waves by giving well-spaced resonances are in the ratio of:

1 : 1.25 : 1.6

Non-parallel surfaces will also reduce this effect.

7

Electronics

General formulae

Ohm's law

Voltage = current × resistance

Power = voltage × current

Power = current^2 × resistance

Voltage in units of volts; resistance in units of ohms; current in units of amps; power in units of watts.

(See audio section for decibel (dB) expressions of power and voltage)

Series resistance
$R = R_1 + R_2 + R_3$

Parallel resistance
$1/R = 1/R_1 + 1/R_2 + 1/R_3$

or for just two parallel resistances:
$R = (R_1 \times R_2) / (R_1+R_2)$

Multipliers

k = kilo = × 1,000 = 10^3
M = mega = × 1,000,000 = 10^6
m = milli = /1,000 = 10^{-3}
μ = micro = /1,000,000 = 10^{-6}
n = nano = /1,000,000,000 = 10^{-9}
p = pico = /1,000,000,000,000 = 10^{-12}

Reactance

$X_l = 2\pi fl$
$X_c = 1/(2\pi fc)$

where f = frequency, l = inductance in henries, c = capacitance in farads.

Resistor colour codes

Colour	As value	As multiplier
black	0	1
brown	1	10
red	2	100
orange	3	1,000
yellow	4	10,000
green	5	100,000
blue	6	1,000,000
violet	7	–
grey	8	–
white	9	–
gold	–	0.1
silver	–	0.01

Note that the value bands start at the band nearest to the edge. The band at the other end, and further in, is the resistance tolerance.

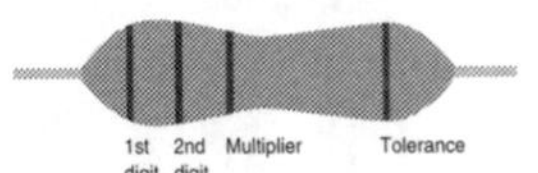

Resistor with 4-band colour code

For four band resistors
band 1 = first digit value
band 2 = second digit value
band 3 = multiplier (for instance, orange = × 1,000)
band 4 = resistor tolerance (see below)

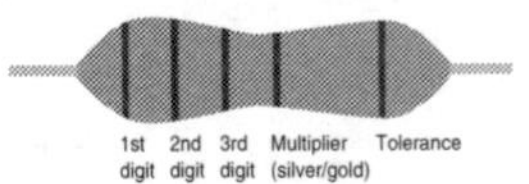

Resistor with 5-band colour code

For five band resistors
band 1 = first digit value
band 2 = second digit value
band 3 = third digit value
band 4 = multiplier
band 5 = resistor tolerance (see below)

Resistor tolerances
brown = 1%
red = 2%
gold = 5%
silver = 10%

Impedance

Series capacitance/resistance
$z = \sqrt{(r^2 + X_c^2)}$
phase angle = $\tan^{-1} X_c/r$

Series capacitance/inductance
$z = \sqrt{(r^2 + X_l^2)}$
phase angle = $\tan^{-1} X_l/r$

Series inductance/capacitance/resistance

$z = \sqrt{(r^2 + (X_l - X_c)^2)}$
phase angle = $\tan^{-1} (X_l - X_c)/r$

Parallel capacitance/resistance

$z = rX_c/\sqrt{(r^2 + X_c^2)}$
phase angle = $\tan^{-1} r/X_c$

Parallel inductance/resistance

$z = rX_l/\sqrt{(r^2 + X_l^2)}$
phase angle = $\tan^{-1} r/X_l$

Resonance

Series resonance

$f = 1/2\pi\sqrt{(LC)}$
impedance at resonance is Z = R

Parallel resonance

$f = 1/2\pi\sqrt{(1/LC - r^2/L^2)}$
impedance at resonance is Z = L/CR

Attenuators

A simple L attenuator pad can be made to connect between similar impedance devices as follows. Note that the parallel resistor B should be 10 times lower than the destination impedance.

Pad	A and B values (Ω)		
10dB	47k/22k	10k/4k7	1k/470
20dB	47k/5k6	10k/1k2	1k/120
40dB	47k/470	10k/100	100k/1k

Audio (analogue) chip pin outs

(LM)741 / (NE)531 / (NE)5534

1 offset null	8 NC
2 – input	7 +ve
3 + input	6 output
4 -ve	5 offset null

(TL)071/081

1 balance	8 NC
2 – input	7 +ve
3 + input	6 output
4 -ve	5 balance

(TL)072/082 /(NE)5532

1 output a	8 +ve
2 – input a	7 output b
3 + input a	6 – input b
4 -ve	5 + input b

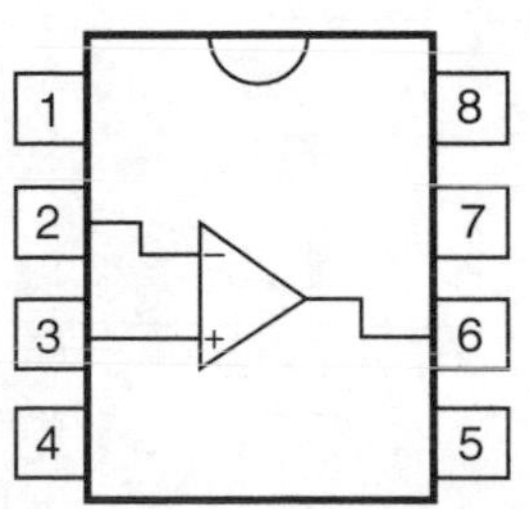

(TL)074/084 /3403/4156

1 output 1	14 output 4
2 – input 1	13 – input 4
3 + input 1	12 + input 4
4 +ve	11 -ve
5 + input 2	10 + input 3
6 – input 2	9 – input 3
7 output 2	8 output 3

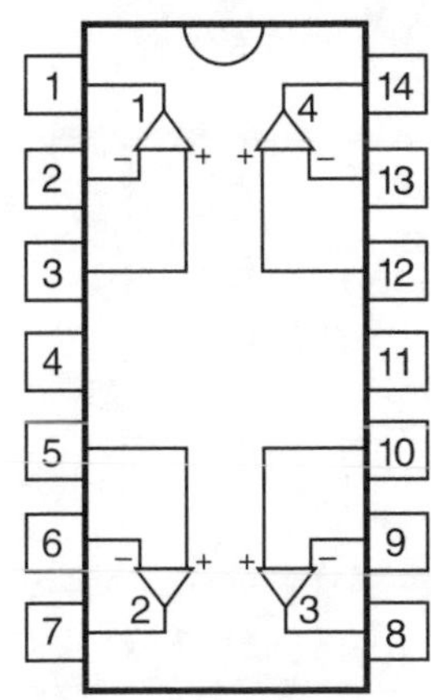

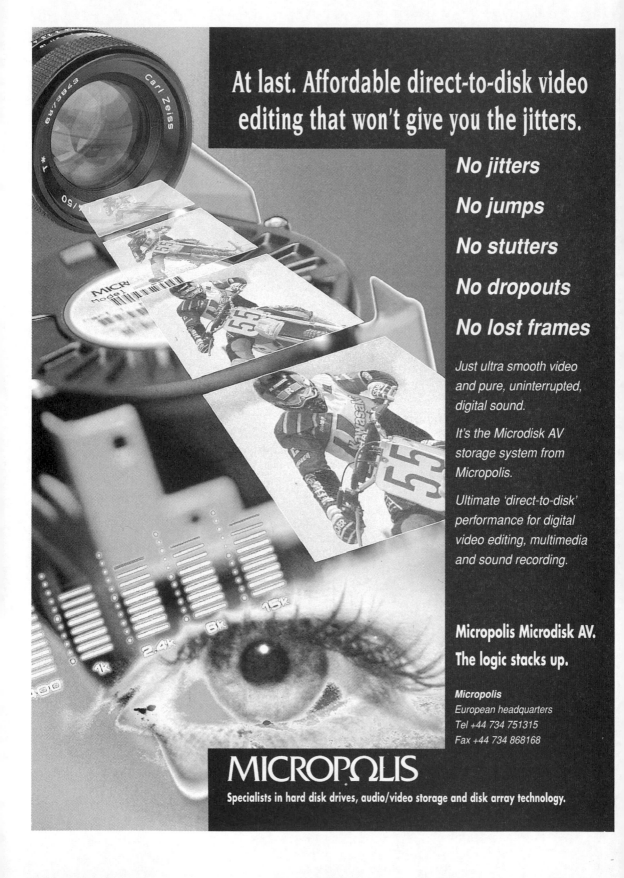

8

Computing and multimedia

What is multimedia?

Multimedia: a system that integrates a number of media, usually under computer control. Can include sound, graphics, video, animation, MIDI files, MCI drivers (such as CD-ROM and laser disk control), text, virtual reality sensors, communications and usually some form of hypertext database control. The degree of interactivity is variable, from simple slide shows to graded course structures.

In the early '90s "multimedia" was a buzz word with little exact meaning. In the later part of this decade, it has become another common term for computing and all the peripheral elements that this encompasses.

Almost all computing platforms have a multimedia capability. Currently the PC (IBM clone) and Apple Mac are proving popular, although dedicated platforms such as Philips CDI and Commodore's CDTV/CD32 had some impact.

In the near future, multimedia will be applied to the concept of home entertainment, including a combined interactive TV/hi-fi/video/games system/ computer – possibly with neural network-type artificial intelligence and automatic program selection based upon personal preferences, user-editable entertainment (for instance, re-mix, edit or create your own version of an existing record, video, or game), home shopping (including software, publishing and music distribution by phoneline), interactive living electronic books and the Information Super Highway (possibly via the Internet system) for global information exchange, world-wide networked games and virtual reality experiences.

CD-ROM

CD-ROM has had a big impact on the multimedia industry. A CD-ROM is simply a compact disc that holds computer data instead of audio information. This data can range from actual software programs (which are usually included on the disk itself in order to access its own contents) to data such as text, pictures, digitised audio or video.

The product has the ability to store some 600Mbytes of information (equivalent to over 600 DD floppy disks) but with a raw manufacturing cost of under £2, and easily distributable with its low weight and small size. Compared with its hard disk equivalent, it offers a very cost-effective removable media storage solution. Its access speed and transfer rate is a lot slower than hard disk (and is not user re-writable).

Current CD technology only allows for WORM (write once read many) access and is cost-prohibitive for an individual to produce. However, with a number of custom manufacturing services and the ever falling prices of the recorders and blanks, this situation will probably change. No doubt a re-recordable domestic system will evolve over time.

CD Book standards

There are a number of standards and formats for CDs defined (by a Philips/Sony agreement) as outlined below:

Book colour	*Application*	*Notes*
Red	CD-DA (digital audio)	74 minutes of 44.1kHz, stereo 16-bit data
Yellow	CD-ROM	
Yellow with extensions	CD-ROM XA	Interleaved vision and audio
Green	CD-I	Philips system (CD Interactive)
Orange	Recordable CD	Kodak PhotoCD and recordable CDs (multi-session)

Data modes

Mode	*Form*	*Application*	*Rate*	*Notes*
1	–	CD-ROM		Uses error correction via main processor
2	1	CD-ROM XA	150kbytes/s	Interleaved. Uses error correction via main processor
2	2	PhotoCD, CD-I	170.2kbytes/s	Interleaved. Can use direct transfer to port

Multi-session disks work on the principle that the previous index points to the location of the next sub index, so that once this has been written, all the data could be located. Without this system it would be impossible to create a table of contents (TOC) in one central place, as it cannot be updated once fixed..

INFORMATION

In order to standardise on the number of possible formats for storing data, a committee designed the ISO 9660 standard (based on an original "ad hoc" agreement called High-Sierra). Most CD-ROM technology is based on this data structure, so that the data can be physically exchanged between platforms, although special translation software may need to be used to interpret that data on a foreign platform.

Philips CD-I ADPCM audio standard

Level	*Frequency bandwidth (kHz)*	*Sampling rate (kHz)*	*Bit rate*
CD-DA	20	44.1	16
A	20	37.8	8
B	17	37.8	4
C	8.5	18.9	4

CD-audio mastering

The process is as follows:

- Creation of material in studio (commercial or otherwise)
- Master tape – analogue or digital format
- Transfer to digital editor for PQ encoding
- PQ encoding to add TOC and sub-frame information
- Production of glass master
- Stampers produced
- Mechanical pressing
- Reproduction of data on domestic system

Multimedia applications/future

Abbreviation	*Application*
POI	Point of information (travel maps, museums...)
POS	Point of sale (interactive store catalogues and sales kiosks – travel tickets, automatic 24 hour car rental...)
CBT	Computer based training, for individually paced tuition/reference, removing the need for travel to conferences...
SIM	Simulation-based training for astronaut, aircraft, train and other driving simulated experiences/tests
VR	Virtual reality, for assessing a real world environment or design, without the expense/time of creating a real world version. Of great use in architecture and product design
DB	Database – living electronic workshop manuals and sales catalogues

Data compression will play a key role in the further development of multimedia. A number of methods are evolving including JPEG (for still photographs), MPEG (for moving pictures), while fractal techniques are being tested.

Compression will allow the use of communication networking for data, real-time video and digital audio networking and conferencing on a global basis.

Computer platforms

There are a number of computer platforms supported by a wider range of manufacturers. Of these, there are currently six major operating systems that are incompatible with each other. Specific versions of a computer program need to be used on each platform, although many software houses publish similar titles for each platform. The data created by a computer however, can often be transferred to a rival platform fairly easily.

Possible ways of transfer include a peripheral port, such as serial modem, parallel printer or SCSI port. Special software is usually needed to support this transfer, such as a BBS terminal emulator. In the case of modem transfer, this can be done via a telephone and BBS service or directly cable to cable, via a special lead called a *null modem* cable (which has its Tx and Rx lines reversed). Another option for data transfer is via floppy, hard disk or CD-ROM.

There are three main factors in data transfer by disk:

- The disk format must be compatible or readable by special software that emulates the format and reads/writes it.
- The data must be in a compatible format. This is usually handled by the specific computer program.
- The file type must be compatible. In many systems a specific file extension will be required, such as "ASC" for ASCII or "TGA" for a Targa graphic file.

The following table may prove useful:

Platform	Floppy disk format	File types
Apple Power PC	DSHD 1.4Mbytes, fixed speed	Data and resource forks. Also PC compatible via SoftWindows and the like
Apple Mac	DSDD 800kbytes, variable speed	Data and resource forks
Apple Mac	DSHD 1.4Mbytes, fixed speed	Data and resource forks
IBM PC	DSDD 720kbytes, fixed speed	Data
IBM PC	DSHD 1.4Mbytes, fixed speed	Data
Atari ST	DSDD 720kbytes, fixed speed	Data. IBM-compatible reading. IBM-compatible formatting from TOS 1.04 (or via a utility)
Atari Falcon	DSDD 720kbytes, fixed speed	Data. IBM compatible
	DSHD 1.4Mbytes, fixed speed	Data. IBM compatible
Commodore Amiga	DSHD 800kbytes, fixed speed	Data. Proprietary FAT. IBM Interchange via programs such as CrossDOS

Note that the Apple Mac uses a different FAT (File Allocation Table) from the PC type. A number of programs are available to convert between the two:

Mac programs	IBM PC programs
Apple File Exchange (Apple)	AccessMac (Avantek) (File exchange only)
(Includes data type change or via ResEdit)	MacSee (PD) (Supports data forks)
AccessPC	
PC Exchange	
SoftWindows (Mac Power PC)	

Also note that there are three types of MIDI file format: 0, 1 and 2 (see Chapter 1) and that the destination sequencer program will have to support this format.

To force your sequencer to save as a format 0 MIDI file (if there is no option) try the following:

- Save your normal copy of the song so that you are effectively using a working copy.
- Normalise all tracks to make any playback parameters permanent (Freeze PP on Cubase and N/Normalise on Notator for instance).
- Merge all tracks by bouncing down to one track. If this option is not provided, turn MIDI thru/echo off, connect the MIDI Out to MIDI In and record an "All MIDI" channel track.
- Delete all other tracks.
- Save this one track as a MIDI file, which should force it to format 0 (one track of mixed MIDI channels).

To transfer a MIDI file from one platform to another, use a program that allows transfer to the foreign format disk. On the destination platform, ensure that the file extension is correct (.MID). On an Apple Mac, the file type will also have to be changed with Res-Edit, or if using AFE or PC Exchange to import from the PC disk directly, the file type (MIDI) will be specified here.

Operating systems

A computer uses a program called an operating system, with which to perform its basic functions, such as a greeting screen, formatting and copying disks and launching applications. The techniques for these vary with each platform. They do however divide into two categories: command line (where you type in a simple but special language which is quite fussy about the spelling and punctuation) and a visual environment called WIMP – Windows, Icons, Menus and Pointing. These are generally mouse controlled and work on a point and click (or drag) principle.

There are advantages and disadvantages to either system and some even offer the choice of both at all times. Even with the graphical systems, there are usually keyboard shortcuts or extra functions when holding certain keys. The following may apply to your system:

Keyboard addition	*Action*
Shift	Select (or deselect) multiple objects or limit cursor movement (proportional re-sizing)
Control	Turn objects into controls or shortcut to menu commands
Alternate	Copy objects or access a menu
Cursor keys	Change the selected object in the cursor direction
Tab	Make the next object active
Return	OK to accept option
Escape	Escape from a command sequence

Useful tips

- Make back-up copies of any important program or data disks.
- Back up your hard drive periodically.
- Use a hard disk defragmentation program periodically.
- Save your work (from memory) to disk regularly – after every important edit or every 20 minutes maximum, whichever is more frequent.
- A hard disk will speed up your computer system operation, probably ten-fold.

It can be very efficient to run programs from a RAMdisk. You must remember to save any data stored in the RAMdisk to a physical disk before powering down or deinstalling the RAM disk, or you will lose it.

When using any computer system, it is important to ensure that the operating system is available all the time. For instance, it may not all load into memory at one time and use the system disks to loop up certain functions making it very memory efficient.

With IBM DOS running from a floppy system for instance, using the Diskcopy command with no system disk inserted will result in an error of Unknown command. This simply means that no system disk was present. Having the system on a hard disk really speeds up such processes and avoids confusion.

9 Contacts

UK

Publishing copyright

Performing Right Society (PRS), 29-33 Berners Street, London W1P 4AA, Tel: 0171 580 5544; Fax: 0171 631 4138

ASCAP, Suite 10/11, 52 Haymarket, London SW11 4RP, Tel: 0171 973 0069; Fax: 0171 973 0068

Mechanical copyright

Mechanical Copyright Protection Society (MCPS), Elgar House, 41 Streatham High Road, London SW16 1ER, Tel: 0181 769 4400; Fax: 0181 769 8792

Performance copyright

Phonographic Performance Ltd (PPL), Ganton House, 14-22 Ganton Street, London W1V 1LB, Tel: 0171 437 0311; Fax: 0171 734 2966

Video Performance Ltd, Ganton House, 14-22 Ganton Street, London W1V 1LB, Tel: 0171 437 0311; Fax: 0171 734 2966

Unions

Musicians Union, 60-62 Clapham Road, London SW9 0JJ, Tel: 0171 582 5566; Fax: 0171 582 9605

British Actors Equity Association, 8 Harley Street, London W1N 2AB, Tel: 0171 637 9311

The Royal National Institute for the Deaf, 105 Gower Street, London WC1E 6AH, Tel: 0171 387 8033

British Association for the Hard of Hearing, 7-11 Armstrong Road, London W3 7JL, Tel: 0181 743 1110

Professional associations

Arts Council of Great Britain, 14 Great Peter Street, London SW1P 3NQ, Tel: 0171 333 0100

Association of Professional Composers (APC), 34 Hanway Street, London W1P 9DE, Tel: 0171 436 0919

Association of Professional Music Therapists, The Meadow, 38 Pierce Lane, Fulbourn, Cambridge CB1 5DL, Tel: 01223 880 237

Association of Professional Recording Studios (APRS), 2 Windsor Square, Silver Street, Reading, Berks RG1 2TH, Tel: 01734 756 218; Fax: 01734 756 216

Audio Engineering Society (AES), P.O. Box 645, Slough, Bucks SL1 8BJ, Tel: 01628 663 725; Fax: 01628 667 002

Association of British Theatre Technicians, 4 Great Pultney Street, London W1R 3DF, Tel: 0171 403 3778
British Kinematograph Sound & Television Society, 547-549 Victoria House (M6-M14), Vernon Place, London WC1B 4DJ, Tel: 0171 242 8400
British Standards Institute, Enquiry Section, Linford Wood, Milton Keynes MK14 6LE, Tel: 01908 221 166; Fax: 01908 322 484
British Phonographic Institute (BPI), 25 Saville Row, London W1X 1AA, Tel: 0171 287 4422; Fax: 0171 287 2252
British Music Industry (BMI), 79 Harley House, Marleybone Road, London NW1 5HN, Tel: 0171 935 8517; Fax: 0171 487 5091
British Association of Songwriters Composers and Authors (BASCA), 34 Hanway Street, London W1P 9DE, Tel: 0171 436 2261; Fax: 0171 436 1913
Incorporated Society of Musicians (ISM), 10 Stratford Place, London W1N 9AE, Tel: 0171 629 4413; Fax: 0171 408 1538
Music Industries Association (MIA), 7 The Avenue, Datchet, Slough, Berkshire SL3 9DH, Tel: 01753 541 963
Music Publishers Association, 3rd floor, Strandgate, 18/20 York Buildings, London WC2N 6JU, Tel: 0171 839 7779; Fax: 0171 839 7776
Sound & Communication Industries Federation, 4-8 High Street, Burnham, Slough, Bucks SL1 7JH, Tel: 01628 667 633; Fax: 01628 665 882
Networking (Women's film, video & TV training association), c/o Vera Productions, 30-38 Dock Street, Leeds LS10 1JF, Tel: 0113 242 8646
Professional Light & Sound Association (PLASA), 7 Highlight House, St Leonards Road, Eastbourne BN21 3UH, Tel: 01323 410 335; Fax: 01323 646 905
Re-Pro The Guild of Record Producers, Directors and Engineers, (A division of APRS Ltd), PO Box 310, London SW13 0AF, Tel: 0181 876 3411; Fax: 0181 876 8252.
Skillset (Goverment training consultants), 60 Charlotte Street, London W1 2AX
Kurzweil Owners Group (K2k), PO Box 907, London SE27 9NZ, Tel/Fax: 0181 761 0178; Email - Compuserve 10033,3701 & phud@cix.compulink.co.uk

UK magazines

Studio Sound and **Pro Sound News**, Spotlight Publications Ltd, Ludgate House, 245 Blackfriars Road, London SE1 9UR, Tel: 0171 620 3636; Fax: 0171 401 8035
Music Week, Spotlight Publications Ltd, Ludgate House, 245 Blackfriars Road, London SE1 9UR, Tel: 0171 620 3636; Fax: 0171 401 8035
Billboard, 23 Ridgmond Street, London WC1E 7AH, Tel: 0171 323 6686; Fax: 0171 323 2314
Sound On Sound and **Audio Media**, Media House, Burrell Road, St Ives, Cambs PE17 4LE, Tel: 01480 461244; Fax: 01480 492422
Future Music, Future Publishing, 30 Monmouth Street, Bath, Avon BA1 2BW, Tel: 01225 442244; Fax: 01225 446019
The Mix, Music Maker Publications, Alexander House, Forehill, Ely, Cambs CB7 4AF, Tel: 01353 665 577; Fax: 01353 662 489
Melody Maker, IPC Magazines, 26th floor, Kings Reach Tower, Stamford Street, London SE1 9LS, Tel: 0171 261 5670; Fax: 0171 261 6706

Kemps, Showcase Publications Ltd, 12 Felix Avenue, London N8 9TL, Tel: 0181 348 2332; Fax: 0181 340 3750
Televisual (pro video/broadcast magazine), Centaur Group, St Giles House, 50 Poland Street, London, W1V 4AX, Tel 0171 439 4222, Fax 0171 287 0768
Audio Visual (AV industry magazine), Emap Maclaren, PO Box 109, Maclaren House, Scarbrook Road, Croydon, Surrey, CR9 1QH, Tel 0181 688 7788, Fax 0181 681 1672
Audio Visuality (high class consumer entertainment technology magazine), Media Communication & Publishing Ltd, Suite 33 Imperial House, 64 Willoughby Lane, London, N17 0SP, Tel 0181 365 0155, Fax 0181 365 0554
The White Book, P.O. Box 55, Staines, Middlesex TW18 4UG, Tel: 01784 464 441; Fax: 01784 464 655

BBS services
Compulink Information eXchange Ltd (CIX), The Sanctuary, Oakhill Grove, Surbiton, Surrey KT6 6DU, Tel (voice): 0181 390 8446; Fax: 0181 390 6561; BBS: 0181 390 1244
CompuServe, P.O. Box 676, Bristol BS99 1YN, Tel (voice): 0800 289 458/0117 976 0680; BBS: 0171 490 8881

USA

American Council for the Arts, 1285 Avenue of the Americas, 3rd Floor, NY 10019, Tel: 001 212 245 4510
Audio Engineering Society (AES), 60 East 42nd Street, New York, NY 10166, Tel: 001 212 661 2355; Fax: 001 212 682 0477
Affiliated Independent Record Companies, P.O. Box 241648, Los Angeles, CA 90024, Tel: 001 310 208 2140
American Federation of Musicians, Suite 600, 1501 Broadway, New York, NY 10036, Tel: 001 212 869 1330
American Musicians Union Inc., 8 Tobin Cl, Durcont, New Jersey, NJ 07628, Tel: 001 201 384 5378
American Society of Composers, Authors and Publishers (ASCAP), Building One, Lincoln Plaza, New York, NY 10023, Tel: 001 212 595 3050; or 001 212 521 6000
American Women Composers Inc., Suite 409, 1600 36th Street NW, Washington DC 20000, Tel: 001 202 342 8179
BMI (music royalty agency), 320 W. 57th Street, New York, NY 10019, Tel: 001 212 586 2000
Central Opera Service, Metropolitan Opera, Lincoln Centre, New York, NY 10023, Tel: 001 212 957 9871
Club Cubase USA
62 Harnworth Drive, Willowdale Ontario, M2H 3C2 Canada, USA, Tel: 001 818 993 4091, Fax: 001 818 701 7452
Composers Guild, Box 586, 40 N 100 West, Farmington, UT 84025, Tel: 001 801 451 2275
Computer Music Association, Box 1634, San Fransisco, CA 94101, Tel: 001 817 566 2235
International MIDI Association, 5306 W. 57th Street, Los Angeles, CA 90050, Tel: 001 310 649 6434
The Just Intonation Network, MIDI Tuning Standards Committee, 535 Stevenson Street, San Francisco, CA 94103

Musicians Contact Service, 7315 Sunset Blvd, Hollywood, CA 90046, Tel: 001 213 851 2333
Musicians National Hot Line Association, 277 East 6100 South, Salt Lake City, UT 84107, Tel: 001 801 268 2000
National Academy of Popular Music – Songwriters Hall of Fame, 875 3rd Avenue S., 8th Floor, New York, NY 10022, Tel: 001 212 319 1444
National Academy of Songwriters (NAS), Suite 780, 6381 Hollywood Blvd, Hollywood, CA 90028, Tel: 001 213 463 7178
National Association of Composers USA, Box 49652, Barrington Station, Los Angeles, CA 90049, Tel: 001 213 541 8213
National Association of Record Merchandisers (NARM), Suite 307, 3 Eves Drive, Marlton, NJ 08053, Tel: 001 609 596 2221
National Association of Schools of Music, 11250 Roger Bacon Drive, Restoo, VA 22090, Tel: 001 703 437 0700
PAN BBS, P.O. Box 162, Skippack, PA 19474, Tel: 001 610 584 0300; Fax: 001 610 584 1038 BBS 001 617 492 9600 OR via internet as Tel:net pan.com
Recording Industry Association of America (RIAA), 1020 19th Street, NW Suite 200, Washington DC 20036
SESAC Inc., 156 W. 56th Street, New York, NY 10019, Tel: 001 212 586 3450
Society of Motion Picture & Television Engineers (SMPTE), 595 West Harsdale Avenue, White Plains, NY 10007, Tel: 001 914 761 1100
Society of Professional Recording Services, 4300 10th Avenue N., Suite 2, Lake Worth, FL 33461-2313, Tel: 001 407 641 6648
Songwriters Guild of America, Suite 306, 276 Fifth Avenue, New York, NY 10001, Tel: 001 212 686 6820
United Songwriters Association, 6429 Leavenworth Road, Kansas City, KS 66104, Tel: 001 913 788 7716
Women in Music National Network, 31121 Mission Blvd, Suite 123, Hayward, CA 94544, Tel: 001 510 471 1752

US Magazines
Electronic Musician , 2608 Ninth Street, Berkley, CA 94710, USA
Keyboard Magazine (MI Hi Tech), 411 Borel Avenue, Suite 100, San Mateo, California 94402, USA, Tel: 001 415 358 9500, Fax: 001 415 358 9527, Compuserve 72662,136
Mix Magazine (Pro Audio), 6400 Hollis Street, #12 Emeryville, California 94608, USA, Tel: 001 510 653 3307, Fax: 001 510 653 5142, Compuserve 74673,3672
Multimedia World (multimedia magazine), PC World Communications Inc., 501 Second Street, #600 San Francisco, California 94107, Subscription enquiries to PO Box 51833, Boulder, CO 80321-1833
NewMedia (multimedia magazine), PO Box 1771, Riverton, NJ 08077-7371, Tel: 001 800 516 0101, Fax: 001 617 749 2018
PC Graphics & Video, Advanstar Communications, 201 East Sandpointe Avenue, Suite 600, Santa Ana, California 927-7, USA, Tel 714 513 8400, Fax: 001 714 513 8612, Compuserve 74771,2521, Subscriptions Fax: 001 503 686 5731.

Recommended Reading

Sound Recording Practice
John Borwick/APRS (550 pages)
Oxford University Press
ISBN 0-19-311927-7

Sound Reinforcement Handbook
Gary Davis & Ralph Jones/Yamaha
Hal Leonard Publishing (400 pages)
ISBN 0-88188-900-8

Illustrated Compendium of Musical Technology
Tristam Cary (542 pages)
Faber & Faber
ISBN 0-571152-51-1

Recording Techniques for Small Studios
David Mellor
PC Publishing
ISBN 1-870775-29-5

Digital Audio Operations
Francis Rumsey (230 pages)
Focal Press
0-240-51311-8

Tapeless Sound Recording
Francis Rumsey (188 pages)
Focal Press
0-240-51297-9

10

Glossary

MIDI

Channel MIDI messages can be addressed to 1 of 16 possible channels specified in the MIDI Specification, all using the same single serial cable. More MIDI channels can be introduced by addressing different MIDI ports. The MIDI channel acts like a unique telephone number where only specified devices (set to receive on the same channel) will respond to those messages. In sequencing, this allows each track to play a separate instrument.

Clock MIDI clock is used to send timing information to other devices so that they can stay in synchronisation with the tempo of the master device.

Controller Used to change MIDI parameters such as pitchbend, sustain pedal, MIDI volume and pan control.

Echo MIDI echo (or Soft Thru) is a sequencer function that takes the incoming data at the MIDI In and sends it directly to the MIDI Out socket (possibly with re-channelisation). This allows a master keyboard to communicate with devices on different MIDI channels, as well as recording into a sequencer.

General MIDI (GM) An addition to the MIDI Specification that attempts to standardise a minimum set of sounds and their location in terms of patch change numbers. This enables sequences recorded on different systems to play with similar sounds on other systems without much effort.

Local mode An internal keyboard function that connects the keyboard keys to the sound-producing section of the instrument. Essential for live playing, but has to be disabled in a sequencing environment when used with a sequencer's "soft thru" function otherwise polyphony halving and continual sound from the master keyboard results.

Merge MIDI is an asynchronous serial system and MIDI data must be combined intelligently under microprocessor control, otherwise the messages can be misinterpreted. A MIDI merge box provides this function.

MIDI The Musical Instrument Digital Interface is an agreement between manufacturers to standardise a method of interconnection and communication between MIDI-equipped devices. It is a serial system, offering 16 separate MIDI channels of information via one cable. A MIDI command often consists of more than one MIDI byte. It is an asynchronous system with a transfer rate of 31.25 kbaud. MIDI does not contain any sound data directly, but merely information about its performance or state (see Sequencer).

MIDI In (socket) Receives incoming MIDI messages. Analogous to a human ear as it listens to the system.

MIDI Out (socket) Used to send MIDI messages to other devices. Analogous to a human mouth, giving instructions and messages to the MIDI system.

MIDI Thru (socket) Duplicates the MIDI In signal and so allows the "daisy chaining" of MIDI units in a system. This system is normally satisfactory for up to three devices, beyond which the use of an active MIDI Thru box is recommended.

MIDI Machine Control (MMC) An extension to the MIDI Specification designed for the control of tape machines and other such devices under a MIDI system.

MIDI Show Control (MSC) An extension to the MIDI Specification designed to include theatrical devices under MIDI control. Applications include lighting, pyrotechnics and stage props.

MIDI Time Code (MTC) A way of encoding SMPTE time code for distribution in a MIDI system. One advantage of MTC is that a sequencer can use its own internal tempo map (which is saved with the song data). As MTC is distributed digitally via MIDI cables, it is less likely to corruption or spill than its audio counterpart. The MTC specification also allows for the use of other commands to be included, such as setting up devices and machine transport control, although the MMC spec. is more thorough in this respect.

Monophonic Of a musical device on which only one note sounds at a time.

Patch change MIDI command used to select a particular location in a MIDI device. There is no guarantee that what is in that location is correct and hasn't been changed since last tested. Applications including calling up synth sounds remotely, changing effects patches and calling up scenes on a MIDI-equipped mixer (audio or lighting).

Polyphonic Of a musical device on which several notes can sound simultaneously. Usually limited to 8, 16 or 32 notes, depending on the particular device.

Running Status MIDI system protocol that attempts to save MIDI bandwidth by assuming that the next message is of the same type as the last one, unless otherwise specified. Unfortunately some devices (in particular, older units) need a full message to function properly.

Sequencer A system that can store and retrieve MIDI information. This usually includes musical performance details (such as what notes were played) but can also store the value of parameters of synth and effects units, or indeed the value of any controls on a MIDI-equipped lighting or sound mixer. A MIDI sequencer does not store sound information itself, only performance data relating to it – the synth unit is always required to play back the performance.

Standard MIDI file A standard way of interchanging MIDI sequencer data between different systems and software products. There are three modes 0 for a single multi-channel track; 1 for multiple MIDI channel tracks; and 2 for pattern-based multiple tracks.

System exclusive Special set of MIDI commands that are unique to a particular make and model of MIDI device. The commands can be used to adjust internal parameters of a synth or effect. This can be used in conjunction with the patch change command at the beginning of a session to ensure that the correct bank of edited patches is in the device.

Switcher A simple device that saves re-patching MIDI connectors for different roles, such as sequencing and editing, or for allowing different MIDI controllers to be used (like MIDI drum pads or keyboard). For any application where the simultaneous use of different devices is not required, a switcher will suffice rather than the more expensive merge box.

Thru box An active device that provides several MIDI Thrus from one MIDI In. Useful for connecting a number of MIDI devices or when a system has more than one unit without a MIDI Thru socket.

Synthesis

Additive A synthesis system that combines a number of simple oscillator elements via their individual VCAs to produce a more complex sound. It works on the principle that all sounds can be described in terms of basic sine wave building blocks at different frequencies and levels.

Amplitude Another term to describe the loudness or level of a sound or waveform.

EG Envelope Generator. An electronic device used to create a varying voltage envelope shape over time. Usually described in terms of ADSR (Attack, Decay, Sustain and Release) elements.

Envelope The change of an entity over time. Subtractive synthesis relies heavily on amplitude envelopes (which change the volume of a sound over time) and the filter envelope (which changes the state of the filter and hence the high frequency content of the sound over time).

Equal temperament The interval and ratio between each note in the scales for western-based music is fixed and evenly spaced. This allows for easy key changing during a piece. See micro-tuning.

Filter A device that can alter the frequency (or harmonic) content of a sound. A low pass filter (LPF) is frequently used in subtractive synthesis to change the brightness of the sound and, in conjunction with an envelope, that brightness over time.

Frequency The periodic repetition of an event. In sound terms, this is perceived as pitch.

Frequency modulation (FM) A type of synthesis, currently patented by Yamaha, that uses the interaction of oscillators to produce new waveforms and harmonics. Similar to ring modulation, an oscillator frequency modulates the output of another to produce new harmonics.

Micro-tuning A system that uses different intervals (or ratios) between notes in a scale. This is quite common in non-western music and arguably produces more pleasing results. A number of micro-tuning systems attempt to reduce beat frequencies introduced by different notes of a chord. Some systems use different numbers of notes in an octave (up to 53). It is necessary to decide on the key before a micro-tuning system can be selected.

Noise An unpitched sound. Often used in synthesis for sound effects such as rain, seashore, laser guns and breath noise of blown instruments. There are two main types used in audio: white and pink noise. See chapter on synthesis for an explanation of the differences.

Resynthesis A form of synthesis/sampling, yet to be fully implemented, which is based on the analysis of sound data which is later used to reconstruct the sound with additional factors imposed, but all in real-time. This means that only small amounts of data need be stored (unlike traditional sampling) and that any parameter of the sound can be infinitely changed. This new technology should allow the faithful recreation of any existing instrument and the creation of truly original sounds and textures. Material construction, acoustic response, perspective, morphing between sounds and transformation (such as blowing a piano) in any dimension will become possible.

Ring modulation A synthesis system where one oscillator modulates another to produce sum and difference frequencies. Unlike FM, the original carrier frequency is not normally present. Very common for synthesis of bell sounds.

Sampling The process of recording a sound and storing it digitally for triggering and manipulation by a sampler. It allows any sound to be treated like a musical instrument.

Subtractive Synthesis system that utilises a fairly basic waveform oscillator/s and modifies it with the use of filtering and amplitude envelopes.

VCA Voltage Controlled Amplifier. An amplifier that can be controlled remotely by a voltage. Used in synthesis to provide level (volume) changes over time when controlled from an envelope generator or LFO.

VCF Voltage Controlled Filter. A filter that can be controlled remotely by a voltage. Used in synthesisers to provide timbral changes over time when controlled from an envelope generator or LFO.

Sampling

ADC Analogue to digital converter. Translates normal waveforms (that is, sound) that vary continuously over time and stores them as discrete steps of a numeric value.

Analogue A waveform that changes continuously over time. This is the natural form of all sound and light.

Bit The smallest quantity in a computer system. Has either a 1 or 0 state.

Byte A collection of eight bits that make up a single character or value code.

DAC Digital to analogue converter, the counterpart of the ADC. Takes digital information and translates it back into an analogue form.

Digital A system where information is stored in a series of discrete numeric values that can be processed, manipulated and stored by a computer system.

Dynamic range The difference between the smallest and largest value of the level of a sound.

Hard disk A device that can store a large quantity of digital information. Used in computer systems to store programs and data. Hard disks provide much faster access to data than a floppy disk and can store many times the amount of information.

Looping the process in sound sampling where a section of a recording is repeated to give the illusion of a longer recording. This saves having to store large amounts of information.

Mapping The process, in sampling, of assigning different samples (sounds) for triggering from different sections of a keyboard.

Sampling rate How often the level of an input waveform is looked at and stored. If the sampling rate is too low, important information will be missed (usually affecting the high frequency response of the sound), but with a higher sampling rate, more (expensive) memory is required to store the values.

Tapeless recording A system that digitally records sound to a medium other than tape. Hard disk is the current medium, but solid state storage will be used in the future.

Quantisation The process of quantifying the value of a sound sample. A finite number of level steps are used on any digital system. Rounding of the true value to the nearest step results in quantisation noise which is often heard by the listener.

Word A usable value in a digital system. In a 16-bit system, two bytes are required for each value.

Music

Bar A subdivision in a musical piece that is used to easily identify the location in a piece. The size of the bar divisions is determined by the time signature. In 3/4 time, for instance, there are 3 beats of a 1/4 value (crotchet) in each bar.

Chord A collection of three or more different notes that sound simultaneously.

Key A name used to describe a scale of notes.

Scale A musical device that stipulates the series of notes from which notes can be selected and played.

Tempo The speed of a song. It is usually taken as the (comfortable) walking or clapping pace or pulse that can run through a piece.

Recording and production

Equalisation (EQ) Similar to the tone controls on a hi-fi, but usually with greater control. EQ is a frequency-selective amplifier that can adjust the volume (up or down) of a certain range of frequencies of a sound.

FASA Acronym for a production method based on the key elements: Frequency, Amplitude, Spectrum and Ambience.

Microphone A device used to convert acoustic sound energy into electricity (analogous in form) that electronic devices, such as a mixer, can understand.

Patchbay A collection of sockets in one common place from which (ideally) all of the connections in the studio appear.

SMPTE Time code named after the Society of Motion Picture and Television Engineers which decided on its format. SMPTE is a system used to identify a section of tape for synchronisation purposes with other devices, including other tape machines or MIDI sequencers (via a SMPTE to MIDI converter). SMPTE is a tone which has the time encoded in it using Manchester bi-phase modulation. The time format is in hours, minutes, seconds and frames, the number of frames depending on the application and country. See Chapter 5 Recording and Production for more details.

Spill The presence of unwanted sound on a signal. Most often caused by acoustic leakage from one source onto a microphone used on a different instrument. Spill is often unavoidable and is not necessarily a problem if it is of a high quality and not coloured.

Tape editing The process of physical cutting a tape to change the order of a recording. For instance, certain words can be removed and the running order changed if desired.

Audio

Absorption coefficient Represents the ability of a material to absorb and reflect sound energy. A coefficient of one means total absorbtion while zero means total reflection. Usually varies with the frequency of a sound.

ADT Artificial double tracking, a technique used to simulate the effect of a repeat performance, producing a chorus-type effect. ADT can be achieved with a slightly modulating delay line (around 50ms). Actually performing twice is often more successful, as pitch and other subtle variations occur.

Ambience The term used to describe the acoustic nature of an environment in terms of its natural reverberation.

Balanced line A connection system, often used on microphones, that employs two insulated interleaved conductors and a common screen. By employing common phase cancelling circuitry at each end of the cable, induced noise on the cable can largely be removed.

Cans Slang term for headphones.

Decibel (dB) A tenth of a bel. Represents a ratio between two values and is meaningless unless the reference value is known. Decibels allow the easy calculation of a system's gain by simple addition or subtraction of the dB values.

Frequency The periodic oscillation of an entity. Interpret as the pitch of a sound.

Helmholtz resonator Structure designed to resonate at a particular frequency and hence dampen or absorb the energy of that frequency in any sound that hits it.

Wavelength Distance measurement between the same point in a periodic waveform. The frequency and wavelength of a sound are related by the formula c = wf where c is the speed of sound (around 1000 feet/s or 330m/s).

Weighted Human hearing is not linear to all frequencies at all volumes. A weighted measurement takes this sonic effect into account when measuring the response of a system. "A" weighting represents the normal response of human hearing.

Electronics

Attenuator An electronic device that reduces the level in a circuit. Devices that operate at different levels can be matched using an attenuator. Often referred to as a pad.

Impedance The resistance to the flow of an AC current. Resistance should be used to describe the opposition to the flow of DC current.

Integrated circuit (IC) An electronic device that contains the equivalent of a large number of discrete devices such as transistors.

Ohm's law Named after its discoverer, this is the physical law that states the interaction between the elements of electricity, linking the flow of current with potential difference and resistance. It also links the concept of power with these factors.

Parallel connection One where a number of paths are available simultaneously and elements can pass together (like a dual carriageway for cars).

Series connection One where only one path exists at any one time (like a one-way single-track road).

Watt A measurement/unit of power in an electronic circuit. The term is also applied to the measurement of sound pressure.

Multimedia

BBS Bulletin Board Service, a system accessed by telephone using computers; provides a means of exchanging files, information and electronic mail messages. Another benefit of a BBS is that as the system stores the data, users need not be on-line at the same time.

CD-ROM A compact disc medium that contains data in a digital format for use in a computer system. Currently, up to 600Mbytes of data can be stored on one disc.

Compact disc (CD) A medium that has audio information digitally encoded on it. Can hold up to 74 minutes of stereo audio.

ISDN Integrated Services Digital Network. A digital communication system that allows high data transmission rates – of at least two channels of 64Kbit per second. This allows very fast transfer of files and opens up a number of real-time transfer options - including real-time videoconferencing. Using two ISDN lines and a special device called a CODEC (Coder Decoder), two way full bandwidth stereo audio can be transmitted. The other advantage of ISDN is that it is supplied as a dial-up service, meaning that the user can simply dial up the destination like a normal phone call.

JPEG Joint Picture Expert Group. A body that defined a standard for data compression originally for still images. Has been extended to M-JPEG for use in random access non-linear editor systems, such as those from Avid and Media Link. Losses are unavoidable but considered acceptable in most people's opinions.

Internet The name given to the worldwide network of computer users accessible from any computer with a modem (via a service provider such as Demon and Pipex, or gateway providers such as CIX and Compuserve). The internet consists of a large number of computer sites (often in Universities) that are connected together globally.

MPEG Motion Picture Expert Group. A body that defined a standard for data compression specifically for moving images. It relies on sending the differences only from the last frame and is hence very efficient, but bad news for random access non-linear editor applications and the like. With compression ratios up to 200:1, offering acceptable compression losses in most people's opinions.

Multimedia Term used to describe a system that combines audio and visual facilities in a computer environment. The term can also be extended to include communication and virtual reality systems.

Video and film

ADR Automatic dialogue replacement. Sometimes called looping. The process of re-recording dialogue while watching the film, to produce a clean synchronised version.

BITC Burnt in time code. A video film that shows the SMPTE time on screen in a window along with the picture. Sometimes called a "window dub".

Blocking Plotting the positions and movement of actors, cameras and microphones.

Control track A dedicated track used on video tape which marks the start of each video frame. Can be used to count time for editing, but is prone to slip and lose count during winding.

DAW Digital audio workstation.

EDL Edit decision list A list of generated cues for video editing. Often created using an off-line system (for economy) and then the EDL list is exported to the on-line system for an "auto conform".

Foley The process of creating sound effects when watching the action. Foley "walkers" work in the Foley stage area to create these effects, such as footsteps - hence the term walkers. Often larger than life to enhance the dramatic effect.

Jam sync The process of regenerating SMPTE time code to a previous reference. Used to recover from drop outs or non-continuous time code caused by editing.

Layback Transfer of the finished audio mix back onto the video edit master.

Layoff Transfer of audio and time code from the video edit master to an audio tape.

Layover Sometimes called layup. The transfer of audio onto hard disk or multitrack tape.

Lip sync The process of matching dialogue sound to the picture.

LTC Longitudinal time code. Refers to SMPTE time code recorded on one of the audio tracks of the video machine. Usually the highest number edge track (at -3dB).

M & E Music and effects track, less dialogue. Used for foreign voice dubbing.

NTSC National Television Standards Committee. The USA TV broadcast standard of 525 lines. The frame rate is 30 drop frame, 29.97 fps.

Offline The video is compiled on a less expensive machine, where only the EDL list is created, but not conformed.

Online The video tape editing is completed from the EDL using high quality equipment.

PAL Phase alternating line. The UK TV broadcast standard. Uses 625 lines at a frame rate of 25fps.

Pilot tone A tone used to resolve the speed of portable recorders to the film.

Post production The process of adding to a production to further enhance it.

Production sound The sound recorded on location during the shoot.

Rushes Also known as dailies. The first print from the lab of the film shot. Used to chart the progress of the film and for preliminary music cuts.

SMPTE Society of Motion Picture and Television Engineers. A body that set the standard for the tone used to synchronise machines (ATR, VTR and tapeless) together. Also extended to synchronising MIDI devices.

Spotting The process in video work of identifying scenes where music cues will take place.

Telecine A machine that transfers film to video tape.

Underscore Music that provides atmospheric or emotional background to emphasise the action.

VITC Vertical interval time code. SMPTE time code recorded as part of the video picture signal. Must be added during video recording but doesn't take up a video track and can be read in varispeed and still frame modes.

Walla Background ambience added to give the affect of an external environment e.g. street noise.

Wild track Audio elements not yet synchronised to the video.

Workprint Sometimes called a slop print. A copy of the original film used as a reference during editing or sweetening.

Index